Trespassing

ʃ Sam Pickering

Trespassing

University Press of New England

Hanover and London

UNIVERSITY PRESS OF NEW ENGLAND publishes books under its own imprint and is the publisher for Brandeis University Press, Brown University Press, University of Connecticut, Dartmouth College, Middlebury College Press, University of New Hampshire, University of Rhode Island, Tufts University, University of Vermont, and Wesleyan University Press.

University Press of New England, Hanover, NH 03755
Printed in the United States of America

5 4 3 2 1

The author and publisher gratefully acknowledge the following publications in which essays in this volume first appeared: *The South Carolina Review, Witness, The Texas Review, North Dakota Quarterly, New England Review, The Missouri Review* (Fall), *Negative Capability* and *The Chariton Review.*

Library of Congress Cataloging-in-Publication Data

Pickering, Samuel F., 1941–
  Trespassing / Sam Pickering.
    p.   cm.
    ISBN 0–87451–640–4
    I. Title
  AC8.P674   1994   93–38325
  ∞

For Mansfield and the

University of Connecticut

—"Sort of like Family"

CONTENTS

Trespassing

5 Magic

*W*hen Hornus Roebuck's chimney began to smoulder, he didn't telephone the fire department. Instead he ran out the back door, leaped over the fence, crossed Grace's pasture, and burst into Noonday, Mother Noon's store on Straddle Street. Mother Noon was Beaver River's conjure woman, selling charms to the love-sick and nostrums to the feverish. For a damp, rumbling January catarrh she sold Hornus a cigar made from mullein leaves. The cigar cured Hornus, and so when flames flickered through cracks in his chimney, association flared like light wood, the smoke from the stove first mingling with the memory of hot mullein then rising before his vision to lead him across Grace's pasture, much like, as Bertha Shifney put it, "that cloud what led the old Jews through the Wilderness." Mother Noon did not like to disappoint customers in search of the miraculous, so she fashioned a prescription for Hornus. "Cut a branch of noisy leaf," she said, "and draw three circles around the house in the dirt, each circle nine hand lengths from the one next to it. Then lay the branch down at the east end of the house, and God will help you." As soon as Mother Noon finished talking, Hornus ran out the door and started for Grace's pasture. At the fence he stopped, suddenly remembering that only alders and red maples grew around his house and that the nearest quaking aspen was in the backyard of the Shore Grocery two miles away. "Mother Noon," he shouted, turning back toward Straddle Street, "I ain't got no noisy leaf. Do you think it would hurt if I dumped water on the fire?" "No," Mother Noon yelled back through the screen door; "it won't hurt none at all. Pour on water. In fact pour on as much water as you can."

The water put out the fire. "It was magical," Hornus later told Bertha Shifney, adding that only four bricks cracked. "Of course," he said, "if I'd had some noisy leaf them bricks wouldn't be bothering me today." Old-time magic was a staple of Noonday. For warts and bleer-eye Mother Noon prescribed a wash made from green flies and apple cider. Hanging above the counter and resembling a litter of long thin peppers was a string of lizards' tails. When wrapped in skin taken from a goat's ear and put on the mantle or, "better yet," Mother Noon instructed, "under the pendulum of a grandfather clock," a tail protected a family from fever during the winter. On the porch by Mother Noon's front door was a reed basket full of chestnuts. "If you carry a chestnut with a worm hole in it in the right front pocket of your trousers," Mother Noon told Hornus, "Cousin Bad Luck will run when he sees you." On the counter of the store sat a squat yellow jar full of what looked like feldspar, or so Hornus thought until he learned the jar contained snake stones, cut from the craws of birds which ate snakes. The stones absorbed poison, and placing one over a wound rendered the wound harmless.

Although the wares for sale in Noonday can still charm a page, they are dusty remnants, relics that no longer astonish or cure. Unlike Mother Noon's nostrums, stories rarely age into artifact. Instead of drying they swell vital and transport hearers into the magical land of Might-Have-Been. None of Hink Ruunt's mates were long-lived, and sometimes neighbors had trouble keeping abreast of the domestic comings and goings in Hink's house in South Carthage. On meeting Hink at a tobacco auction, Googoo Hooberry inquired about Hink's wife, whose name Googoo had forgotten, somewhat understandably because she was the sixth Mrs. Ruunt. Having spent the previous week in Nashville, Googoo did not know that Mrs. Ruunt had died on Wednesday. "Hink," Googoo said when he ran across Hink looking at sprays for tobacco worms, "you are looking mighty good, and how is that fine wife of yours?" "Well, Googoo," Hink replied, pausing and pushing the plunger on a spray up and down, "to tell the truth I'm kind of out of wives just now."

Not long afterward on some Caucasian holiday, Robert E. Lee's or St. Patrick's birthday, Hink went to Nashville himself. Whether the trip was provoked by grief or, as some said, a quick payment from the life insurance company, isn't known. What is certain, however, is that Hink spent much time drinking along lower Broadway in the gritty bars near the river. One night Hink wandered up town into a better drinking establishment on Church Street. Hink was a prodigious chewer and spitter. What was fine for sawdust floors a few fathoms above the Cumberland River wouldn't do, higher up under the shadow of the War Memorial Building. And when Hink started spitting, a bartender fetched a spittoon and set it down near Hink on the floor. Hink looked at the spittoon then turned away and spat in the opposite direction whereupon the bartender shoved it closer to him. For a moment Hink looked back and forth, first at the bartender then the spittoon. But finally he shrugged and digging a hunk of tobacco out of his jaw pushed it around in his mouth, his cheek resembling the sail of a boat scudding through small-craft warnings. As Hink's cheek fluttered and billowed, the bartender kicked the spittoon right up against Hink's chair. Hink eyed the spittoon again, his cheek slack for a moment. Then he looked the bartender in the eye. "Fellow," he said, using his tongue as a tiller and steering the tobacco up under his ear, "if you don't take that thing away, I'll be hanged if I don't spit in it."

Along with being unsophisticated, Hink was lazy—spoiled, Turlow Gutheridge said, "by all them adoring wives." According to Turlow, Hink was so slovenly he wouldn't go to the door to see if it was raining. Instead he just whistled for Buster his dog, who slept under the front stoop. When Buster came into the house, Hink ran his hand along the dog's back. If his fingers got wet, Hink knew it was raining. Like many lazy people, however, Hink became energetic when he thought of an unscrupulous way to make fifty cents. Once he found a bucket of yellow paint at the dump, and when the patients from the school for the afflicted in Buffalo Valley came to Carthage for their half-yearly outing, he painted his mule and shutting it up in his barn charged the poor souls five cents to see, as the sign he hung up declared, "the camel without no hump."

The trip to Nashville changed Hink, however. Nobody knew what happened. Perhaps he drank too much or "bit off more than he could chaw," as Googoo put it. Whatever the case, on returning Hink pronounced himself a Christian and started attending Slubey Garts's Tabernacle of Love. When Pharaoh Parkus came over from Memphis to hold a baptizing, Hink was waiting on the riverbank. Hink knew almost no doctrine, and when Pharaoh asked him if he believed in Original Sin, he answered, "yes, if it's lived up to." "The cerebellum don't keep the keys to the white gate; many a plodding soul has been sucked up the heavenly flue," Pharaoh was fond of saying, and after nodding to Hink, he turned to the congregation and said, "Is there any reason why I shouldn't baptize this man?" For a few seconds the crowd was silent; then from way back came a voice. "Go ahead, reverend, but you've got aholt of an old sinner," the voice declared, "a little dip and scrub won't do him no good. You're going to have to anchor him far out and let him spend a night or two in the deep." Pharaoh was a trifle deaf, and although he smiled, most likely he did not hear the advice. In any case he ignored the voice, and turning away from the bank seized Farr Stonebridge, the man standing next to Hink, and pushed him under the water. He held Farr down for fifteen seconds, and when he let him loose, Farr flailed up, spewing water and words. "Praise God," he shouted, "I seen Jesus sitting on the great throne. All the angels was playing their harps, and the virgins and poets was dancing in their birthday suits. And that ain't all," he continued, digging a wad of red clay out of his ear, "I heard the amethysts in hell, suffering and just crying and begging for water." After the ladies in white handed Farr a towel and led him into the shade, Pharaoh dunked Hink. After Pharaoh released him, Hink did not come to the surface right away. Instead he swam about a bit as if he were searching for something. He didn't find what he was looking for. "Hellfire," he said when he finally came up, "I didn't see no virgins. All I saw was a tractor tire, a catfish, and a goddamn big old mud turtle." What was magical for Farr was ordinary for Hink, and in truth magic may lie in the eye of the beholder. Indeed it probably resides in the plastic power of the mind, enabling a person to transform a catfish into Jesus, a tractor tire into angels, and then amid the slow wash of a river to hear the sad moans of sinners far from their God.

"When I read a book," Eliza told me last month, "when I read more than three pages, it feels like I disappear. I just go inside the book." Since Christmas Eliza has baptized herself in books, disappearing beneath the covers of Frances Hodgson Burnett's *The Secret Garden* and *A Little Princess* then swimming through a shoal of Laura Ingalls Wilder's tales. Turning pages is sleight of hand, creating illusion and transforming the self and the world. "Now you see me, now you don't," Eliza said, opening *Little House on the Prairie* and shutting the door to her room. Much as magic shines from story, so it radiates from the bindings of life. Many old ailments blind: pin and web, squint-eye, convention, and habit. Occasionally, though, one bathes in one of Mother Noon's washes, and for a moment imagines that days are stitched together not by dull task, but by a sharp wand, rippling the air and teasing glee from an hour.

I have taught for twenty-five years, and teaching has become routine. Last month at a university open house when a man asked what my students taught me, I responded automatically. "Nothing," I said. "Look," I continued, "I am fifty years old. Most students are teenagers. Even if they had something to teach I wouldn't want to learn it." The man looked disappointed and started to respond, but then he thought better and was silent. "Damn these sentimentalists, romanticizing youth and the inarticulate," I muttered to myself and turned away. My reply did not win a friend for the university, and later I felt guilty, so much so I reviewed the semester, turning memory like pages of jottings in a spiral notebook. Much as a student trying to write what his professor wanted I searched for a reply that would please the man. Suddenly halfway through the semester I found an answer, not the stuff of the old educational shell game, a soft, uplifting inspirational response, but the sinew and gristle of real learning. From Ian I learned "the rectovaginal technique of artificially inseminating cattle." "All these books we have read about Nature are fine, so far as they go," Ian said to me, "but you need hands-on experience." Hands-on turned out to be hands-in. That afternoon I met Ian in the dairy barn. Over my left arm I put a plastic sleeve. Thirty-seven inches long, the sleeve reached from shoulder to fingertips. Loose-fitting, the sleeve was ten and a half inches wide at the shoulder while the distance between the end of the thumb and that of the little finger was eleven inches. Ian demonstrated the technique on a Holstein. The cow was skittish, so he suggested that I practice on another of "the ladies," a quiet, tawny Jersey with a plastic identity tag stapled through her left ear. Printed on the tag was the name Cheryl and the number 874. I lubricated the end of the glove with soap and water. Then pushing my fingers together into an arrowhead, I leaned against Cheryl and eased my hand into her rectum. For a moment Cheryl tensed and her muscles contracted, squeezing my arm, but soon she relaxed and my arm slipped deep inside her. Then I, too, relaxed. As I rubbed the base of her tail, heat from her body washed through my arm, eroding and softening the sharp pain of arthritis. "If you can't find me some afternoon," I told Josh the next day, "look in the dairy barn. I'll be up to my shoulders in arthritis cure-all." In order to find the cervix, which lay just under the "rectal floor," I scooped several handfuls of manure out of Cheryl. "Once you get that field butter out," Ian said, "push down and you will discover the cervix. It feels like a turkey neck." In my right hand I held a foot-and-a-half-long plastic rod with a plunger at one end and a dollop sperm at the other. Carefully I inserted the rod into the vagina. The going wasn't easy. I steered a slow course, but eventually I tacked through the rings of the cervix and docked at the uterine horns. "Nothing to it," I said the next morning in the Cup of Sun, "give me a mug of coffee and bring on the whole damn herd." "Artificial insemination? Did I hear correctly?" a woman sitting at a nearby table asked Josh after I left. "It won't work," she said; "it won't take. The cow's body will reject it. He ought to know better," the woman continued, pausing to chew the matter over, "he's a professor, isn't he?" "I explained to her," Josh recounted, "that you were not quite so intimately involved in the procedure as she thought. Still," Josh continued, "she was naive, particularly when it came to that bit about your being a professor. The only thing that saves the bovines around this university is that the professors are so busy screwing each other they don't have time for higher forms of life." Josh's bile was understandable. A colleague had just hammered his latest book in a big review, calling Josh himself mundane and self-serving and categorizing the book, which I thought pleasant and even sweet, as belonging to "the Obejoyful, swift-footed earthworm, cornpone school of writing."

If "learning experiences," as my questioner at the open house would label them, rarely occur in the classroom, memorable moments do happen on the campus. Not long ago I corrected a student's manners. "You need," I said, "to learn civility." The girl looked puzzled. "Civility?" she responded, "what's that? I'm not an English major." In case any of the saved needed resuscitating, Dr. Sollows attended Pharaoh Parkus's baptizing. Googoo Hooberry had recently come down with the croup, and seeing Dr. Sollows standing by himself on the riverbank, he approached, and after chatting for a while about the weather and then the state of dry unsanctified souls, he asked Dr. Sollows to recommend a medicine for croup. Dr. Sollows obliged and wrote Googoo a prescription. A week later Googoo appeared in Dr. Sollows's office. "Dr. Sollows," he said, "when you prescribed this medicine you said it was good for the croup." "Yes, I did," Dr. Sollows answered; "there's nothing better." "Well, then," Googoo said, "I'm still ailing. How about you giving me something that is bad for croup. This here sickness has been humored long enough." As not all magical things said are polite or sensible, so many transformations lower rather than elevate. In spring when flowers push through the dirt and burst into bloom, aspiring almost to spiritual beauty, I sink earthwards, braying and kicking up words. People who tolerate me fall and winter bolt in the spring. A decade and a half ago the university administration decided to raise money by building an incinerator atop Horsebarn Hill. For a fee the university planned to accept and burn low-grade hazardous waste, generated initially from within Connecticut but then later, "after the kinks were worked out," from all over New England. The environmental impact would, the university assured townspeople, be negligible. Part of the incinerator would consist of a tall chimney, from the mouth of which ash would be dispersed and blow far and never near. The proposal did not fly. At a town meeting citizens burned a crate of statistics, turning the university's proposal itself into ash. The reluctant spokesman for the university's "position" was a man who after scraping the cinders from his hide became dean of arts and sciences. "Congratulations, on the deanship, Frank," I said, ambling into his office one April morning, "I forgive you for trying to shrink my testicles, but, by God, don't you try anything like that again." Each spring I drop by the dean's office. Although his lights are usually on and his desk cluttered with paper, I rarely catch him in. Once I saw him through a window. He even waved at me. By the time, though, I entered the building and reached his office, he had vanished magically, leaving behind a fresh cup of coffee and a pipe full of tobacco.

Platitude often starts me bucking. In kinder moments of self-awareness, I think myself kicking through jargon and hollow phrase much as spring bursts clamoring and vital through the gray woods under Horsebarn Hill. In truth, however, braying is in my nature, and I enjoy burrs under my tail. I'm on the local school board, and recently when a principal said she appointed a "task force" to examine the curricula of the school, I interrupted. "Task force," I exclaimed; "I'd prefer a committee. The idea of a task force sailing up and down Hunting Lodge Road and shelling Eastwood and Hillside Circle makes me damn uncomfortable." That evening, I am afraid, I strayed far from stall and paddock. Last year the board set seven goals for the school system, one of which was to increase children's "Motivation to Learn." One principal provided a list of things done at his school to increase motivation, including "Personal Safety Curriculum," "Shared Decision Making in the Classroom," "Youth Services Bureau," and "Here's Looking At You, 2000, Health, Safety and Self-Esteem Program." The word *curiosity* did not appear on the list, and most of the activities were directed toward producing happy rather than intellectual surroundings. Feeling comfortable does not necessarily make a person thoughtful, and when I saw "Greeting Students When They Arrive at School" on the list, I spoke. "What sort of greeting do you use?" I asked. "Do you say 'Good morning you little son of a bitch?'" When the principal looked startled, I forged on. "When my children get off the bus in the afternoon, I say 'welcome home you little bastards. How was the Hell Hole today.' And," I continued, "I'm giving my babies something important: the ability to deal with the unexpected. In contrast to all those other children who are greeted by a bland, simpering 'Good morning, Johnny' or 'Did you have a nice day, Sally,' my babies are learning to cope. Instead of being startled and knocked off stride by the unforeseeable, my children will hunker down and batter ahead, straight through to success." Often, of course, I bridle my tongue and spit the bit out only in imagination. Not long ago a parent whose child attends school in another town came to see me. In discussing reproductive matters with a seventh grade class of both girls and boys, a teacher had unravelled a condom over a banana. I liked the parent, and knowing she was upset, I was sympathetic. "How very common," I said shaking my head, trying to confuse a small voice who was on the verge of seizing my tongue and asking, "Was the banana peeled or unpeeled?"

Always fast and loose with event, memory resembles a flim-flam artist. Still the shell games memory plays are often magical. On rainy days when recess is canceled at Northwest School, the children watch movies. "Edward," I said one night in March, "I don't care what everyone else is doing, including the teachers. When recess is not outdoors, you go to the library and read. I never saw a film the whole time I was in school. For that matter," I continued, putting down my fork, "I don't think the school owned a movie projector." "Well, then," Francis said, "what did you do when recess was rained out?" "We stayed in our rooms and . . ." I began. Then I paused. Instead of finishing my sentence with *read*, I smiled and said, "and played the eraser game." "The what?" Eliza said. "The eraser game. The greatest game in the world," I replied. "Don't they teach you anything in that school of yours?" Two children played at a time, the chaser and the chased. Both had blackboard erasers on their heads. Through the aisles they ran, one pursuing the other until somebody's eraser fell off or the person chased was caught. The winner played another round while the loser retired to his desk. "Daddy," Edward said, "were you the best in the class?" "No," I answered; "I was good, but I wasn't the best." "Who was?" Edward asked. "Hayes," I replied without pausing. "Hayes had a flattop, and he was the best." Suddenly Parmer School popped out of the past and into the present, bringing with it a classroom filled familiar faces: Hayes, Eddie, Barbara, Alice my girlfriend, Mary, John, Jack, Bill, and Garth. The old hocus-pocus of memory made me sad. I longed to see those children again, to chase someone across the front of the room before Mr. Bass's desk, to race past the radiators, the rain ringing on the windowpanes above, no one behind me and nothing ahead except the long future and one laughing boy or girl.

At the end of March I actually saw myself running, albeit not in fifth or sixth grade but as a senior in high school. Stored in the gymnasium of Montgomery Bell Academy in Nashville were films of high school football games. For twenty-five dollars the alumni association wrote that I could buy a copy of MBA's 14–12 victory over Springfield in 1958. The showing occurred at four-twenty one Tuesday afternoon, before Vicki started dinner and just after Edward and Eliza got off the school bus. For me the film was wondrous. Thundering, or so I said, across the screen were Carl Babb, number 70, John Clay 77, George Creagh 81, Jackie Hooper 65, and, of course, good old 75. The film did not entertain the other members of the audience as much as it did me. "Daddy," Edward said, "why isn't this in color?" "Where are you, Daddy?" Eliza said. "Right there on the ground," I said pointing to a pile in the lower left-hand corner of the screen. I spent most of the game on the ground. At the time I imagined that I stripped blockers from the running backs. What I now saw was that the runners were far from my grasp, and on almost every play I was knocked on my bottom, so often that the seat of my trousers was black. Still, I played, and that was all that mattered; I even played some offense. I wasn't quick or graceful; in fact Mrs. Carter, the headmaster's wife and a family friend, told me years later that "we often wondered how you managed to run without falling down." I ran because I was a poor athlete, and like many people I wanted badly to do the things for which I was not suited. From football I learned that playing, not winning, was important, and through the years whenever I have coached from the front of a class, I've tried to play everybody: both the student with the agile leaping mind, and the plodder, tripping over every clod of thought. Like that field in Tennessee, the classroom is a place where games are played, a grassy area in which children tumble and block and where coaches encourage, sometimes by sprightly malice, more often by kindness.

The film was short. "Guys," I said at the end, "What did you think?" "All right," Edward answered, "but I thought this was going to be professional, or at least college." "You were wonderful," Eliza said, hugging me, "the best daddy football player in the world." "I saw a 1958 Chevrolet under the goalposts," Francis said; "it was two-toned." "My heart was just in my throat watching it, Sam," Vicki shouted from the kitchen, having left at the end of the first quarter to start dinner. That night when I snuggled up to Vicki in bed, she pulled away saying, "I am too tired to be Hovercrafted." "All right," I said, turning the other way. Soon I was asleep. I dreamed I played football. Instead of a helmet I wore an eraser. I made more tackles than anyone else on the team, and my eraser never fell off.

"Which is more useful, the sun or the moon?" Quintus Tyler asked his class in the Male and Female Select School in Carthage. "The moon," Billie Dinwidder shouted, "we couldn't get no wheres at night without it. The sun," he explained, "don't do us no good because it's naturally light in the daytime." My students are too cagey to be spontaneous, and rarely do I get such magical answers in class. Still, last Thursday Ian startled me. "I had a course with a professor who," he said, "began each class with an awful joke. I got tired of pretending to laugh, and one afternoon I went to the library and taking down the record of state employees looked up the professor's salary and the number of courses he taught. Then I estimated the time he spent grading papers, preparing lectures, and doing research, and added them to the hours he spent in class and in his office. Next I converted everything to minutes, and after dividing the minutes into his salary, I discovered that each joke cost the state thirty-five dollars." "Every man may have his price," I quipped when Ian finished, "but how many of them are worth it?" "For that wonderful joke," I said when the class looked puzzled, "the state got a bargain: nine and a half cents."

Forever pulling lively surprises out of the academic hour, Ian was a joy. Usually, however, mail and telephone startle more than the classroom. In February a writer in Georgia sent me his review of my latest book and then a selection of his essays. "I feel like a novice addressing the master," he wrote in his covering letter. "That's the stuff," I thought, picking up the article, "this review will be special." It was. "Pickering loses his way," the caption read. In the *New York Times* a reviewer discussed my being the source of the John Keating character in the movie *Dead Poets Society*, and as a result I received bundles of mail. "From the article," a woman wrote from Chicago, "I conclude you have lost your enthusiasm. Professor Pickering," she declared, "I am going to give you some free advice. Don't be afraid to be young even though you are not the youth you were twenty-five years ago and not even if you have twenty children and a harem of wives. Don't be afraid to stand on your desk again. You must give students advice. I know from the movie that the last time you gave advice you got into a lot of trouble. But don't give up. You don't have to settle for the conventional even when defeat has you by the throat." From Norfolk a man wrote saying I was his "mentor." "I was on the docks," he said, reading Walt Whitman's poetry, and rain started to fall. "It was a sign that I was destined to be a great poet. Soon I will come to Connecticut to sit at your feet." "I respond by return mail," I wrote in reply, "because unfortunately my feet will soon be out of Connecticut. By the time you receive this letter I will be in Britain. I am writing a book and must remain there for at least two years in order to do research." "Your real mentor," I stated in conclusion, "cannot be me or any stranger. Instead your mentor should be your imagination. Coupled with hard work, imagination brings success." Addressed to "Non-Finalists," a university informed me that "as of January 30, your application was removed from the Committee's file of applicants under consideration for the presidency." "We remain grateful for your interest," the letter ended, "and we wish you the best as you pursue your vocational goals in other settings." Sometimes letters are so magical that I am not sure what settings I frequented in the past, never mind settings in the future. "I was thrilled to see your name in the *Constitution* several months ago," a woman wrote from Atlanta; "I sent the clipping to my grandson and he was impressed that I knew you." After telling me about her grandson, the woman ended, asking, "Do you ever get to Atlanta any more? We'd love to see you. I remember fondly the time you lived in this house while in school at Emory University." Unfortunately I did not know my correspondent. I have spent only two weekends in Atlanta in my life, and not only did I not attend Emory, but I have never even visited the campus. I was not sure how to respond. I did not want to embarrass my correspondent who seemed old and kindly. "Your letter," I eventually began, "brought back wonderful memories of days long past." I complimented the woman on her grandson's successes then concluded by thanking her for her "warm and gracious letter." To confuse one person with another is commonplace, but in the commonplace lies magic. To discover it one needs only to observe, or listen. An hour after I replied to the woman from Atlanta, KOPE radio in Medford, Oregon, interviewed me. The program lasted an hour. I talked to the host and answered questions from listeners for part of that time. Lengthy advertisements broke the show into segments, and while the advertisements were broadcast, I sat in the study, holding the telephone in my lap. At first I ignored the advertisements, but then I heard a man say "at least honk your horn" and I started to listen. At the Door and Window Store, next to the brewery in Grant's Pass, Fred waited for customers. Fred was a convivial sort; in fact, the advertisement declared, he "just loves helping you." After buying blinds from Fred, one could eat lunch at the Applegate River Ranch House, seven miles from Roque on the Applegate River. Entrées started at $7.95, and Fred's friends could chose from a wide range of "Texas Frontier and Blue Hawaii Cuisine."

Last spring I was on a program celebrating fifty years of graduate study at the University of Connecticut. Participants rode a bus from Storrs to Hartford. I sat next to Virginia Pyle, professor of music. Virginia had just begun work on Mozart's *The Magic Flute*, the first full opera ever produced by the School of Fine Arts. To bring the opera to the stage would take a year, but she was excited, she said, and looked forward to the challenge. When I said, "That's wonderful," she asked if I would like to appear in the production. Accordingly I began rehearsals the first week in March. Not since Ransom School and Nashville had I been on stage. In second grade I was a wiseman in the Christmas pageant. One of the other wisemen, Sarah Ann MacKenzie, froze on stage. After disappearing behind the curtain I had to return, and creeping up behind Sarah Ann grabbed the sheet she wore and tugged her into the wings. In *The Magic Flute* Tony Dibenedetto, a chemical engineer and sometime acting head of the university, and I were "honor attendants" to Sarastro, high priest of a mysterious, quasi-Masonic brotherhood. Tony and I had "cameo," non-singing roles. Near the end of the opera I placed a hedge of plastic privet on the head of the hero Tamino. Then in the finale I handed Sarastro a gold crown, decorated with colored glass resembling hard candies: raspberry, grape, orange, and cherry flavors. My first appearance lasted sixteen seconds; the finale, forty-eight. For my minute on stage I put in sixty and a half hours of rehearsal. While acquaintances spent spring vacations wandering white sands and sipping planter's punch, I strode the intoxicating boards. The hours Tony and I put in made us part of the company. The lead singers rehearsed for a year, and if I had devoted less time to the opera, I would have been not simply a ringer but a charlatan. The first rehearsals I attended were held in the auditorium of the agricultural school, and feeling like an outsider rather than a participant, I only observed. Pasted to the doors of the Agronomy department were bumper stickers: "Let's Stop Treating Our Soil like Dirt," then "Plant a Tree," followed by "Have You Planted *Your* Tree Yet?" Students in the cast wore the equivalents of bumper stickers, tee-shirts with names or slogans printed on them: "National Music Camp,"

"Where the Wild Things Are" stamped in yellow under a sketch of the old library, "Greenpeace," and then across the back of a black shirt, white letters reading NINEINCHNAILS. Since the boy wearing the shirt had a long blond pony tail and looked Scandinavian, I thought the phrase Finnish or perhaps Norwegian. A student enlightened me. Nine Inch Nails was a musical group, "probably not your kind of group," the girl told me. When not performing, students read or did homework. I saw a boy race through the crossword puzzle in the *New York Times*. During two evenings Courtnay, a girl in my course in nature writing, and a tree then the belly of a dragon among other things in the opera, read John McPhee's *Pine Barrens*. Because rehearsals were new to me, I did not know how to occupy myself. To fill the hours I jotted down observations, once noting that "the role plays the person, not the person the role." By the third night, however, I began to think myself part of the production, and instead of standing aside, I was drawn into the performance. Not only did I begin to cheer the students' improvements silently, but my own small role became important, not for myself but for others. I did not want to let the cast down. I wanted to be good enough to slip on and off the stage unnoticed. Tony felt the same way, and endlessly we discussed entrances and timing. Several times we walked the stage, measuring my long stride against his short one.

Three thousand people attended the two performances. "The evening was magical," Vicki told me later. The magic resulted from hard work. As I choreograph the flow of noun and verb through paragraphs, so every moment of the performance was planned. Late each evening Paul Phillips the conductor and Nafe Katter the director dissected the rehearsal. Nafe spared no one, and as he churned through the rehearsal and approached my entrance, I shrank in my seat. I was back in third grade. I had forgotten to bring my homework to school, and knowing that the teacher was going to call on me, I tried to be inconspicuous. I failed. Nafe saw me step on the train of Tamino's robe. He saw me catch my toe under the corner of a board and stumble. The day after he told me to pretend to sing, the *Willimantic Chronicle* ran an article describing Nafe's methods, noting that among other things he encouraged "English professor Sam Pickering to lip sync the arias so he" was not "the only one on stage not moving his mouth." For the next four nights I stood before the mirror in the bathroom watching myself praise Isis and Osiris. In performance I was not bad, and if the article had not appeared, friends might have thought I sang. Indeed during the week after the performances a woman came by my office. "I just wanted," she said, "to tell you what a beautiful voice you have." On my confessing that I only pretended to sing, she got huffy. "Look," she said, "anyone with a voice as lovely as yours does not have to be modest."

For the opera I grew a beard. Despite the explanation that the beard was a prop for *The Magic Flute*, friends insisted that I was making "an unfortunate fashion statement." "When the magic goes down," I told Mike, Pat, and George one Saturday at the Mansfield Parents' and Children's Basketball Game, "You guys won't be there; I will." And it was magical, in great part because it took so much work. Of course I also had fun. Printed on white tape above two hooks in the dressing room was my name. Not since football at MBA had my name appeared above a hook. Never had I worn so much make-up, and for dress rehearsals and performances I became a greasepaint native of Asia Minor. I caked "Golden Tan" on my skin, worked "Negro" through my beard and eyebrows, filled the lines on my face with black, and rubbed white on my cheekbones, eyelids, down the ridge of my nose, and over the knobs on my brow. For two evenings I strode out of the Arabian Nights, and in my imagination thundered through Tabriz and Samarra, Kish, Dizful, and Kirmanshah, a sword whirling yellow above my head, cutting through air like birdsong. The costume also transformed me. I wore a dark blue velour tunic, trousers, and boots. Over them draped a loose sandwich board of golden cloth, decorated with bright stitching at the neck and along the sides. I enjoyed swishing about in the costume. Although the outfit was designed for the Opera Theatre of St. Louis twelve or so years ago and was battered, probably having been seen on stages in Birmingham and Knoxville, Toledo, Ames, and Bismark, the clothes made me feel exotic, just the fellow to have a harem of wives and not twenty children but forty, fifty, maybe even seventy-five. "The flute's magic sound," as my "aria" put it, even made me think better of the university and of myself. Would that an invisible hand could have scrawled advice for all students across my sandwich board, something like, "Work hard and take advantage of the university so that when the magic occurs, you, too, will be part of it."

At nine, the morning after the second performance, I went to the Campus Barber Shop, and George cut my hair and shaved my beard. Never before had a barber shaved me. I associated such shavings with the assassination of big-city crime bosses, bodies lumpy in chairs, faces bound in towels, and blood seeping through sheets and pooling in catchments behind clots of hair. Being shaved was a treat, almost worth the inevitable bullet, I thought as George wrapped hot towels around my head, then pulled and massaged, the sharp razor mowing across my skin. Afterward came brisk wintergreen and a soothing cloud of powder. I floated home, my face and imagination tingling. Eliza, however, pulled me back to earth and to Bic and Gillette Foamy. "Daddy," she said, opening the kitchen door, "You look so dorky." Despite the shave and my ordinary outfit of sport-coat and trousers, costume remained on my mind. Three hours later I boarded a flight for Rockford, Illinois. Two rows up from me in an aisle seat sat a man wearing an expensive shirt. While the collar was white, the body was striped, blue alternating with white. After every forty stripes a broad green band appeared, slicing down the body of the shirt like a drainage ditch through a contoured field. On the empty seat beside him the man put two carousels of slides. He was a dentist, and throughout the flight he raised slides of mouths up to the light and peered at them intently. The slides were colorful and from a distance resembled coral reefs, the teeth white and glowing, black holes appearing where hunks had been whacked out. The reefs must have lain off a big city, for trash had been dumped on them, here a bicycle pump, there a pitchfork. The trash attracted fish, and the eyes of many small creatures glowed from crevices. Fish were not the only animals drawn to the reefs. Near the end of the flight a stewardess knelt in the aisle beside the man and resting her left arm on his seat, cranked her head back, opened her jaws, and with the index finger of her right hand pointed to something behind her upper incisors. Although I undid my seatbelt, hunkered down, and scanned her mouth carefully, I was able to obtain little more than a fleeting glimpse of dark enamel. The stewardess, though, and her masticatory problem became pulp for thought, returning to mind the following morning as I ate breakfast in the Geneva Room Breakfast Shoppe attached to the Holiday Inn in Rockford. I was hungry, and although I suspected I was making a mistake, I ordered eggs benedict. Alas, the Hollandaise sauce was thick and pellucid and clung to the roof of my mouth like plaque. I did not finish breakfast and left the shop bilious. Music, though, bubbled to my relief, not the "flute's magic sound" but the Rockford Alpine Kiwanis Club, singing "Ida, sweet as apple cider, sweeter than all I know." The words were familiar, and I followed my ear into a meeting room and joined the cast. This time I did not pretend. I sang: "Blue Moon," "I'm Always Chasing Rainbows," and the finale "American, the Beautiful."

Back in Connecticut the "fruited plains" were still tightly budded, but the warm abracadabra of spring was on the wind. Two days later a red-shouldered hawk hunched on a limb above the woodpile, the cere sunny above its beak and its orange breast blowing and rippled by waves of white feathers. At the sheep barn lambs cried, and starlings hopped through the froth of wool along the backs of ewes gathered at the feeding troughs like matrons around bridge tables. Woodpeckers drummed in the woods, and in lowlands frogs rang and snapped, sometimes sounding like castanets, other times like tambourines. Robins appeared and ran through the damp furrows of the Ogushwitz Meadow. Frozen wetlands melted, the ground first cracking underfoot then splaying out into soft, sucking patties. Buds of alders turned a gentle purple, and thorns on honey locust seemed less stark. In the hills creeks lost their fangs as the ice rolled into globes resembling bright candies or bumpy platters of nuts.

The real clairvoyant does not envision the distant; instead he discovers enchantment in the familiar and the immediate. Sometimes I think I have wasted most of my life, blinded by the faraway and the unimportant. Bewitched by grades and the desire for a Phi Beta Kappa key, I collected A's, not learning in college. In April I flew to Tennessee and Sewanee to lecture. Whenever I was free, I slipped idea and thought and wandered down the Cumberland Plateau through Shake Rag Hollow. Ledges had broken from the sandstone bluffs, and unlike the smooth, almost polite hills of Connecticut's Eastern Uplands, Shake Rag was bony and arthritic with spurs. Curving beneath an overhang wind blew fast and cold. Far above buzzards glided over the valley. Pouring through cracks in the sandstone, water washed out limestone, forming caves that gaped and drew me. There are no caves in Mansfield, and lacking mystery the landscape is almost too benign, or so I thought in Tennessee. Perhaps I was spellbound. Copperheads and canebreak rattlesnakes live amid the boulders of Shake Rag, and although the weather was not warm enough for them to leave their dens, the possibility of seeing snakes made me more observant, if not careful, and increased the magic of my wandering. Except for the distant rumble of a jet airplane, the hills were silent, birdsong tagging across the slopes and the throaty rush of streams not seeming noise but notes of a visual symphony. A blue and gray flycatcher leapt off a branch and exploded in a flutter of quarter notes. A winter wren popped in and out of rocks, almost ringing. Warblers skittered through the trees: yellow throats, black-throated greens, and then a flock of myrtles, their yellow rumps clapping in the sunlight.

The steep bluffs resembled hanging gardens. Under ledges near the top were the remnants of the nests of dirt daubers, the tops eroded and the bottoms resembling the imprints of long, thin fingers. Wedged in a crevice a pod of spider eggs swelled. Ridges of iron cut like veins through the sandstone. Lower down the slope, water dripped forming lilypads of moss, and often the ledges seemed giant shells gathered about seaside pools. Lichens blossomed in bouquets of white, gold, green, purple, and rust. Grapevines tangled through the tops of saplings then stretched upward into tall oaks. Down the bluff basswood was as big as walls, picket fences of suckers rising around them. Buckeyes towered in columns, their bark plates more elegant than dining room and cupboard dish. Leaves had not appeared on the big buckeyes, but about them saplings had broken into leaf to gather light before the high canopy formed a basin and caught the sun. Clinging to fists of dirt along the bluff were marginal woodfern, mountain spleenwort, and walking fern, banners of this last waving over the ground then digging tips into the soil to start new plants. Early saxifrage grew on the ledges, and I chewed its leaves and then those of sweet cicely.

A thick, wet snow fell in Connecticut the day before I flew south, and I spent the afternoon walking around Tift Pond. The snow turned twigs into soft muntins and the spaces between into panes, pulling sight into hard, clean channels. In traveling to Tennessee

I quick-stepped into spring, and instead of being drawn taut my sight flowed, ebbing and spreading like a pool across the forest floor, catching leaf and flower but always lapping outward. Fern-leaf phacelia covered the tops of boulders in a blue haze. Along the ground ran bloodroot, gill, larkspur, great chickweed, white trillium, geranium, violets both blue and yellow, rue anemome, crinkleroot, and toadshade, the blossoms of this last fragrant as bourbon and its red patches so dark they seemed aged. The fuzzy stems of hepatica snared sight and shined like silver fur. Under the shadow of a rock were minute shakers of pepper and salt. Along the bank of a stream wood poppies bloomed, resembling yellow saucers from a child's tea set. A blanket of dutchman's breeches wrinkled down a shady slope; through seams in its fan-like green leaves trout lilies dangled in trumpets. A white butterfly bobbed swiftly past; a brown dusky wing spread its wings in bloom. A spring azure tumbled by, resembling a fragile scrap of blue paper. May apples grew together in green puddles, the leaves spreading out and down in umbrellas.

I almost lost all fear of snakes when I saw the May apples. According to Mother Noon tea made from them purged venom. In fact the wares of the hollow could have stocked Noonday. Dutchmen's breeches were good in poultices, and a wash made from the roots of toadshade cured pink eye. Bloodroot removed warts, and hepatica cured both piles and persistent coughs. The tonic I found in the woods was not of Mother Noon's making, though, but of spring itself, not something to make me stand on desks again, as my correspondent from Chicago urged, but something to clear the eye and give a bounce to the step. I doused myself in Shake Rag Hollow, and four days later when I returned home, spring was in the house. "Daddy," Eliza said, "you don't look dorky any more." "You obviously had a good trip," Vicki said. "Yes," I answered, "a magical trip. But then, all this is magical, too," I added, the faces of Francis, Edward, and Eliza blooming around the kitchen table. "Mr. Pickering," Lew said stepping into my office the next morning after class, "my father grows daffodils for a hobby. Each year he cuts at least ten thousand blossoms. Most he gives to hospitals and nursing homes. He says he likes to bring sunshine to people. Anyway," Lew continued, suddenly shy as he opened a box and handed me an armful of spring, "he wanted you to have these."

�“ Peculiar

"*W*riting," Vicki said as she pulled up her bedsocks, "has made you peculiar." The next morning as I sat at the card table in the living room, George at my feet, a yellow pad in front of me, and a boom of number two pencils keeping a lake of tea from washing into my lap, I thought about Vicki's words. For seven years I have written an essay month. Although essay-writing has not made me peculiar, it has influenced my life. Never have I had an original idea. In truth I find the limitations of my mind comforting. Prejudice reassures me, and each year when I discover it sprouting familiar like an ancient lilac, I am pleased, glad that I have not faded out of individuality into compost. The perennial thoughts that reassure a person, however, can undermine the writer. If an essayist wants to keep readers for longer than two or three books, he must grow different ideas or at least nurture the illusion of change.

By altering perspective one creates the appearance of originality. In my essays I forever change perspective, crawling, for example, through the yard trying to imagine how a bug sees life or spending nights roaming woods in hopes of getting a different view of familiar path and creek. After years of writing essays I now change perspective unconsciously, habitually twisting vision and challenging opinion in hopes of seeing something extraordinary. Alas, I rarely discover anything unique. Instead I have become unpleasant, not willing to let even mundane statements pass unexamined. Last week at a dinner party, a woman said she was worried about the Japanese buying land and businesses in Connecticut. "Soon," she said, "they will own the state." "That's all right," I answered, "what frightens me are not Japanese but Americans. Can you imagine what this country would be like if Americans owned it? Indeed," I continued, noting a pained expression on the woman's face, "I have written the governor asking him to sponsor a bill which will limit the amount of property Americans can own in Connecticut." The woman replied, but I did not listen. Essay-writing has made me unpleasant but not contentious. As the form of an essay is short, preventing a writer from examining any subject in depth, so I have grown flexible, rapidly shifting premises and never committing myself to particular views.

Changing perspective is a trick, and if used too often in books can itself turn into dull convention. To avoid appearing bound by contrivance as well as by thought, I have created fictional characters who wander my writings. They toy with ideas and enable me to change the point of view without involving myself in after-dinner conversation. In general the characters are bolder and less tolerant of platitude than I. Because I have lived with them for years they have shaped my character. Although I disagree with much they say, I admire their outspokenness. As a result I speak more freely and am less concerned about offending than I was before I began writing. "Don't worry," Josh told a basketball fan last spring, "education at the University of Connecticut will never dilute the quality of Big East basketball." Josh believes athletics corrupt education. For months he has preached the subject to me, so much so that when the University of Miami joined the Big East basketball conference, I dropped in on the dean. Miami, Josh informed me, was an institution that had labored hard, and successfully, to distance itself from matters intellectual. "I come to reassure you," I told the dean; "contrary to rumor Somers Prison will not be joining the Big East next fall; this despite," I added, "a catalogue of programs of which any university could be proud, programs in penalogy, abnormal psychology, criminology, and rehabilitation. Of course," I said as I left the room, "a promoter in the athletic department did tell me that because Somers could guarantee a large attendance at home games it was a most attractive institution, one, he was sure, some conference would snap up in the future."

Later, on pain of banishment from my essays I forbade Josh to mention basketball again. The night after I lectured the dean I dreamed about basketball. A kindly woman named Sarah Hedding died from a heart attack while watching a game. Even worse, I was the star, and she died applauding me. With basketball killing dream people, the time had come to purge the game from my head. Oddly, though, writing essays may also have been responsible for turning my thought nightmarish. Essay-writing is more mechanical than inspired. The writer sketches, outlines, gathers tools and supplies, draws up a time table and then sets to work: pouring verbs and nouns, sanding clauses, and hammering adjectives and adverbs. Only in dreams do my thoughts become odd. Almost as if the mind were compensating for the drudgery of essay-writing, my dreams seem creative, especially after a long day's writing. Two nights ago I dreamed that each fall a duck died, tumbling down from the sky and falling into a black pool. Gradually the duck decayed. As the duck's sinews loosened and pieces broke off, fall became deeper and colder. When nothing of the duck remained except shreds of feather and bone, winter arrived. Toward the end of February, however, a man started fishing in the pool. Instead of perch or bass, he hooked pieces of the duck. Slowly, he put the duck back together, and spring budded. By the time the duck was whole, summer was flowering. The man then tossed the duck into the sky, and it flew off, vanishing through the horizon, its wings slipping out of sight like the long gold and pink bands of sunset. Last night I dreamed I owned a magical Pembroke table. Anything shut into the drawer could be shunted back and forth through time from 1948 to the present. If he chose to do so, the person placing an object in the drawer also traveled through time. In the dream I returned to 1948. In my parents' old apartment on West End Avenue in Nashville, I found a fat yellow Persian kitten resembling Winkie, a pet I owned as a boy. Thinking that Eliza would like the kitten, I put it into the drawer, and we traveled to the present. When I opened the drawer to give Eliza her kitten, I found a small pile of dust. For a moment I was puzzled. Then I realized that even if the cat had lived for a dozen years, it would have died in 1960. Quickly I shut the drawer, hoping a kitten would crawl out into 1948.

Much as the form of an essay determines content, forcing the writer to narrow focus and preventing him from pursuing a grand vision, so writing has influenced the way I see life. I take short views, thinking days paragraphs linked not by some fundamental unity but instead by transition or contrivance. For me life now seems a series of snapshots and moods, even dreams. As an essay runs quickly to a conclusion, so I have come to believe that everything is fleeting and that people ought not to blot their few pages planning the future but should instead color the present. As careful outlines for essays are sometimes discarded, so parents cannot determine a child's future. Instead of planning distant happiness and saving money for college, I have decided to give my children present happiness and send them to summer camp in Maine. If their moments are enriched, maybe their essays in life will be successful, the moods of their paragraphs joyful, the transitions smiling.

The implications of taking short views are many. For the novelist perhaps, that person attracted to the long or large vision, the short view not only limits but depresses. For me, belief that nothing lasts is freeing, enabling me to escape ambition. Certain that my writings and people's thoughts about them will rapidly disappear, I don't suffer when critics attack me. Consequently fear of offending does not make me geld unappealing characters such as Josh. Even better, dignity is not a concern, much less a burden. Early in December a woman wrote me from Oregon. "For Christmas," she said, "I would love to present my friend Tom with your signed picture." Since I do not stock pictures of myself, I drew one. Round and squat my chest resembled a beefstake tomato. About it I planted a garden: above, an eggplant for a head, below, a turnip behind. My legs looked like anorexic cucumbers, thin and hairless, and my arms cooked, stringy okra. I dressed myself in short pants and a striped tee-shirt, the picture, Josh said, of "hermaphroditic middle-age, a man without radishes enough to criticize an athletic department."

Essay-writing has made me a collector, not of the large and the abstract but of the small and particular. As life seems a series of brief events, so my essays are composed of little things. These I sort and arrange, using words to fabricate relationships. Writing has also made me observant, often strangely so. When I receive mail, I read first for oddities, not for gossip or information. "It is an open question," a man wrote me from Oklahoma, "if the sudden collapse of the government of Margaret Thatcher had anything to do with my repeated complaints about the plagiarism in *The Works of Charles Babbage*." After Bruce Willis's office inquired about an option on the film rights to my latest collection of essays, I mentioned it to the dean, saying "if you see me strolling around with Cybil Shepherd under one arm and a Tommy-gun under the other, you'll know that I am beyond basketball and education." Of course the truth is that I find hermaphroditic middle-age comfortable, and neither guns nor Sibyls, ancient or modern, interest me. Of course the vegetative side of my nature occasionally sends out a green runner. In 1955 when I was a high school freshman I took Doris to a dance. At the dance our picture was taken. Doris wore a white formal gown that left her shoulders bare. In the picture she stood straight and stared at the camera. I leaned to the right, head tilted and eyes digging a warm channel under the front of her dress. This fall I saw Doris at a book festival in Nashville. Immediately I remembered the picture. I wasn't embarrassed. I still wanted to look down the front of Doris's dress, a feeling, I thought, that stripped years away and spoke well for both of us. Because essay-writing has led me to take short views, I enjoy discovering, indeed fashioning, links to the past, be that past fleshly or intellectual. Just after Christmas I read *Through the Looking Glass* to the children, not for the story but because I found the copy given to Vicki's father by his "Aunt Janet" on Christmas Day, 1918.

To build essays I collect not simply oddities from letters and glimpses of the past but forgotten lore. I wander libraries, and some months read more old than current newspapers. Often I learn things. Because I want Eliza to enjoy a fruitful marriage, turnip greens will not be served at her wedding reception. Moreover Eliza's wedding dress won't cost a penny. If she bites the head off the first butterfly she sees in the spring, soon afterwards she will receive a dress colored like butterfly's wings. If Dr. Dardick's medicines don't cure the croup, jaybird soup will. For his asthma Edward can smoke a hornets' nest in a clay pipe. I have also told Vicki I want to be buried barefooted. At the Resurrection animals will need their skins. If I am shod in leather, some poor creature will be forced to endure a cold and shivering eternity.

Along with lore I collect the doings of daily life. Instead of fit, I keep observant. This afternoon I was early for class so I sat on a bench outside the Wilbur Young Building and studied students. In a conversation lasting one minute and twenty-eight seconds, a girl used the word *like* fourteen times, or one *like* every 6.3 seconds. Gathering the everyday for my essays peels boredom from the hours, in the process making ordinary life interesting. Rarely do I dream about distant lands, and in the small doings of my household I find matter for essays, and more importantly, contentment. This December Christmas "flu" past as all of us except Francis were ill. Edward missed the last three days of school before vacation, and on Christmas Eve Eliza's fever climbed to one hundred and four. Sitting by her bed I wasn't really worried until she turned to me and said, "I'm not going to see my daddy ever again, and I love him." Shortly thereafter I put her in a cool tub. That night the fever broke. She recognized me, and although she did not bound downstairs the next morning, she managed to open her presents just as fast as Francis and Edward opened theirs. Christmas is for children, and I receive few presents, something I rarely think about. Still, this year as I sat shaking in the living room, I thought, "with a 103 degree temperature opening the presents you don't get isn't much fun."

As my thought was garbled on Christmas morning, so recording ordinary life distorts, making the normal seem feverish. My dog George has reached puppy puberty. "My god, he is just a you-know-what with four legs," Vicki said the other morning after the children got on the school bus. I did not respond. Instead I picked George up and scratched him behind the ears. "He's your dog all right," she said; "he resembles you." I remained silent. People who have been married for a good while do not have to speak to communicate. They can quarrel without saying a word. I knew what Vicki thought and decided the silent response better than the spoken one. With silence I always get in the last word. From writing I have learned that the truth can rarely be told. Instead the writer must create the illusion of truth. My marriage is good, and I have long wanted to write honestly about the conversation of happily married people. Rarely does a writer capture the stable humor of bedtime talk, those biting conversations which seemed fanged but which are really friendly nibbles. If I recorded the things Vicki and I said, readers would misunderstand. In November my legs begin to dry out, and by mid-January I have "the winter itch." Last Wednesday the itch was so bad I removed my trousers and ate dinner in boxer shorts, something I have never done before. I kept my shirt and necktie on, and Vicki did not notice my bare legs, probably because she was exhausted, having spent most of the day on a field trip with Edward's second grade class. That night in bed I told her I ate without trousers, adding that I was astonished that she had not noticed. "I'm beyond noticing," she said, reaching up to turn off the light; "there's nothing I want to notice any more."

Would that I could blame the itch on writing. Like the itch my writing is seasonal. During summer I write little. Instead I roam our farm in Nova Scotia, sketching plants and insects and jotting down observations about the natural world. In September I organize my observations into essays and begin writing. By winter I have exhausted my notes, and I start scratching about for new material. Sometimes I have to dig deeply, this year, for example, keeping track of the various lotions I used to battle the itch: Lubriderm, Suave Aloe Vera, Bag Balm, Oatmeal Bran Bath Treatment, and Rainbow Golden Moisturizing Oil, this last a blend of almond, olive, and peanut oil. "You will love using" Rainbow Oil, an advertisement on the bottle stated, "on yourself and on someone you love." I read the advertisement to Vicki, but she said nothing, Rainbow Oil and its applications not being things she cared to notice.

Although essay-writing can turn brown days golden, it also makes one aware of his weaknesses. The examined life always has flaws. The night before war began with Iraq, there was a prayer vigil at St. Mary's Church in Willimantic. For a moment I considered going, but then I paused. Where, I wondered, would I park? I wasn't sure, and so I stayed home and read Montaigne. The print was small, and I couldn't read much. By ten o'clock I was asleep. This past weekend four bus loads of people drove to Washington for a peace march. The buses left Willimantic at twelve o'clock Friday night and were scheduled to be back by one Sunday morning. The outbreak of war sickened me, and I knew I should go to Washington. However, I did not try to book a seat on a bus until Thursday afternoon. By then the buses were full. The trip to Washington would have been tiring, and I delayed on purpose, hoping I wouldn't be able to get a seat. That way I gained credit for good thoughts without having to be inconvenienced.

Although I neglected to wear trousers at dinner, I would not have forgotten to take a pencil and notebook to Washington. Indeed, to excuse my remaining at home I have questioned my motivation. I would have made the trip, I sometimes now think, for the wrong reason, not because of a moral commitment but only to gather material for an essay. The vagaries of the mind are curious, twisting weakness into strength. By refusing to exploit the peace movement for my writings, so this reasoning goes, I denied myself. Instead of

being too weak to sacrifice convenience for principle, I was strong
enough to resist ego and temptation. Maybe I am too hard on myself. Essay-writing forces life under the microscope, and although
study can bring knowledge, it can just as easily lead to self-deception.
No matter the occasion or the lack thereof, I carry paper and pencil
with me. Since a grand vision is beyond my essays, I sweep up small
details, gathering dust from the corners of days. Two months ago
the publicity department of the university asked me to appear in a
television advertisement. Never before had I worn makeup, and so I
took notes. While the makeup was applied, I sat on a stool in a small
room. Before me was a rectangular mirror surrounded by twenty
bright bulbs; under it was a blue and white sink. The woman applying the makeup carried her wares in a black bag. The bag resembled
a toolbox, opening up and out into a series of trays above a well.
In the box was a jumble of cans, curlers, rags, and jars: Sheer Mist
Hair Spray, Pritt Glue Stick, Hollywood Extra Cold Cream, Q-tips,
and Lip Medex, on the side of which was printed "Helps Heal Cold
Sores." Clustered in a row in one tray were jars containing "color
foundation" for skins variously described as Golden Tan, Western
Indian, Chinese II, Sumatra, and Toasted Honey. On another tray sat
squat bottles of Lydia O'Leary Covermark: Peach and Rose Beige,
Tea Rose and True Brown. Framed on the wall outside the room was
Serenade, the sort of picture found hanging over beds in motels. In
Serenade a violin and a bow lay on sheets of music while rose petals
tumbled down in pale, red dapples. Across the corridor beside the
door leading into the film studio was a picture depicting peacock
feathers in a round, blue vase.

Rarely can an essay describe in profound detail, and I accumulate
clutter in hopes of gathering the stuff, not of completeness but of
mood or distinguishing characteristic. Observation is not easy. As I
think platitudinously so I see conventionally. Because I went to the
film studio only once, my observations were flat. Usually I revisit,
on each occasion laboring to see, if not differently, at least different
parts of the same scene. To an extent essay-writing has turned life
into a series of short, repetitive walks. Day after day I take the same
walk, trying not only to collect a mass of detail but also to see new
detail. After an ice storm in January I wandered my neighborhood.
For a week until the ice melted I walked behind my house along

the cut for the power line to the marsh south of the high school baseball field. I walked to see January and the ice. Often a red-tailed hawk soared over the baseball field. In the afternoon titmice and chickadees appeared, small flocks hunting through brush. On windy mornings tall exposed trees clicked; those lower to the ground where the wind twisted in currents seemed to ache and moan. Under the hard surface of the stream caddisfly larvae fed on moss and algae. The larvae cut squarish bits from fallen leaves and, binding them into piles, fashioned houses. Drifting under the ice the larvae resembled stacks of minute green newspapers. Once the ice melted the larvae would become difficult to see. In March my attention would pitch and run with the stream, and looking under the surface of the water would demand concentration. Now the stream was asleep, ice covering it like a silver blanket, the plants near the surface immobile, one-dimensional decorations visible in the cold silence.

Ice stiffens and defines. In December the plants of marsh and streambank appeared nondescript: a low shadow cast by the heavy gray sky. Now separated by ice individual plants stood out: steeples of hardhack; somber, beaded strings of sensitive fern; dock rising in fingers; purple clusters of maple leaf viburnum; balls of sweet fern and then rushes arching, the heavy mass of spikelets first brown then yellow. As the sun broke and bent though the ice, spidery cups of wild carrot turned pale blue. Behind the carrot, cattails glowed red. Walking was easy. Brambles lost their bite as ice belled out from their stems, covering thorns. On the ground grass rumpled in flaky mounds, the nests and runs of voles suddenly apparent.

I looked carefully at grasses. After the ice melted I examined stalks under a hand lens. Rarely was I able to identify a species, concluding only that some resembled panic grasses. The essayist is a generalist, not a specialist. Because the essay is short, the writer does not have space enough to probe deeply and as a result concentrates on appearances. Surface truth may, however, be the only truth. Writing essays, of course, has shaped my opinion. More often than not depth now strikes me as misleading and contrived, even fabulous. Moreover in comparison to that of the generalist, the world of the specialist seems constricted. Unlike the specialist who knows his subject and appears intelligent, the essayist often seems fumbling, unable even to identify common grasses. Where the specialist wanders a landscape with eyes only for particular knowledge, the essayist feels compelled to observe everything. Unlike the specialist, though, whose learning can delude him into satisfaction and pride, the essayist is humbled, forever feeling ignorant and planning new study. During January I examined buds on trees. How could I have lived almost fifty years, I marveled, and not have noticed buds. Beneath the ice the twigs of swamp dogwood burned red, resembling narrow luminous torches. At the end of segments round like the jointed body of a caterpillar were the russet buds of black birch. The purple buds of speckled alder hugged twigs while catkins hung in frozen brown tassels. Along twigs of spicebush flower buds rolled in small green balls. Like a rake, battered and stuck handle-end into the ground, the buds of clammy azalea clawed upward, each at the end of its own tine and yellow lines slicing it into purple diamonds. In looking at buds I found other things: on willows, pine cone galls then splattered against a fork in an alder, regurgitation, small yellow bones buried in a bundle of gray fur.

Before I wrote essays I paid little attention to the structure of writing. Now form seems as important as content, and I labor over my essays, crafting beginnings, middles, and ends. Shaping essays has influenced my literary taste. I am now more interested in story than poetry, in particular preferring compact tales with clear divisions, endings, for example, which complete and do not stretch beyond tale into provocative mystery. As the truths described in my essays vary with place, time, and perspective, so I like tales which don't preach. Much as I wander Storrs looking at buds or listening to conversations, so I collect stories and include them in my essays. In essays I blend fact and fiction. Believing that words cannot capture reality, I pass old tales off in my essays as truth, assuming readers resemble me and care little about the arbitrary border between fact and fiction, thinking, if they think about it at all, that it is a matter for specialists to squabble about. Since my essays are short, I only squeeze brief tales into them. Still, I am careful about the stories I include. In an essay rough words sear. In the novel multiple event sweeps over roughness like Rainbow Oil, cooling vulgarity and making it seem a fitting part of life, an itch belonging to the long year of the narrative. In an essay vulgarity rises larger and often seems carbuncular, plugging mood and blocking enjoyment.

People suggest tales to me. Although entertaining in the telling, most are not suitable for an essay. Last Monday a university official who knows I enjoy country matters told me a story. Although a little crude, the story, she said, was funny, adding that "if you expand it, it might do." The story won't do. Lavernia Perleigh, a widow in Ashford, the story began, had three sons: Azra, Elijah, and Mustard. Every spring Lavernia cleaned the insides of house and boys, thoroughly washing the floors and windows of the first and giving each of the second a dose of castor oil. As Lavernia quickly mopped the floors pushing the dirty water out the kitchen door, so the castor oil ran swiftly through the boys, sending all three dashing for chamberpots at the same time. Azra got the one in the parlor, and Elijah the one on the second floor landing. There were only two pots in the house, and in desperation Mustard threw open the window upstairs over the front door and thrust his bottom out. Unfortunately at that very moment a lightning rod salesman stepped onto the stoop and started to knock on the door. The salesman was relatively inexperienced, and usually his knock was timorous. This time, however, what began softly quickly turned into a pounding. "What is it," Lavernia said, opening the door and fanning herself with a dust cloth. "Somebody done crapped on my head," the salesman shouted. "Oh, my," Lavernia said, crooking a hand on her hip and looking thoughtfully off toward the Hope River. "Let me see. It couldn't have been Azra because he's in the parlor. It couldn't have been Elijah, either; he's on the landing. It must have been Mustard," she said, pronouncing this last name louder than the others and with a sense of triumph, almost as if she had solved a difficult puzzle. "Mustard!" the salesman exclaimed; "Mustard! I'll be damned if this is any mustard. This is pure shit."

The doings of Mrs. Perleigh's family are too highly seasoned for the plain fare of my essays. Less aromatic and more palatable are the goings-on in Carthage, Tennessee, the inhabitants of which wander my writings adding a homey flavor binding feeling to place. Late one January Hoben Donkin and his wife Clulee traveled to Limestone for the funeral of Philo Ruddle. Clulee's sister Delldeena was married to Clardy Ruddle, Philo's second son and a chairmaker in Limestone. Shortly after the funeral and before Clulee and Hoben started back to Carthage, a winter storm blew up. Six inches of rain fell on Smith County. Goose Creek flooded, washing out the bridges at Sandy and Brick Chapel, forcing the Donkins to return home by way of Liberty. What with the going and coming, and waiting out the rain, the Donkins were away four days. In December Hoben brought a stray kitten home. Clulee didn't like cats, but she tolerated the kitten, hoping it would occupy Hoben and keep him from bringing home something bigger: a crippled crow or maybe a fice from the trash heap behind Barrow's store. Hoben was soft on animals, and no regimen of scolding changed him. Hoben was "the weakest, most tender-hearted, chicken-livered man imaginable," Clulee told Delldeena. "Once when he found his dog sleeping in the coal bin he ordered a ton of soft coal." When Hoben saw an animal being mistreated, he bought it from its owner. Hoben didn't pay attention to what he paid, and Clulee accused people of taking advantage of Hoben, complaining to Delldeena that Hoben was the only animal she knew that could be skinned more than once. Before going to Limestone, Clulee spent the morning churning. She made a three pound cake of butter and in the rush to leave forgot to put it in the root cellar. She also forgot to turn the kitten outside. No food was left for the cat, and when the Donkins returned to Carthage, the butter had vanished. Clulee was angry and wanted to drown the kitten in the washtub. Hoben hesitated. "How much did that butter weigh," he asked. After learning that the cake weighed three pounds, he put the kitten on the scales. When the kitten also weighted three pounds, he rubbed his hand across the back of his head, spreading his fingers and pushing hair oil into his palm. "Well, Clulee," he said slowly, looking at his palm; "I guess what you say is true. The three pounds of butter are here all right. But what I want to know is where's the cat?"

Clulee was a specialist at nagging, and occasionally Hoben was forced to leave home, and pets, for an afternoon, even a day or two. At such times he went fishing at Dunphy's Pond. Hoben prepared carefully for fishing. Always handy in the toolshed were poles, hooks, a blue Maxwell House coffee can full of damp black dirt and worms, and then under a loose floorboard behind the scythes a big jar of Enos Mayfield's best yellow whiskey. Hoben never failed to drain the jar and to catch a bucket of fish. The jar was large, and Smith Countians often speculated how Hoben could drink so much whiskey yet still catch fish. "He gets help," Turlow Gutheridge told the lunch crowd at Ankerrow's Cafe, "help from snakes." The last time Hoben went fishing, Turlow recounted, pushing his soup bowl aside, a water moccasin curled alongside him to take a nap. Hoben had saved many a snake from being run over on the highway, and having a snake against his thigh didn't bother him. For a while the snake dozed, but then he flicked out his tongue while dreaming of a nest of quail eggs and caught a whiff of Hoben's jar. That woke him up, and to get Hoben's attention he began to twist, first one way then another. Finally he tied a knot in his tail, reared, and opened his mouth wide. His throat was white and dry as a starched sheet. "That poor serpent was so thirsty," Hoben said, "that he couldn't say a word. All he could do was hiss, so I grabbed him around the neck and poured a stiff drink down his throat." After shaking his fangs back and forth and gulping a little, the snake crawled into the pond. Five minutes later he was back with a six pound catfish in his mouth. He dropped the fish in Hoben's bucket then heisted himself up for another snort. According to Hoben, Turlow continued, chewing a mouthful of rice pudding, "this went on the whole afternoon, the snake catching fish then taking a drink afterwards." "After three or four hours," Hoben said, "the serpent commenced to wander. The forks of his tongue stuck together. He chipped a fang on a flat rock and then he bunged himself against a stump, tearing a hunk of scales out of his hide." Finally, when the snake brought up a rusty trowel, then a boot, Hoben tried to stop his drinking. Getting a drunk snake to follow the straight and narrow is impossible. "I couldn't leave the poor serpent," Hoben explained; "he was so far gone he might have bit himself. I thought about bruising his head with my heel and knocking him out. Finally, though, a blackberry bush along the bank shook, and two of his buddies dropped out. One wrapped his tail around my fishing companion's neck while the other twisted about my friend's middle. Together they raised him up and crawled off, stopping every few slithers to let their old buddy hiss and hiccup." A group of truant schoolchildren were in Ankerrow's Cafe and heard Turlow's story. "Daddy," Billie Dinwidder said to his father that night, "does Lawyer Turlow ever tell the truth?" "Great God, son, of course he does," Billie's father answered; "lawyers will do anything to win a case." Essayists resemble lawyers. I will do anything to make writing work. I often lie or at least exaggerate. Occasionally I even tell the truth despite the risk of being thought peculiar.

9 Belonging

*I*n the seventeenth century John Locke argued that childhood education shaped adults, making nine people out of ten "good or evil, useful or not." Instead of being born into a rich tableau of gene and root, fibers of landscape and heredity binding and nourishing personality, children entered the world as blank tablets. Dissociated from dark, haphazard nature, children were slates on which dreams could be drawn. With the right education a person could achieve any aspiration. Now the bedrock of educational philosophy, Locke's thought supports a heavy framework of extravagant hope. To confident youth before whom the future rolls lush with promise Locke seems sensible. By middle-age, however, the cant of life and thought have changed. Years ago when my path turned upward toward drier, rockier slopes, away from the soft green plain of youth, I jettisoned the heavy burden of aspiration. Not education but heredity and luck, I now believe, determined the course of my days. No longer does the landscape ahead shimmer with promise. Instead of imagining a future in which I become luminously different, I thrust future out of mind. In hopes of traveling a little longer in the present, I labor to belong, wedging myself between mood and event, anything, I sometimes think, firmer than the soft chalk of education.

The two great hobbies of middle-age are genealogy and gardening. In gardening people attempt to plant their ways back to Nature, that sustaining habitat which Locke erased from the tablet of life. Unlike education which locates the sources of personality in the immediate, genealogy stretches through generations, family lines twisting through history like roots, drawing sustenance from the deep past and providing comfort by making one seem part of an enduring biological process rather than short-lived pedagogical method. I consider New England home, having lived here for twenty-two years. Because I have a southern accent, people ask me where I am from, not once a week but sometimes twice a day. When I first moved to Connecticut, remarks about my speech made me feel out of place. Now questions no longer bother me. Genealogy has put me at ease. "I was born in Tennessee," I answer, "but the Pickerings originally come from Salem, Massachusetts. I am," I continue, "a wanderer returned home." In 1637 John Pickering appeared in Salem. He had two sons, John the eldest his namesake, and then Jonathan Pickering, my ancestor. With Jonathan's son Samuel, the wanderings began, taking us through Bucks County, Pennsylvania, Hopewell, Virginia, and Belmont County, Ohio. After the Civil War, Great-grandfather settled in Tennessee. Four generations later my Pickering children were born in Connecticut. Without southern accents no one asks them where they are from, and they, and I, belong.

Three years ago Mother died; last year, Father, and this spring, Aunt Amanda. In middle-age the fallings from us of family and friend change from the occasional tumble into a landslide. Stripping away shallow-rooted dream, death exposes mortality, that hard reality which runs under days like granite beneath the hills of eastern Connecticut. After death passes, however, bits of lives remain behind, blown into crevices and caught in the seams of bare rock. For me these remnants provide assurance, and I gather them in hopes of creating continuity and place. In January, Vicki, the children, and I visited her parents in Princeton. Vicki's father wanted the children to have some books which he read as a child. "Grandma Johnson" gave him *The Arabian Nights*. "To my dear little grandson, Edward Dudley Johnson," she inscribed, "For his first birthday, November 29, 1912." Beneath the title she wrote poetry, "I would flood your path with sunshine; / I would fence you from all ill; / I would crown you with all blessings, / If I could but have any will; / Aye! but human love may err, dear, / and a power all wise is near; / So I only pray, God bless you and keep / you through the year." The books were in a cardboard box in the basement. On a shelf above were oddments, pieces of lives forgotten. From the shelf I brought a selection of things back to Connecticut: *The Bric-a-Brac*, the yearbook published by "The Junior Class of Princeton College" in 1886, and then the Jones Family Bible. Although the bible was battered and watermarked and worms had bored through much of the New Testament, the Family Record ran clear for one hundred and forty years beginning on September 22, 1796, with the marriage of Charles and Rosanna Atchison and ending with the death of Francis Marion Jones in Paint Township, Madison County, Ohio, on February 22, 1936. In part I brought the bible back with me because it fell open to *Ecclesiasticus* when I picked it up. In the third chapter someone had circled the nineteenth verse, "Many are in high place, and of reknown; but mysteries are revealed unto the meek." In offering consolation to the humble the verse is more sentimental than truthful. Yet it appealed to me, for dearly would I like to believe that the path of modesty leads to the palace of wisdom.

Beside the bible was *Martine's Handbook of Etiquette and Guide to True Politeness*, "A complete manual for those who desire to understand the rules of good breeding, the customs of good society, and to avoid incorrect and vulgar habits." Published in New York in 1866 and sold for fifty cents, the book measured four and a half by six and a half inches and was one hundred and sixty-seven pages long. On the front a tall, dapper, mustached, cane-carrying man-about-town raised his top hat to a young woman wearing a flowing red dress. Standing envious in the background was a pudgy yokel in a rumpled coat and porkpie hat. Vicki's great-great grandfather George W. Lattimer wrote his name so neatly on the title page that at first I thought he stamped his name in the book. Chapters of the *Handbook* focused on topics such as Marriage, Dress, Habits at Table, Evening Parties, and The Art of Conversation. Much of the advice was aphoristic: "Never ask a lady a question about anything whatever" or "Think like the wise; but talk like ordinary people." Despite the informal tone of his advice, Martine was more attracted to etiquette than to its relaxed, more substantive relative, manners. "If a lady waltz with you," he wrote typically, "beware not to press her waist; you must only touch it with the palm of your hand, lest you leave a disagreeable impression not only on her *ceinture*, but on her mind." Only in the discussion of conversation did the book have a gamy, informal flavor, and even then the wit hung too long, aging out of bite into decay. "The egotistical bore," Martine declared, was "the very *Boa-constrictor* of good society; the snake who comes upon us, not in the natural form of a huge, coarse, slow reptile, but Proteus-like, in a thousand different forms; through all displaying at the first sight the boa-bore, ready to slime over every subject of discourse with the vile saliva of selfish vanity."

More appealing than Martine's advice was the list of his publisher, Dick and Fitzgerald. At both the end and beginning of the *Handbook*, Dick and Fitzgerald advertised one hundred and thirty-three books, writing a descriptive paragraph about each and assuring readers volumes would be sent "Free of Postage at the Prices annexed." Some books were novels, tales of *The Pretty Milliner* and *The Orphan Seamstress*, even *The Matricide's Daughter*. Others were self-help manuals ranging from guides to ballroom dancing to "ready-reckoners," "lightning calculators for traders and housekeepers." *Mind Your Stops* made punctuation plain while *The Poet's Companion* contained "all allowable rhymes in the English Language." *How to Cook Potatoes, Apples, Eggs and Fish Four Hundred Different Ways* was especially suited for "those who are often embarrassed for want of variety in dishes for the breakfast table." Many books contained jokes and comic illustrations. Pickle the Younger wrote *Broad Grins of the Laughing Philosopher* while *The Plate of Chowder* was "A Dish for Funny Fellows." *Yale College Scrapes; or How the Boys Do It at New Haven* described escapades of students at "Old Yale." The Young Reporter taught shorthand; Ann Stephen, crochet; and The Wizard of the North, magic. Prices were various. *Rarey and Knowlson's Complete Horse-Tamer and Farrier* cost fifty cents; *Spayth's Draughts or Checkers for Beginners* was twenty-five cents more. *Courtship Made Easy; or The Art of Making Love Fully Explained* was cheap, only thirteen cents, a penny more than *Courteney's Dictionary of Abbreviations*. Costing two dollars and fifty cents, the most expensive book was *Duncan's Masonic Ritual and Monitor; or, Guide to the Three Symbolic Degrees of the Ancient York Rite*.

Books were not the only thing I brought back to Connecticut. On the back left-hand corner of the shelf was a child's alphabet plate, "Crusoe Finding the Foot Prints." The plate was seven and a half inches in diameter. Printed around the edge were the capital letters. In the center of the plate was a colored sketch of Robinson Crusoe and his goat, discovering a footprint. The footprint was green and looked like a hand lopped off at the wrist. In his excitement the goat resembled a shaggy ballerina, pirouetting and tossing its horns like locks of hair. Growing in the foreground of the illustration was a plant resembling a yucca with a tulip blooming on top. Behind the flower, sand stretched green down to a gray sea. For his part Robinson Crusoe wore furry brown clothes made from animal skins. Over his left shoulder he carried a homemade orange umbrella; on his right a gun rested stiffly, almost as if he were on parade. Dangling from Crusoe's waist was a sword while a wicker basket looking like a fish creel hung down his back. Crusoe's shoes were astonishingly well-made, resembling high-topped Victorian button shoes. Above them were blue puttees, "shin guards," Edward explained when he saw them, "the sort I wear when I play soccer. But, Daddy," Edward said, "Did Robinson Crusoe play soccer on the island? I thought he was alone." "Yes, Edward, he was alone," I said, then quoting Martine, added "a well-dressed man does not require so much an extensive as a varied wardrobe. He wants a different costume for every season and every occasion." "But what does that have to do with Robinson Crusoe?" Edward asked. "A lot," I replied, picking up the plate and starting out of the room before I turned, continuing, "when you are older, you will understand these things."

Feeling, not understanding, provoked my concern about belonging. In February I went to a funeral at the White Church in Storrs. Snow fell the night before, and behind the dairy, Horsebarn Hill loomed against the cold sky. Around the church windows, Chinese witch hazel bloomed yellow and fragrant. Tapered columns supported the balcony inside the church, and the red covers on the hymnals had aged into a quiet orange. The organist played "In the Garden." The familiar tune brushed softly against the bare pews and through my mind, raising prickly thoughts of that time when the dew was still on the roses and I never missed Sunday school. A voice whispered in my ear, not that of the son of God, as the hymn puts it, or even that still, small voice of calm, but instead a nagging, doubting voice. For a moment I felt out of place. Not only had I drifted from the faith of my fathers, but I had left the South. Suddenly I longed for something other than the spare, cool dignity of the Congregational Church. "Brothers and Sisters," I imagined Slubey Garts shouting, "the buzzards ain't circling just to get a suntan. There ain't no use in asking the cow to pour you a glass of milk. No, sir, you got to be doing. You got to repent. When the little train with the black engine starts across that trestle over the Jordan, you want to be on it, not strapped to the back of those red mules headed for that hot place where the stones in the creeks burn and shout for water."

Slubey's church was garish and tender with story. Occasionally Loppie Groat appeared on Sunday. Loppie was simple, and doctrine lay beyond him. One Sunday Slubey asked Loppie, "Where is the Lord?" Puzzled, Loppie looked down at the callouses on his hands and was silent. "He's everywhere," Slubey announced, waving his arms like blades on a windmill. Later that week Slubey saw Loppie sitting on a bench outside Read's drugstore, eating peanuts and drinking a Coca Cola. Thinking to drive his Sunday lesson home, Slubey accosted Loppie and repeated his question, "Where is the Lord?" To gain time to think, Loppie put down the Coke and took a peanut out of his mouth, rolling it about between the thumb and index finger of his left hand, studying it almost as if it could provide an answer. Suddenly he brightened, and flipping the peanut over the back of the bench, looked up at Slubey and in a concerned voice said, "My word, am He lost again—if that just don't take all dog." Although people often testified to the truth of the doings in Slubey's church, some accounts belong in the Apocrypha. Every Sunday night Deacon Yowsely and his daughter Cora Ann attended meeting. Instead of going by the road, they usually took a short cut, following a path that ran from their farm in Bible Hill down through Sevier Hollow and then up the ridge to South Carthage. One week a wildcat was seen in the hollow, and Cora Ann urged her father to avoid the short cut. "God takes care of his children," the deacon said; "I don't care nothing about no wildcat. In the valley of the shadow the Lord will be there with a big stick." Cora Ann could not dissuade her father, and so on this particular Sunday they went separately to Slubey's tabernacle. Despite going the long way around, Cora Ann arrived at the church before the deacon. The congregation was busy hollering and testifying how Jesus had saved them from fire and flood, drink and sweet women, when the back door of the church banged open and the deacon tumbled in. He'd been scalped. Blood ran down his face; the hair on the back of his head had been torn off, and his right ear dangled loosely like cud hanging from the jaw of a cow. "Oh, Brother," Slubey shouted, staring at him, "praise the Lord. Testify." Eyes rolling, the deacon staggered to the Mourner's

Bench. "Jesus," he began, supporting himself with a bloody right arm, "Jesus is mighty good with the little things. He can save you from tornadoes and hurricanes. But good as He is, I'm here to tell you He ain't worth a tinker's damn in a wildcat fight."

Although I liked the serenity of the White Church, I missed the extravagance of story. Still, as fond as I was of Slubey's congregation, I had long since slipped out the door. I resembled the man from Mississippi who moved to New York. After he made a big success, several people from Yazoo City asked him to return and help out his old friends. "Let me talk to the Lord about it," he said, "then I'll get back to you." Two days later he telephoned Yazoo City. "The Lord and I have talked. I told Him folks in Mississippi needed me," he recounted, "and asked Him if he would come south with me. After I spoke there was a pause. Finally the Lord cleared his throat and said, 'I'll go with you as far as Memphis.'"

One of Vicki's relatives underlined the first verse of the fourteenth chapter of John: "Let not your heart be troubled." In his funeral address the minister of the White Church quoted the verse, and when I left the building, I felt at home. Although I erased much from my life when I left Tennessee, I sketched in other things. Instead of Slubey and Loppie, I now thought about Bertha Shifney and Beaver River, Nova Scotia, where we have a farm. Bertha was sick this past winter and when Dr. Gatch examined her, she told him, "The only reason I am clinging to life is to see what in the hell is coming next." Bertha's language was contagious, and the doctor caught a dose. The next time Bertha rang his office, demanding that he visit her, he agreed, saying, "I have to see Green Malone in Salmon River, and so I'll drop by and kill two birds with one stone."

Despite spending much time by myself I am rarely lonely. Whenever days become blank I sketch a tale. Often I draw it over the telephone. "Jay," I said last week, "I'm tired of essays. Let's buy us a cadillac convertible, a long red one with fuzzy seatcovers, and get a couple of young friends and head for The Land of Enchantment." "Right," he said; "we could let our hair grow and wear it in buns." "Yes," I said, "and eat cactus and see things." We talked for ten minutes, writing a story about middle-aged men on the road to Santa Fe, young friends under their arms and cholesterol forgotten. We planned meals and stops, but then, of course, we had to return to work. "I guess I had better get back to the screenplay," Jay said; "the deadline is coming up." "Lordy," I said; "I have to finish this essay by Saturday." "Anyway," Jay added; "our hearts would not have lasted past Allentown." "That's for sure," I answered, "and who knows how good doctors are in Pennsylvania?"

Much as educators try to shape personality by marking tablets so I create belonging by filling the calendar. One Thursday night at the end of March I attended the "Invention Convention" at Northwest School. A sundae cost a dollar, and except for Francis we all ate hot fudge sundaes, mounds of vanilla ice cream chunky with chocolate and awash in whipped cream. Although the cream was natural, Francis would not eat it, and instead of dumping fudge on his ice cream, sprinkled strawberries over it. Eliza's classroom was locked, and Mr. Flynn was cleaning Edward's, so we visited Francis's room. Mrs. Titchen's goldfish and turtles were healthy, and Siobhan, the brown and white guinea pig, seemed pleased to see us and chewed up a great hunk of newspaper. Unfortunately the white mouse had died on Wednesday. Round pink warts popped out all over his stomach and he stopped eating, Francis explained, showing us the empty cage, then adding that the guarantee from the pet store was still in effect. Mrs. Titchen told the class, he said, that she would return the body over the weekend and pick up a new mouse. Before leaving school we looked at the inventions. Three won prizes: a wooden rack on which to hang wet mittens, a windshield wiper with an ice scraper attached, and for cooking marshmallows in bulk, a metal "stick" with four prongs instead of one.

This past Saturday was the Little International Livestock Show at the School of Agriculture. Students competed against each other, exhibiting pigs, sheep, horses, cattle, and chickens. I was entered in the Celebrity Swine Showmanship Class. I wore L. L. Bean boots, a white Hathaway shirt with a buttondown collar, a curly green wig, a pink and yellow necktie four inches wide and purchased in 1967 at Saks Fifth Avenue, and then a pair of red trousers, last worn in 1969 at the Princeton-Rutgers football game, celebrating the hundredth anniversary of college football. Too young to realize that I dressed to win, Eliza was embarrassed by my appearance and refused to enter the Ratcliffe Hicks arena with me. I was one of nine competitors and around my waist wore a tag with number 208 printed on it.

Blue Seal Feeds furnished the numbers, and on each tag was a blue rosette, the logo of the company and the slogan "Mark of Quality Since 1868." My pig was number 79, a seven-month-old Yorkshire gilt weighing 225 pounds, a gilt being, as I explained to Francis, "an unmarried lady pig." In exhibiting a hog the idea is to show the animal's hams to best advantage. To do so one keeps the hog between himself and the judge. Each showman carries a cane and a brush. With the cane he strokes the hog on the stomach to calm it down or whacks it on the hocks to steer it toward the judge. With the brush one rubs the hog's shoulders and flanks, or, if need arises, pushes aside any matter that might suddenly appear on the animal's backside. The serious, or unscrupulous, exhibitor, and of the latter I am one, observes his competition carefully and always flicks this matter at his nearest competitor. Pig-do splattering on the chest, or better, against the brow, can undermine the poise of even the most experienced showman. My competition was inexperienced and sensitive. For a while my friend Neil matched me shank for shank, but then I maneuvered near and he suffered a soiling, dislocating accident and slipped to third. "Daddy, you won," Eliza exclaimed, "I can't wait to show Rebecca your ribbons at my birthday party."

Wednesday was Eliza's birthday. At noon, ten six year olds got off the school bus at our house. Vicki hung balloons from the ceiling and piled peanut butter and jelly sandwiches on the dining room table, along with bowls of potato chips, black olives, celery, and carrots. On the sideboard was a Carvel cake, decorated with a pink unicorn. At breakfast Vicki told Eliza the cake had a black rhinoceros on top, and Eliza cried. The afternoon, though, was sunny and cloudless as the children played musical chairs and pin the tail on the donkey and threw beanbags through holes in a wooden clown. Only when they attacked a piñata hanging on the clothesline in the backyard did the sky become overcast. The piñata resembled Humpty Dumpty, and Eliza slept with it on the foot of her bed for a week. When Bethany knocked his left arm off, Eliza's face turned red. Then when Devon punched Humpty's head into the forsythia, Eliza burst into tears and ran into the woods. I lured her out by eating a bug—well, not a real bug, but the castoff shell of a dragonfly nymph. An inch and three-quarters long with six spidery legs, the shell was dry and crumbly. What the shell lacked in flavor, however, it made up for in effect. My munchy made Vicki queasy, and she sat down on the grass and hung her head. The children, though, thought the snack great, and later during the week their mothers called Vicki. After complimenting her on the party, they eventually said, "my child told me Sam ate a bug. I told her she must be mistaken, but she insisted, saying it was big and brown. Tell me the truth. Sam didn't really eat a bug, did he?"

The shell saved the party for Eliza, and she went to bed that night smiling, Humpty Dumpty forgotten. The workings of the mind are peculiar, however. Three years ago Mother died on Eliza's birthday, April 3. Caught up in preparations for the party, I forgot Mother. That night, though, I dreamed about her and woke up in the dark crying, a line from an old song running through my head, "Precious memories, how they linger, how they linger in the soul." Mother died on Easter, that "welcome happy morning." This April, Easter fell the week after Eliza's birthday. On the Saturday before Easter the children dyed eggs and left them in a basket in the garage for the bunny to hide in the yard. Crows nest in the woods behind our house and are fond of the eggs. Two years ago the bunny slept late and hid the eggs hurriedly. By eight o'clock when the children began their hunt, crows had already found thirteen of the thirty-six eggs. This year I got up at five-thirty and hid the eggs carefully, wedging them in trellises and drain pipes and piling tents of rocks around them. As a result crows stole only five eggs.

I have mixed feelings on the children's birthdays. Because I have survived another year I am thankful. I don't want a long life; I only want to live until my babies are old enough not to need me. Strangely, what brings happiness also brings unhappiness. As the children grow away from me toward independence, I am sad as well as thankful. The children define me. They need me, and I have duties. When I am no longer necessary to them, I fear that I'll have no reason to live, no reason to struggle against grim mood and the pain burning down my back. Still, I am needed now and will probably be needed for a snap of time more. For Edward I am writer as well as daddy. Edward wants to be a writer when he grows up, and this year he wrote eleven books, among them: *Pig and Mouse*, *The Story of Sir Small*, *Lots of Pets*, *HALLOween*, *The Adventures of Fred*, and *This Is Your Life Hank House*. The books ranged from four to sixteen pages in length and were different sizes. Two were the size of sheets of paper, eleven inches tall and eight and a half wide. Most of the books, however, were wider than they were tall, often measuring three inches in height but running six or seven inches in width. All the books were illustrated. On the back of *Pig and Mouse* was a blue table, in the middle of which sat a round, yellow pizza. Along the near side of the table were two dinner settings; stamped in the center of the left-hand plate was M for Mouse; in the center of the right-hand plate was P for Pig. While ghosts rumpled down the margin of *HALLOween*, bats flapped across pages. Although his head resembled that of an alligator and black weeds sprouted from his skull, the creature in *The Monster* wore purple and blue chainmail and waved a red spear. Edward often combined fairy tale and medieval romance. On his charger Mousekin, Sir Small fought Hoghead the giant and Hothead the dragon. When Sir Small entered Hoghead's cave, he "herd Hoghead muching on human bones. It made Sir Small shiver to think of being eaten. Sir Small sneaked under the table. Sir Small had to watch out for falling bones." In *The Adventures of Fred*, Fred's father was a "macanic" and the inventor of a time machine. One day Fred pushed "the start button by acsadint." Shortly thereafter he fought dragons and met dinosaurs and cowboys. The dinosaurs were friendly, but a "brotasarusis" almost stepped on him. The cowboys were also pleasant; unfortunately they cared little about their health, and after greeting Fred saying "hody kid how your dowing," one offered him a "sigaret."

Edward dedicated *Lots of Pets* to me and to George, our dachshund, writing "for daddy and George. This really is my dog." The dedication pleased and reassured me. Not all the children's concerns are so comforting. When George dies, Eliza told me last month, she wants to hold a funeral in the backyard. Alongside George, Eliza said, she would bury his toys: the knotted socks, the red and yellow miniature jogging shoe, his tennis ball, Francis's old green slipper, the clear plastic bone, and his sticky blue football. "We won't bury his collar," she said; "we'll hang that on the Christmas tree." She then paused and after looking at me continued, "Don't worry Daddy, when you die, we'll bury things with you, too." "What things?" I said. "Oh," she said brightly, "your teacup, the one with the cat standing on the chair and typing on a blue typewriter. Then a brush because you never brush your hair and God wants you to be neat in heaven. Then your daffodils. You could help Adam and Eve in their garden." Just that morning I ordered bulbs from Grant Mitsch in Oregon: joyous, misty glen, sunny thoughts, and a selection of pink seedlings. Since I have lost strength in my right arm, I did not buy so many flowers as in the past. Still, I ordered a few. Planting bulbs in October is part of the ritual of fall, contributing to my awareness of season and making me feel as if I belong to soil and place.

Habit fosters belonging. If I did not plant flowers in October, the month would be unsettling. People resist difference, I suspect, because it disturbs the mental landscape. In spring when daffodils bloom in the dell, I look beyond blossoms. Not only do I see a landscape which I have created, but I envision a world of which I am a part. Whenever I travel I carry habits of sight and thought with me and seeing only the familiar rarely feel out of place. In February I wandered Beacon Hill in Boston. Accustomed to roaming Mansfield studying trees and flowers, I barely noticed the steep streets and red brick houses. Instead I saw ailanthus trees, their seeds crushed into cracks in the sidewalk and then one tree, a black iron spike atop a railing pushing deep into heartwood, being absorbed yet being thrust back too, the fence swelling outward and breaking from the ground under pressure from the tree. In Mansfield not only do I see the same things, but I stamp pattern on my life. Each day I make rounds. I start with coffee at the Cup of Sun. From there I walk to Arjona and visit the English department. Then I go to Brundage gymnasium and swim, on the way dropping in at the graduate school to chat. After swimming I go to the Co-op bookstore. From the bookstore I start toward the Agricultural School where I meet classes; on the way I pop into Wood Hall to bother deans. My path is regular, so much so the secretaries of the honors program in Wood have posted a sign on the door reading, "This is not Sam Pickering's office." Of course I go into their office and say, "I'm looking for Sam Pickering. Has he come in yet?" On my rounds I harvest observation and quotation. "How are you this lovely spring day?" I said to a student last week outside Arjona. "I've just had my heart broken," she answered; "but it's not going to stop me from getting my mustache waxed." "I can't talk this morning," a woman said to me in the bookstore; "I'm going to Pennsylvania on Tuesday and have to go home and wash my underwear. You know how that is." As could be expected most of the statements I harvest are homegrown. "I know it's not a smoky man or a man who takes drugs that I'm going to marry," Eliza said Monday, adding, "I like men more when they have a mustache. I like you, too, though you do have a big nose." Recently a woman came to talk to Vicki after arguing with her husband. The woman was upset, and feeling sorry for her Edward tried to reassure her, saying, "Mommy and Daddy have set the world record for yelling at each other without getting a divorce."

Words fill days and push troubling thoughts from the mind. Unlike silence they rarely cause melancholy. Awash in words I feel at home on my rounds. When the rounds are dry, I sprinkle days with words. From responses I often reap quotations. In March I wrote the Copley Plaza Hotel in Boston, explaining that in May I wanted to write an essay called "In a Good Hotel." Prices at the Copley Plaza are thicker than my wallet, and so I asked the hotel to give me and my family "a deal" for both room and restaurant. Along with the letter I sent a copy of my latest book as bait. Although the hotel did not rise to the lure, the manager did bite, not at my proposal, though, but at me. "Unfortunately, we cannot participate in your generous offer," he responded; "May is our busiest month and we never give any discounts or complimentary accommodations or meals as we are always fully booked. Thank you for considering the Copley Plaza and thank you for the book. It is now part of our library in the Presidential Suite." Having a book in a presidential suite ought to satisfy me. It doesn't. Instead of my words on a shelf, I'd prefer me in a bed. Still, last Monday I did have a memorable conversation with Governor Weicker in the Old State House in Hartford. I spoke there as part of a program celebrating fifty years of graduate study at the University of Connecticut. I was standing near the front door when the governor came in. "Good morning, Governor Weicker," I said. "Good morning, Sam," he answered; "how are you?" "Fine," I said; "how are you?" "Fine," he answered.

"That's all," my friend Scott said after I described the conversation. "That's it," I replied. "Oh," Scott said, pausing, "I guess things were fine." "A-ok," I said, "just dandy." "But," Scott continued, "how did the governor know your name?" "Come on, Scott," I said in exasperation; "everybody knows me. One of the governor's aides told me later that the governor came early hoping he'd get to talk to me. Besides," I continued; "he is thinking about appointing me to a post in state government, a position almost as big as the one I have been offered in New Mexico." "Holy cow," Scott said; "I guess you really are well-known." "Old buddy, you better believe it," I said, standing and turning to walk out of the office. "Who knows what's next, maybe a big, red cadillac, a convertible," I said, pushing my right hand into the pocket of my jacket then jerking it out, having forgotten that after my speech I'd stuffed in a name tag, one with a sharp safety-pin catch and with "SAM PICKERING" printed on it in thick blue letters, letters big enough for a middle-aged governor to read at a glance.

I speak often. No matter where I travel, I don't feel out of place. Of course most places I visit are college towns and the sights are familiar, their buildings airport-academic, concrete bunkers sunk into bare hills or low boxes with gravelly roofs and long racks of symmetrical glass windows. One Saturday late in April I traveled to Greeley, Colorado. I got up early Sunday morning and roamed the town. Streets ran parallel and perpendicular and were numbered, not named. Along the sidewalks silver maples had just burst into bloom, their blossoms dark clumps against the blue sky. The light was pale and slight, and instead of rolling the clouds drifted, ducks occasionally rippling under them in black eddies. Across the plain, mountains rose in purple lumps. Behind the library, Long's Peak was snow-capped and as hard as bleach. The air was fresh and washed, but then in mid-morning the wind changed, blowing through stockyards thick with hoof and bone. In a spring pasture damp with dandelion and winter cress, manure is sweet. In Greeley "rendering" burned moisture out of the season, and in the still afternoon the air was ashy and choking. As I roamed the town, I looked at signs. On the south side of the sign for Winchell's doughnuts, the *n* was missing. Alberto claimed he served the "Hottest Green Chile in Town." I stood at a crossing and watched a train pass, traveling north into Wyoming. Four orange diesel engines pulled one hundred and ten empty coal cars, most owned by the Union Pacific. I went to the student center, and in Pike's Peak Ballroom where I was slated to speak found a stack of programs. On Saturday the Conditioning Spa had sponsored the

"1991 Mr. & Mrs. Natural Northeastern Colorado Body Building Championship," proceeds from which were donated to the "Right to Read Program."

Before dinner I went to Gunther gymnasium and swam. I was the only person in the pool, and two boys acting as lifeguards watched me. I did not have a towel and the university did not furnish them. The home of the president of the university was nearby, just across a broad lawn, and thinking to dash across and beg a towel, I climbed out of the pool. "Sugar," I said to one of the lifeguards, "what's the name of the president of this university." Neither lifeguard could remember the president's name, and so like a dog I shook myself and did without a towel. "Can you imagine," I told Vicki when I returned to Connecticut, "the students' not knowing the president. That guy hasn't made much impression." "No," she said, "nothing compared to the one you made. You probably scared those boys out of their wits, and they forgot the name." Vicki does not keep abreast of academic fashion. If she did, she would realize that if a man refers to a woman as honey pot, sweetie pie, or sugar, he is liable to be accused of sexual harassment. Nothing will happen to him, though, if he applies such endearments to males. Indeed social engineers will praise his advanced thinking and commitment to diversity. Consequently I have revised my speech. No longer do I address men as sport and old horse. Instead I wink and call them snookums and dreamboat. I keep up with trend so that I will be part of contemporary academic life. Vicki cares little about such matters. "Lordy," she exclaimed when I explained why I now addressed males as sugar, "you've gone off the deep end again." Vicki's statement irked me. "Deep," I said; "I don't know anyone intelligent enough to go deep. I have gone shallow. Bubba," I continued, looking at Vicki, "I have just begun to change my speech. Instead of going off an end, I have returned to the beginning."

Beevie Povey was a friend of Beagon Hackett, the minister of the big Baptist church in Carthage. Shortly after Beevie's son was born, Reverend Hackett christened him; in fact, little B.H. was the first baby christened in the new marble font. Unfortunately neither religion nor education took, and after the third grade B.H. quit school and began to hang around Enos Mayfield's Inn in South Carthage. One afternoon just after B.H.'s eleventh birthday, Turlow

Gutheridge caught him smoking a cigar and shooting craps in the alley behind Ankerrow's cafe. When Turlow told Beevie, she didn't know what to do. "Trust in the Lord," Vester McBee told her, "and He'll send you a sign." That evening Beevie got her sign, an actual cardboard sign. Billie Dinwidder had spent the day hanging posters around town, announcing that on Sunday Pharaoh Parkus, the evangelist, was coming over from Memphis to hold an old-fashioned baptizing. Billie traveled around Carthage on roller skates, and just in front of Beevie's house he tripped and dropped a stack of posters. He found them all except for one which fell behind the big sugar maple by Beevie's front door. When Beevie discovered the poster, she hurried off to see Slubey Garts whose Tabernacle of Love sponsored Pharaoh's appearance. Beevie wanted to sign B.H. up for the baptizing, but she hoped, she told Slubey, that B.H.'s previous experience in the Baptist church would not lessen the effect of Pharaoh's ministrations. "Lord, no, sister," Slubey exclaimed; "can't nobody be washed too much in glory. Besides," he continued, "little B.H. has only been dipped. This here is a real choke and blow your nose river dunking. When Pharaoh sanctifies a soul, it stays sanctified. Why," he said; "if Pharaoh had baptized Adam, you wouldn't of found him hiding in the bushes pinning leaves on hisself. No, sir, he and Eve would have been shouting in the sunshine, naked as jaybirds and stomping on Satan, their precious jewels free and just blowing in the breeze."

Beevie promised to bake B.H. a jam cake with caramel icing if he would go to the baptizing. B.H. was easily persuaded. Pharaoh's preaching was famous, and knowing that much of Carthage would be at the river bank, B.H. thought he might be able to play a few hands of poker, reckoning the pickings would be fat, particularly among those brethren preparing to renounce earthly possessions and sink their anchors in Canaan's straight and narrow channel. B.H. hid a deck of cards under his white robe, and when Pharaoh called him forth, he was dealing behind a blackberry patch. He barely had time to cram the hand down his shirt before two of the sanctified hauled him off to the river. "In the name of the Father," Pharaoh shouted as he pushed B.H. under the red water, then pulled him up, the boy snorting and the ace of diamonds swimming up beside him. "In the name of the Son," Pharaoh continued, sinking him again, the ace of

clubs foaming up as B.H. flailed his arms. "And in the name of the
Holy Ghost," Pharaoh said, pushing him down firmly and shaking
him about, this time both the ace of hearts and the ace of clubs rising
out of the depths. "Oh, Lord," Beevie moaned when she saw the
cards, "little B.H. is lost forever." "Sister, don't you worry none,"
Pharaoh said standing up after studying the cards, "with a hand like
that he's anything but lost."

Gambling can blot a copybook or a blank tablet almost as badly
as shaking sweetener on the wrong sex. Still, if one wants to belong,
not only should he keep his hand in but he ought to play through
his days, observing and collecting. He ought to fill the calendar. If
he does so, he will be happy. He might even belong. This morning
I read two articles written about my essays. One said I was "Connecticut's Agrarian politician" while the other labeled me "a serious
voyeur." The pieces puzzled me, and I wanted to ponder them. But I
didn't have time. Today is Francis's birthday. He is having a party at
Lucky Strike Lanes in Willimantic. Once the party is over, I intend
to think about the articles, provided, of course, that something else
doesn't mark my slate.

5 Pace and Quiet

"*I* don't know why it is," Raymond said, "I just want everyone to go away." May had begun. Term papers, examinations, and committee meetings broke days into slivers. People gossiped and told terrible jokes. "The horse," Tom said, stopping me in the English department "doesn't care whether his meals are served à la cart or table d'oat, just so long as he gets his baled hay à la mowed." By June classes were over, and days were whole. Jokes languished in the loft, and friends tumbled into summer's quiet, ambling pace. Since elementary school did not end until the middle of June, I hurried about for two weeks longer than Raymond. A juggler performed at the picnic at Northwest School. For a contest he drafted eighteen fathers to balance peacock feathers on their chins. I finished second and would have won had I not tripped over a first grade girl. At the picnic six collections of books were raffled. Our family won twice. I kept a picture book, Graeme Best's *Animalia*, but thinking it unfair for one family to take home two prizes, I gave the other collection to Katherine and Elizabeth Jordan, twins in Edward's second grade class. I had read two of the books in the collection to our children and did not think giving them away would upset anyone. I was wrong. As soon as we started home from the picnic, Eliza burst into tears. "I put all my luck on that prize," she sobbed, "and you gave it away and didn't even ask me."

That Thursday school ended. Grades and competitions, including raffles, stopped, and life slowed. Twice the following week, once on Sunday and then again Friday, we picked strawberries at Pleasant Valley Farm, the first time bringing home 9.8 pounds in a cardboard tray twelve inches wide, eighteen long, and three and a half high. The second time we picked a mound of berries weighing 12.7 pounds. I spent Saturday afternoon at the Benton Museum looking at the paintings of J. Alden Weir, an American Impressionist who painted pictures of Windham County and the textile mills in Willimantic. Weir's colors turned slowly like leaves in a breeze, small brush strokes flowing through patches into quiet harmony. That night Vicki, the children, and I ate dinner in Willimantic at Norma's Taste of the Island. For a treat I ordered a big bowl of "cuajto con guineos," pigs' ears and potatoes served in an orange sauce. Edward and Eliza would not taste them, and Francis and Vicki had only one bite apiece. Chewing took effort, and the ears tasted piggy. Still, I ate them all. I had settled into the summer mood of being satisfied with what life and restaurants served me. During the school year when days crack into shards, my taste is sharper, and I am brittle and critical, resembling Hoben Donkin's wife Clulee.

Clulee was so fractious that store owners in Carthage grimaced when she walked through the door. Lowry Barrow kept mail-order catalogues at his grocery, and his clerk Gerald helped people order goods for kitchen and home. One winter Clulee ordered an iron skillet. When the skillet arrived, she looked it over carefully, turning it from side to side as if it were awash in bacon grease. "This ain't the skillet I ordered," she said finally, dropping it onto the counter. "Yes, it is, Clulee," Gerald said; "the picture is right here in the catalogue." For a moment Clulee was silent as she looked at the catalogue. Then she spoke, "That's the one all right, but this here on the counter ain't it. I ordered a skillet just like that one in the picture, filled with fried chicken. This skillet you're trying to sell me is empty," she said, walking toward the door, "and I ain't buying it."

Above the front door of the Tabernacle of Love was a transom. On hot June nights Slubey Garts opened it with a long pole. Unknown to Slubey and his congregation a big black crow often sat on the sill outside the transom. Intelligent and a good mimic, the crow learned words from Slubey's sermons. One night when Slubey was shouting about Doubting Thomas and Wrestling Jacob, the crow flew through the transom and lighting on the Mourner's Bench cawed, "Repent, repent!" Up from their knees the congregation rose. "Pilot me to the shore," Clevanna Farquarson shouted, raising her arms above her head, then bringing them down to push aside Vardis Grawling who had stumbled and was moaning, "Lord, I'm coming. Show me the way." "Clear the path to glory, sinners," Slubey shouted, hurdling a pew, "I'm done toiling here." Like Pharaoh's soldiers in the Red Sea, the congregation vanished. Only Googoo Hooberry remained behind, unable to make his legs work. Cocking his head left then right, the crow stared hard at Googoo. Then as if it had made up its mind about something, it flew across the church and landed on Googoo's shoulder. For a few seconds it strolled about, examining Googoo's earlobe and pecking at a wart. But then it stopped and gathering itself rocked forward and cawed, "Repent." "Brother," Googoo said, his voice a whisper, "You are mighty kind to take such particular care of me, but this ain't my regular congregation. I'm just a visitor here. Normally I prays with Reverend Hackett in the Baptist Church up on Main Street. There ain't but one preacher there telling folks what to do, and I can handle it just a little better. But I tell you what, just as soon as I get out of here I'm going to think about what you've said. And I want you to know that I'm awfully obliged to you for taking the trouble to talk to me."

When Googoo finally laced up his traveling shoes, he high-tailed it out of the door and down the street. In his place I suspect I would have done the same, even though the month was June. Still, I might have walked out of the church. My Junes are calm, and I work to keep mood quiet and pace ambling. Shortly after Northwest School shut for the vacation, I bought a mountain bike at Scott's Cyclery right across the street from Norma's. The last bicycle I owned was a three-speed Raleigh bought when I was a graduate student at Princeton. Fifteen years ago when I moved to Storrs, I gave it away. Bicycle prices have risen since 1966. My new bicycle cost $370.40. The price included a forty dollar helmet, a bell, lock, and chain, and then attached to the front handlebars a heavy-duty basket. I only wanted three speeds, but the bicycle has eighteen. "The most reliable bicycles," Scott explained, "have lots of gears." I spend days roaming the woods surrounding the university farm. Dirt roads lead to the woods, and I needed a durable bicycle to carry me and George, the dachshund. On the bottom of the basket I lay a gray sweat shirt with Princeton Tuna Team printed on it in black letters. On top of the shirt I put George. He stretches out and despite the bumps, dozes. Near the shed where the university stores hazardous waste before shipping it to South Carolina, I chain the bicycle to a tree. Then George and I wander. No matter the temperature I wear heavy clothes: boots so I can cross wetlands; jeans; to protect myself against brambles and deer ticks, high, tight socks; a tee-shirt, usually an old running shirt; and a white sweat shirt tucked into my trousers. Over the sweat shirt I wear a work vest. The vest is orange, and when friends in the English department see me in it, they often ask if I repair roads in my spare time. The vest is practical and has nine pockets and a built-in back pack. In it I carry pencils, pads, a hand lens, glasses, wallet, pocket knife, and plastic containers for insects. During a walk I fill the deep inside pockets with plants to identify later at home. Over my shoulder I sling binoculars. In the woods I wear a floppy sailor hat. While riding the bicycle I wear my helmet. The helmet is black and white and oval-shaped, and when I rode past Tom on Tuesday, he shouted, "There goes Mushroom Man to the rescue."

As I age my thoughts about Nature change. For a long time I considered the natural world the garment of God, this despite my not believing in a deity. Now I sometimes think the whole world the body of God. If people thought this way, then perhaps they would treasure field and hill and also treat each other with reverence. In a June wood thought softens and becomes sentimental. The ideas which infect the day, raising lumps of angry tension, drain clean, and when I get back on the bicycle after a hot four-hour ramble, I am cool and refreshed, maybe even a little better. In the woods I examine things, bits of canvas, for complete pictures lie beyond my vision. Along the creek behind the high school baseball field I looked at galls: at first old ones on the gray stems of goldenrod, then willow pine cone galls, and on the ground last year's oak apple galls, the spongy inside dried to brown threads radiating out from a hard seedlike center. On new leaves galls rose in a variety of shapes and colors. Some were brown and nutty; others red and yellow. Eyespot galls spotted maples while galls resembling drops of green chocolate splattered hickory leaves. Sometimes resembling tubes, other times balls, glistening red swellings inflamed the tendrils of grape.

In quiet June the small flat surfaces of leaves suddenly became deep with life. Along with galls I found tussock caterpillars, often the castoff skins of pale tussocks but also other kinds of tussocks, dark, dappled tufts of hair rising from their backs like brooms. On beech leaves green and yellow striped cankerworms reared up while sawfly larvae circled white birch leaves, their bodies curved upward, heads attached to leaves and tails thrust out forming a live moulding. Side by side platoons of scarlet oak sawflies stripped the leaves of white oak. Resembling small slugs the sawflies glistened with slime, their heads bulbous and yellow, a dark tube running through their mid-sections, and their sides pale and trailing off thinly almost as if everything behind the head was an afterthought. Jutting out at 45 degrees between the veins of alder leaves were case bearers, sawflies which build protective tubes around themselves. On every branch leaves were rolled, folded, or tied together, forming shelters for worms.

Like worms, spiders bound leaves together, mostly small crab spiders but occasionally a big orange nursery web spider. If I tapped lightly on the nest with a pencil, often the nursery web spider rushed out aggressively. The world of leaves was large with life. Ants herded aphids, and lady bugs bustled along stems. Horned tree hoppers resembled thorns until they popped from sight. Leaf-footed bugs lumbered onto shrubs, the lower parts of their hind legs resembling gnawed hunks of leaf. Dragonflies hunted around me: white tails slipped neon through the air and then at water's edge pale, pink damselflies, their wings fluttering slowly like the blades of stalled helicopters. Busy with insects I paid little attention to birds. Warblers tumbled through shrubs about me, however, and once when I looked up, I watched a red-tailed hawk spiral high until he vanished over a ridge. Another time a broad-winged hawk flew over me, a small snake curling in his bill.

Rarely did I do more than observe. Until eight years ago I had never seen a warbler, and the closest I had ever come to a yellow bird was in a pet store. When young I rushed through day and place unobservant. The pace of my life has changed. A bad back has slowed me. Forced to pause, I now see, and as I notice comfrey at the edge of a field and smell hayscented ferns on the breeze, I think these days the richest of my life. Of course observation takes work and makes a person active. Often activity of one sort leads to activity of another sort. For some time my university has planned to build an industrial park on farm and woodland. The economic recession has stalled the plans, and a broad road linking the Middle Turnpike to the North

Eagleville Road has been abandoned, half-built. Cutting deep into a rich forest the road suddenly stops. Beyond it at the edge of the wood bluebirds nest. Beneath the trees moss-covered stone walls roll cool and green. Beside them grow huge sugar maples. University developers have not, alas, jettisoned their plans, and throughout the woods numbered stakes stick out of the ground and orange tape covered with obscure calculations circles trees. Whenever I am in the woods, I shift stakes and remove tapes, twisting the road into knots. Vicki disapproves of my actions, saying I am breaking the law. Despite its library of words, law is finally a matter of perception. For my part I no longer look through the little filter of precedent and book, but through trees and across fields. The real criminal is not the person removing stakes, but the person removing forests, bulldozing maple and oak, burying the water vole's stream in a pipe, poisoning the green world and blighting budding souls.

June has shaped my perspective. Behaviour that may be cussedness I think high-minded. Certainly life is nicer if one misinterprets the wilful. Although a good worker, Loppie Groat's mule Jeddry was the most ornery animal in Smith County. Some mornings Jeddry refused to work, and on several occasions he wandered off into the woods and stayed there for three or four days, returning home when it suited him. Loppie, however, was proud of Jeddry and always found an excuse for the mule's behavior. One day Googoo Hooberry saw Loppie ploughing Battery Hill. Jeddry was giving Loppie trouble, ploughing for a few steps then stopping. "What's the matter, Loppie?" Googoo said, squatting under a hackberry tree, "Is Jeddry sick?" "No, Googoo," Loppie answered, "he's fine." "Well, then," Googoo asked, "is he stubborn?" "No, not Jeddry," Loppie said; "he's just too sensitive. He's afraid that I'll say 'whoa' and what with the jangling of the harness and all he won't hear me so he stops every once in a while to listen."

When I was not examining leaves, I looked at flowers. Near the storage sheds on the ridge below the sheep barns, mayweed bloomed. Atop a mound of manure, nettles stood six feet tall. At the foot of the cut for the power lines a dry, sandy field was my garden. Around the edge sweet fern blew balmy through the air. Beside it rose sharp pinks. Across the rise in the middle of the field was a thicket of black locust, surrounded by a wall of raspberries, both red and black. Below the raspberries crown vetch grew in a thick circle, the center bare and the vetch pitching outward and piling two feet high around the rim. Fleabane, golden ragwort, and black-eyed Susan grew in bright patches, the disks in the middle of the black-eyed Susans almost purple in the sun and all the flowers having thirteen yellow rays. On bush clover a few last orange trumpets pushed upward. On a slope near the power line shafts of mullein turned buttery while daisies and birdfoot trefoil faded out of sight. Nearby, St. Johnswort bloomed hairy and golden. Purple and yellow clover wilted but rabbit's foot clover blossomed in a pink carpet. At the edge of the field was rough-fruited cinquefoil, the flowers more delicate than their name, five creamy yellow hearts around a bushy center. In the grass stood white beard tongue and yarrow bloomed in flats, spicy in the hot air. At the edge of the wood was showy tick-trefoil, the flowers pink in the sun then purple in the shade. At the top of the cut for the power line spires of staghorn sumac had burned beyond orange into red and a sweet cherry fragrance. Along the road to the beaver pond grew mint, whorled loosetrife, and self-heal. Beside the pond cattails flowered. When I shook them yellow pollen blew over me in clouds.

Looking at flowers I noticed little else. I heard deerflies zinging about my head, but few bit me. One afternoon George found a dead mole alive with maggots and rolled over it, one of the mole's front paws wrapping over George's shoulder and resembling the hand of a small, fat elf. At the end of June swarms of Japanese beetles appeared. Occasionally I saw a grasshopper, but the horde of late August was still distant. Warblers and sparrows dipped through shrubs, and red-winged blackbirds nagged me. High in an oak two rose-breasted grosbeaks hunted, but most birds remained invisible in the trees. At least while I bent over flowers I did not see them. Of course I often heard them and many days stood and listened to veerys. Their morning song seemed different from that of the evening: instead of chilled shafts of blue night, the song twisted like light through an icicle, refracting color and laughter. I cannot identify the songs of many birds, and listening I imagined a ballet of small girls, pink tulle around their waists, puffed satiny sleeves, epaulets of green petals at their shoulders, stems slicing across their flat chests, and red roses waving in their hair. Each girl danced oblivious to her companions, but parents glowed, and the ballet startled and charmed.

Occasionally I found flowers I had never seen before. One morning in the field I noticed two: spiked lobelia, slender shafts of pale blue, and viper's bugloss, a garish bristly plant, the stems green and speckled, the blossoms luminous purple horns with reddish stamens protruding like unruly hairs. Later that morning alongside the road to the Ogushwitz Meadow I saw poke milkweed. The plant was smaller than common milkweed, and instead of rising in pink balls, its blossoms dropped in loose creamy-white clusters. In the meadow itself common milkweed bloomed in ribbons stretching the length of the field, the fresh blossoms brisk and pink then tumbling and turning yellow as they aged. Along one side of the field, Canada thistle bloomed, fritillaries darting over it, their wings winking like orange flowerheads tossed in a wind. Below the thistle red admirals fed on the green blossoms of false nettles, and silver spotted skippers hung on vetch. Swallowtails fluttered around milkweed, one yellow swallowtail as big as my hand, the five black lines falling down each wing like drops of paint running over then drying on clapboard. A newly hatched Baltimore dried in the sun, its wings black fields, orange shrubs blooming around them and white dots like boulders speckling them. Large wood nymphs hurried past, eyespots at the edge of their forewings staring out from yellow bands. On the ground at the damp side of the field sat a painted lady. On a leaf a banded hairstreak preened, its minute tails quivering and draining into pools of blue and red at the tip of the wing.

On the bank above the Fenton River vervain rose high in bright pitchforks of blue. Behind it grew elderberry, the bushes white with blossoms. In the tall grass water hemlock bloomed, most of its umbels containing twenty clusters of flowers but occasionally one containing twenty-five. Behind it and low to the ground was forget-me-not, the blossoms delicately blue and yellow. Near the dirt road crossing the field tall meadow rue burst into starry bloom. Early in the morning red-top gathered dew and bent toward the ground in a pink haze. Beside the road itself soft spikes of Timothy shined silver, then blue, the spears fat with blossoms.

Although June was hot, the weeks did not burn. Like a slow fan, life seemed to turn through a circle, one lasting not a fraction of a second or even a week, but thirty years and blowing cool satisfaction through the days. During the summer of 1960 and for four summers afterward I was a counselor at a boys' camp in Maine. When I was twelve, Grandmother sold her farm. That summer my parents offered to send me to camp. I refused to go. My Nashville friends had attended camp for years and already knew how to sail and shoot bows and arrows. Not only was I seasons behind them in skill, but as a poor athlete I knew I would never catch up. For me camp promised embarrassment and frustration. Eight years later in Maine camp was sheer joy, and I decided that if ever I had the means I would send my children to camp, not at twelve but earlier so they would start level with other campers. This past year I spoke at several universities and made money enough to send Francis and Edward to my old camp, Timanous in Raymond, Maine. At ten and eight the boys were the right ages. At six Eliza was too young. Late in June, Vicki, Eliza, and I drove the boys to camp. When we arrived, the day was sunny, and Panther Pond shined blue. The smell of pine rippled in the air, and as I looked down the hill by the dining hall through the bunkline, memories of summers dark in the past suddenly flickered golden through my mind. Francis was assigned to Eagles, the cabin where I had been head counselor. Under a beam I found my name, "Sam Pickering, Nashville, Tennessee—1960, 61, 62, 63, and 65." I showed the inscription to the boys. At that moment I understood the satisfaction of the alumnus whose children decide to attend the college he once attended. Desire to send a child to one's old school has little to do with academic matters. A child's admission links generations and is affirmation of vitality, a visible sign of continuation and steadiness in an unstable, fragile world, a world beset by developers, bulldozers uprooting maple trees and ordered decency, paving the landscape with theory and tar.

"Spinach," Eliza said to Edward outside the dining hall, "I hope they make you eat spinach for breakfast, lunch, and dinner." Although variety is not the spice of camp meals, the food at Timanous is good, and when spinach was served, I assured Edward, another vegetable appeared with it. Vicki, Eliza, and I left camp at noon, before lunch. Slow June was in the air, however, and instead of rushing back to Storrs, we stayed in Portsmouth, New Hampshire.

In March I spoke to a convention of school administrators there. I liked the town, and repeating the visit would, I thought, be satisfying. We stayed on the waterfront in the Sheraton, the same place I stayed in the spring. In March salt was being unloaded from a freighter and piled on a pier. Now a small mountain, the pile had been covered with tarpaulins and rubber tires. Three months, though, had brought little change to either the town or my behavior. We roamed streets, looking at buildings and rummaging through shops: along Market and Pleasant, down State toward the river, and up Daniel and through Penhallow. In Prescott Park Vicki and Eliza ate Eskimo pies. Because Eliza likes Chinese food, that night we ate dinner in the Szechuan Taste. We had spring rolls, the house fried rice, chicken with garlic ginger sauce, and then beef with scallions "in Mongolia Sauce." As usual Vicki and I ate too much, and so after dinner we walked some more. At nine o'clock we went to the Café Brioche. In March I bought a chocolate croissant there and watched a steeple-jack paint the tower on the North Church across the street. Earlier in the afternoon Vicki and Eliza sat on a bench outside the church and watched a wedding party arrive in limousines. By evening all croissants had been sold, so I had a piece of German chocolate cake, and Vicki and Eliza split a hunk of chocolate mousse cake. By ten we were in bed. Although Edward's and Francis's arrival at camp rounded off thirty years, the short visit in Portsmouth helped dispel the few worries I had about them. Once I was at home, worry vanished completely. In the mail was a letter from a former camper, a "boy" whom I had not heard from since 1963. "Do you recall," he wrote, "the time in Eagles when I challenged you to a pushup contest? I was ahead until you told me it was lights out, and you forced me to go to bed. Then when I was safely tucked away, you did enough pushups to claim victory. What a dastardly deed!"

The letter cheered me. I imagined the boy in Eagles to be Francis, vexed at losing the contest but delighted too. With the boys in camp and classes over, I had time to wander, not only to the Fenton River but through the currents of my days. During the week following the return from Maine, I studied my mail, hoping to see viper's bugloss or find a bright swallowtail. Like life itself, though, the pace of mail had slowed, and the things I received were ordinary. World Wildlife asked us to increase our donation from three hundred to five hundred dollars. The March of Dimes urged us to renew our twenty dollar membership. The Connecticut chapter of the National Abortion Rights League thanked me for a ten dollar donation, and the University of Connecticut Foundation acknowledged a contribution to the Milton R. Stern Fund. From Blue Cross came a statement listing payments made to Dr. Raynor for cleaning the children's teeth. Blue Cross paid forty of the fifty dollar charges for both boys, and fifty-six of the seventy dollars for Eliza who had x-rays in addition to the cleaning. The Health Services Corporation of Massachusetts General Hospital acknowledged receiving my check for eleven hundred dollars. In May I went to Boston and the hospital photographed my bad back with a Magnetic Resonance Imaging machine. The MRI, as it is called, cost eight hundred and fifty dollars, and the doctor who read it charged two hundred and fifty. I received few bills. The week before I made advance payments on my income tax for 1991 to both state and federal governments. Distant bureaucracies intimidate me, and I always overpay my taxes. This past year was the first in which I made quarterly payments to the Internal Revenue Service, and when I figured my income tax in March, I discovered I had paid twice as much as I owed. The only bill in the mail was that for the Citibank Master Card, $803.56: $42.61 to Forestry Suppliers for an "Astro Disk" showing the constellations and which I can't understand how to use; $49 for admissions fees to Old Sturbridge Village, thirty miles away in Massachusetts, then $627.40 to the Prince of Fundy Cruise Line in Portland, Maine. The day after camp ends we plan to take the ferry to Yarmouth and spend two weeks on our farm in Beaver River, Nova Scotia, before returning for school. Also on the statement was an $81.05 charge from Williams-Sonoma. Before catching the bus back to Willimantic from Boston after the MRI, I bought Vicki a set of picnic bowls and saucers. At the time Vicki "oohed" over them, but now they are in the attic. Vicki wears a ten and a half shoe and has trouble finding shoes locally, and the final charge on the statement was $71.50 from Johnson Brothers Shoes in St. Louis. Unfortunately the shoes did not fit, so Vicki sent them back, and we received a credit of $68 on the statement, the difference of $3.50 being the postage charge. I paid the bill the day it arrived. I always pay bills immediately and have never paid interest on a charge card. Not to pay on time seems feckless, an emblem of a developing, irresponsible age.

During the week I received one check, a payment of $19.78 from Dominion Resources, a dividend from stock Grandmother gave me many years ago. In contrast to the single check, I received a bundle of advertisements. From September 18–22, I could attend "The Taos Conference on Writing and the Natural World" for $595, excluding transportation. Filling out a travel survey would bring me, Sears promised, "complimentary Travel Coupons from major airlines and hotels with a guaranteed value of over $75.00." Chrysler Corporation reminded me that the Plymouth needed servicing and sent a book of coupons. With a coupon, tuning the engine cost $49.95. Servicing the cooling system was $48.95, and having the car greased and oiled and getting a new oil filter installed cost $18.95. Declaring that the "University's aim" was to receive donations "from 60% of the alumni by June 30th," Sewanee, my undergraduate college, urged me to contribute to the Alumni Fund. A retired dean announced publication of his memoir, the proceeds from which went to a scholarship fund. I wrote a puff for the memoir, and in his announcement the dean cited my remark and then George Bush's statement, "It was kind of you to think of me."

Catalogues were out of season, yet a few lingered like the last trumpets on bush clover. Claiming to be "America's Oldest Mail Order Company Since 1865," Orvis sent its fall catalogue. I did not look beyond the cover. Similarly I did not go beyond the table of contents of the *South Atlantic Review*, an academic journal. Of the seven literary essays and twenty-four reviews, five of the former and seventeen of the latter had colons in the titles, and I avoid reading articles with colons in titles, the colon being a sure indicator of learned illiteracy. I wanted to throw away the policy book of the Mansfield School Board, fifty-eight pages of legalisms that block discussion of education and children. Since I am a board member, however, I was obliged to keep the book. I stuffed it in the lower right-hand corner of my desk, knowing that I would never open it. What I did look through was the Smith & Hawken summer catalogue and the "1991 Fall Wholesale List" of the Daffodil Mart. Among the bulbs on the list was the Mount Hood, an old standby white daffodil. A hundred "top size" bulbs cost sixty dollars, and I longed to buy them. Planting hurts my back, however, so I controlled the longing. "Crafted of Plantation Teak," a five foot long Giverny Bench in the Smith & Hawken catalogue appealed to me. The bench curved high in the middle and unlike the bulbs would have supported my back. Unfortunately it cost $595 and buying it would have given me a pain in the lower back, in the wallet area. If the bench were mine, I would put it in the dell where I plant daffodils. In spring I would sit on it, look at daffodils, and catch up on magazine reading. I subscribe to many magazines, most of which I don't get around to reading. During the week *Time, Smithsonian, Audubon,* and *World Wildlife* arrived. I stuffed them in a wicker basket in the dining room. They will stay there for six months after which I will pile them on a shelf in the study and the children will slice them up, recycling them in collages.

When *The Scroll*, the alumni magazine of my college fraternity, arrived, I looked at the obituaries, "The Chapter Grand," as the column is called. I also looked at the section listing people who contributed money to the fraternity in 1990. Among the twenty-one alumni from Sewanee who contributed, I recognized five names. I thought about flipping through the magazine and examining pictures in hopes of seeing an old friend, but I did not. Thirty years changes people, and I knew I would not recognize anyone. Numbers interest me. When *Humanities News* published by the Connecticut Humanities Council came in, I ignored the articles. Instead I read the list of contributors and among the three hundred or so names recognized eighteen. Ten years ago the University of Tennessee Press published one of my books, and I looked through the press's "fall/winter" catalogue. Typically entitled *Narrating Mothers: Theorizing Maternal Subjectivities*, most of the books seemed incomprehensible. Beside the advertisement for *The Hippies and American Values* was a photograph of three boys with long hair standing in a patch of marijuana. From the distant perspective of now, the late 1960s and early 70s look harmless, even naively moral. How, I wondered, had I lived through the 60s and missed the hippies. To be sure, I ate in restaurants named Stone Soup or Wonder Bread and danced around Maypoles with thin girls wearing loose dresses and Aquarius buttons. Once I went to a wedding in a corn field and skipped down a furrow, a blue balloon tied to my wrist. Still, I did such things for carnal, not cultural, reasons.

The week brought few personal letters. A friend wrote that she was going to Romania to adopt a child. From Oregon a man sent an account of a dog catcher's chasing his daughter's poodle. Swept up in the spirit of the chase, the dog catcher bounced over curbs and drove through yards, even crossing a playground and disrupting a children's basketball game. Not until neighbors got into their cars and pulled out in front of him, poking along at ten miles an hour, did the dog catcher give up, and even then he said he stopped only because his shift ended. A teacher sent a copy of a final examination a student wrote on Shakespeare's *King Lear*. "Lear," the student began, "is a play that start apart and all come together at once. This play finishes totally oppisite of the way it begins." This spring in his school journal, Edward wrote, "We took daddy to the airport early so he would not piss the plane to Pittsburgh." Edward wrote quickly, and influenced by the p's in *plane* and *Pittsburgh* carelessly turned an *m* into a *p*, recording more of the truth perhaps than he realized. At Timanous campers write letters home on Sunday. Even though the boys had only arrived on Saturday, they wrote. "I love this camp," Edward declared while Francis said, "I think I am going to be happy here." "Hallelujah," Vicki exclaimed.

Only a couple of pieces of mail were odd. From Atlanta a friend sent a postcard. On the front was a photograph of a statue, a woman holding a bird above her head. The woman was bare-breasted, and the bird looked upward, its bill an arrow cleaving the horizon. The statue, the card stated, represented the Phoenix and was "the symbol of resurrected life," the "rebirth of Atlanta from the burned ruins left by General Sherman's troops." "Observing this woman performing an unnatural act with a bird," my correspondent wrote, "I naturally thought of you." From New Hampshire came a review of my latest collection of essays. "This man's mind is a lively, if somewhat bizarre place," the reviewer stated; "you wouldn't want to live there, but it's a fascinating place to visit." "Listen to this," I said to Vicki; "the reviewer says I am fascinating." "Not to me," Vicki answered, chopping up sausage for dinner, "I live next door." Explaining that Storrs could be dull in the summer, a friend in the English department sent me photocopies of some of the official stationeries he collected over the years. "They are useful," he wrote, "for crank letters." Among the papers were letterhead sheets for The New York Public Library, The Fluvanna County Library in Fork Union, Virginia, and from Inyo County, California, sheets off the desk of Thomas J. Sawyer, Director, "Substance Abuse Services."

Suggestions can be addictive. Suddenly June seemed slow. The next morning I got up at 4:30 and loading George into the basket rode off to the woods. At sunrise mist hung over Valentine Meadow like a blanket, shreds of wool dangling down into the creek or blowing over the trees. At six o'clock I was at the beaver pond watching a beaver slap its tail on the water and then dive only to surface three feet away, a thick stump rising from the bottom. Two kingfishers chattered through the trees, their breasts feathery white cutaways. I had never seen a beaver in the wild before, and for twenty minutes I watched silently. But then as the beaver continued slapping and diving, I thought of professors swimming laps in Brundage pool. "Lord," I exclaimed; "summer is really dull. I can't stand it any longer." At ten o'clock I was in the Women's Center, harvesting vocabulary. "What are you doing?" Josh asked when he saw me leaving the building. "Just trying to perk things up," I answered; "June would bore the behind off an elephant."

The next morning I mailed a letter to the Willimantic newspaper. "I read," I wrote, "that the League of Women Voters is studying the school systems of Willington, Mansfield, and Ashford in hopes of bettering the education of children and the finances of towns. In a time of enlightened sensibilities I find it scandalous, indeed wounding, that a credible organization retains a sexist name. The very name institutionalizes sexism, invalidating males, dehumanizing them as others. By its exclusive nomenclature the organization disparages the minority gender. Must men be forever marginalized as gardens of delights, playmates, little frogs to be turned into princes then back into frogs as the whim of a matricentric society? Such sexual privileging has educational costs, devaluing an entire gender and drilling helplessness into character. In a better world of global humanhood there will be no place for gender segregationists or sexual supremacists." A week later the letter appeared in print. That night two men called to tell me, as one put it, "right on, brother." Three days later

I received a letter from an officer of the League, urging me to join and help change the world. Otherwise, she said, I would forever vent "my anger and frustration" in the local newspaper. I wrote back, thanking her for the letter, but declining the offer to join the League, explaining that changing the world was not "my thing." I wanted to leave that, I said, "to the boys, and the gals, in the backrooms." And that was that. Not another word was said. "What did you expect," Josh said; "June is slow. Nobody gets angry now. You should have written in November."

9 Outrageous

Since the letter was short, I read it to Vicki. "I am writing in response to your talk in Pennsylvania. I believe you are a very intelligent person and most erudite. Your presentation helped me see that there is another dimension that needs to be added to your life. You have a need for an additional person to come into your life. That person is Jesus." He signed his letter, "A Caring One." For a moment Vicki was silent. Then she exclaimed, "That's outrageous." Bold, tasteless, concerned, the letter may have been, but it wasn't outrageous. This past year I spoke many times. Before I traveled, I assumed that most people thought as I did. Now I realize that the Connecticut I inhabit resembles an island, not one surrounded by rough, tossing seas, but a place nevertheless cut off from the main.

I am an old-fashioned conservative, believing government ought to limit its meddling to public policy and leave private lives private. Although not an activist I support unrestricted access to abortion, thinking the individual, not the state, ought to decide whether or not she has a child. Fifteen years from now, I occasionally say in a talk, if my daughter Eliza becomes pregnant no one will force her to have a baby if she doesn't want to. After I spoke in Pennsylvania, a man approached the lectern. "Doc," he said, "half the people who walk into abortion clinics don't come out alive. Think about it," he said, pointing the index finger of his right hand at my bosom. Never had I met anyone opposed to abortion, or at least anyone who said so openly, and I was at a loss for words, and if the truth will out, for mathematics also. At first I couldn't figure out what the man was talking about and thought my high school knowledge of fractions and percentages had finally fallen out of memory. "You should have quoted Tennessee Williams to him," a philosopher at the university later told me. "You should have pointed your middle finger at him," she explained when I looked puzzled, "and said, 'Screw you.'"

"Nice people, the right sort," Vicki said, interrupting my reverie, "don't discuss religion, or for that matter, any high-minded topic. The letter is outrageous." "No," I replied, "what's outrageous is something I did last month." While on a speaking trip in Nebraska, I taught a class in composition. For me words resemble lumber, and writing is a matter of carpentry, not inspiration. Planing and squaring, the writer creates effect. He builds deceptive haha's. To break a long expanse of trimmed words, he sets out window boxes and tosses a prefabricated gazebo into the middle of a paragraph. Under the rug of prose lies plywood, not hard wood, flooring only strong enough to support the light glance of everyday reading. For the regular teacher of the class, writing was elevated and almost mystical. Words came trailing clouds of glory, and, she seemed to think, as the bible put it, "In the Beginning was the Word." As I demystified writing, turning it into a dirty, everyday activity of joists and rafters, stories framed with levels and T-squares, the teacher grew restless, and frowning made her displeasure apparent. As the speech in Pennsylvania moved "A Caring One" to write, so the teacher provoked me. Although I often hung humor about the walls of my essays, some jokes, I told the class were too rough to use. "In the name of clarity," I said, "let me give you an example." Because she felt poorly, a man, so the story began, took his wife to the doctor. The doctor examined her carefully, and afterwards conferred with her husband. "Mr. Richards," he said, "your wife is basically in good health. What she needs is more sexual intercourse, and I am prescribing it three times a week." "Well, that's just fine, doctor," the man said, nodding, "just fine. You can sign me up for every other Thursday." "Now that," I told Vicki, "was outrageous." "No," she answered, "silly, and maybe a little naughty, but not outrageous." Nebraska, though, is not Connecticut. When I finished the story, the teacher rose from her desk and, like that biblical carpenter Jael delivering the children of Israel from the Canaanite Sisera, dismissed the class, her voice sharper and more pointed than a ten-penny cut nail.

Writing has made me aware of detail. When I see a brick wall, I look beyond height and color to pattern: basket weave, running bond, whorling square, and Jack-on-Jack. Observation has become habitual and changed my vision of the world. Instead of reflecting a period such as Georgian or Federal, life now seems a mass of distinct details, many odd, some even outrageous. On my travels I note detail. In Pennsylvania I addressed the annual convention of the School Counselors' Association. The counselors met at the Milton Hershey School, and before talking I ate lunch in the Camelot Room, the school cafeteria. The room resembled a medieval banqueting hall. Students ate at round tables. Shields hung on the walls, and the Middle Ages had even been baked into plates. In the center of each plate was a knight jousting. Around the rim of the plates were medallions of romance, the heads of Merlin, Sir Galahad, the Lady of the Lake, King Arthur, and then, appropriately enough, between the King and Guinevere, Lancelot. In the lobby outside Camelot was a fair of exhibitors. A good many advertised schools: Keystone Junior College, Triangle Tech, Empire Beauty Schools, the Pittsburgh Institute of Mortuary Science, and the Diesel Institute of America. From the booth of this last school I picked up souvenirs for the children: flat black and white magnets cut in the shape of big trucks. Printed along the side of the trailers was the school's slogan, modeled after signs on the Interstate, "Enter To Learn" and "Exit To Earn." Accelerated Development, Inc., of Muncie, Indiana, published books. I stopped at their booth when I saw the title *The Psychology of Creative Dating*. How, I wondered, did creative folks spoon in Indiana. The front of the book jacket was red. Across the middle the title ran in yellow script; beneath it bloomed a rose, white and thornless. The authors, the jacket stated, had "extensive exposure to a broad spectrum of people through their chosen careers" and had compiled their data through "personal experiences as well as discussions and surveys." What, I pondered, would the old Hoosier poet James Whitcomb Riley have thought. The frost was clearly off "the punkin." Life along the Wabash had speeded up, and "Little Orphant Annie" had lit out for the singles' bar, tossing her stories about "the Gobble-uns" into the garbage can by the back door.

A little success can make seeing true detail difficult. When I travel people often show me sided experience. Despite my insisting that old beams and battered subfloors interest me, I am taken to paneled restaurants and driven through split brick neighborhoods. In May I gave the commencement address at Missouri Western State College in St. Joseph, Missouri. I arrived in St. Joseph early in the evening. The town looked interesting, and thinking that I might not have a chance to explore during the next two days, I wandered the night, from third to tenth street and back and forth along Faraun, Jules, Francis, Felix, Edward, Charles, and Sylvanie. Pony Express riders began their runs in St. Joseph, and a gigantic iron figure galloped past Hardee's, headed not for the plains of Kansas but a flat parking garage. Over the squat modern buildings downtown, nighthawks dipped, twisting through the lights after insects, their cries shrill and the white bands on their wings blinking in and out of the dark. I ate dinner at Johnny Fry's, a hamburger and Mexican restaurant in the Wholesale Row, a block of warehouses built in the 1880s. I had a taco salad and a Boulevard Wheat beer. Since I was the only customer in the restaurant, I poked about. Johnny Fry's was named after the first Pony Express rider, a boy later killed during the Civil War. Mounted on walls were the heads of animals: buffalo, deer, elk, and then a mountain goat, its horns thick, tight spirals. A turkey stood alert on a platform while a Canada goose tilted down over a table and a bass rose open-mouthed for a fly. The bar itself was cherry and weighed two tons. Made in Philadelphia, it had been shipped to Chadron, Nebraska, in 1871. Above green and red stained glass on the left side, the waitress told me, were two bullet holes. I examined them. They were big enough to stick my thumb through and looked drilled rather than shot. If they were bullet holes, they were so high above the bar that the person shooting was either a terrible shot or was aiming at a basketball player, a professional one and not a guard either, but a center, a giant raised on bonemeal, nitrogen, and peat moss.

During the next two days talks and receptions filled my schedule. The people at Missouri Western had, however, read my books, and they provided time for me to roam. They even furnished guides. Sheridan Logan, a banker who had retired home from New York and had written a book about St. Joseph, showed me the city. The great stone homes downtown had run to boarding houses, their cornices chipped and channeled by time and change like the red bluffs north of town. Spring had been wet, and beneath the bluffs the Missouri River flowed muddy and orange in the sun, the surface broken by rolling gnarls of roots. In the distance Kansas stretched silent to the horizon. Rattlesnakes and copperheads lived beneath the bluffs, and I longed to wander through the brush along the river, startled by stirs in the grass or stones unwinding. I went to the old cemetery; iris and peonies were blooming, most of the former blue and the latter pink or white. One man had achieved, his tombstone stated, "sweet oblivion of self," a state of being, I thought wistfully, beyond the essayist, forever stamping the hours with words.

The next morning John Rushin, a biologist, took me for a walk along a nature trail established by both the college and the Missouri Department of Conservation. Near a pond a rat snake pulled itself through leaves. Perched on a dead limb was a bluebird, a caterpillar curling in its bill. A brown thrasher bustled through trees, and a great crested flycatcher sat quietly in the shadows, its breast pale yellow. In the distance a cuckoo sang; farther off a meadowlark seemed to answer. I ran my hand across the deeply rippled bark of a hackberry; nearby in the shade honey locusts were dying. Because I could not spend long on the path I looked mostly at plants. A last showy orchis glowed purple and white. Spring onions were high, and in the grass at the edge of woods bladder campion, black mustard, goat's beard, and spiderwort bloomed. Milkweed and musk thistle pushed up, and under a railing beside a road field bindweed raised its small pink trumpets.

After lunch Sue Robinson drove me to the cattle auction in Atchison, Kansas. The auction was held in a creamy yellow, metal-box-shaped building across the railway tracks and beyond and behind grain elevators. The holding pens gleamed silver in the light. Parked about them were rows of heavy-duty pickup trucks; a sticker on the rear bumper of one truck read, "Have You Hugged Your Tractor Today?" Many trucks pulled trailers. Sue's husband Tom brought two cows to the auction: a tired, bony Hereford and a sleek Angus who had lost her calf and wasn't worth feeding for another year. In the pens cattle bunched in calm groups. Occasionally a lone cow became frightened and shied against the rails, eyes spinning white then dark like windows on slot machines. Two men riding mules drove the cattle down chutes to the auction, after which they drove them back to the pens. The inside of the building resembled an amphitheater. In front center was a small dirt enclosure fenced about on three sides by wooden rails. The back side of the enclosure was concrete and formed part of the side of the building. Above it was the auctioneer's box, really a small room. Cattle entered the pen from a gate to the auctioneer's left. Three men with whips kept the cattle moving and after they were sold drove them out a gate to the auctioneer's right. On the wall to the side of the exit gate was a sign reading, "All Guarantees & Statements Are Based on Information Received From Livestock Owner." The words "Are Based on Information Received" were printed in black letters, the rest in red. On the other side of the auctioneer was an electric sign divided into four parts: Headcount, Average Weight, Total Weight, and Price. When, for example, two Hereford steers were driven in the pen, the Headcount registered two; the Average Weight, 627, and the Total Weight 1255. The price reflected bidding, and the steers sold for 87.50 cents a pound. Most of the cattle sold were old cows and young steers. Many were mixed breeds, but a goodly number of Angus, Hereford, and Holstein appeared, these last, Tom said, destined for McDonald's. Bidders held small cards marked with red numbers and flicked them unobtrusively when they wanted to buy. Tom's cows sold for $1200, and he bought ten steers for $4300. Grass in his fields was high and plentiful, and he would graze the steers summer and winter, selling them the first Saturday in January. During summer they would put on a pound and a half a day. "Money in the field," he said, "is better than in the bank."

Buyers sat on steep concrete rows built up and around the pen. Every eight or so feet was a spittoon, a large yellow and black can which once contained six pounds and fourteen ounces of Nugget Chili Beans or a red and yellow can which held seven pounds two ounces of Hunt's Tomato Ketchup. Everyone in the building seemed a farmer or, like Tom who was an engineer, a part-time farmer. Most wore seed company caps, the one-size fits all kind. I wore the same type of cap, one given to me by the man who rebuilt the foundation of our house in Nova Scotia. The cap was claret. Stamped on it in white letters was "Charles F. Winship Contracting South Ohio, N.S. 742-5784." Although I wore jeans I did not look like a farmer. Machines break people, and many of the men watching the auction were bent or twisted. One man had lost half his right foot, and several others were missing fingers. Still, I felt at ease, and I clambered about chatting ignorantly about cattle and manuré, as I said fancy city friends pronounced it.

The trip to St. Joseph was a high point of spring, in great part because I had never been to a cattle auction before. Familiarity, of course, reduces the exotic to the everyday. At a dinner not long ago I was served by a waiter wearing rings on all his fingers, thumbs included. On my remarking that *Goldfinger* must be his favorite movie, he misunderstood, thinking I asked where he bought the rings. "At Wholesale Jewelers," he said, "on Harkridder, next to the Piggly Wiggly." When I heard *Piggly Wiggly*, the waiter and his hands almost became ordinary. On the flight to St. Joseph, I sat beside an eighty-eight-year-old woman. During the trip she told me about the death of her husband three years earlier. She described his funeral and then that of her son who died in infancy at eleven months. Two years ago her grandson died from cancer, and now his father, her son-in-law, had it. She said she was in good health although both hips had been replaced and she had recently had laser beam surgery on her eyes. Out of context the conversation seems grotesque. But it was not. She reminded me of all the grandmothers and great-grandmothers I have known. She was returning to Missouri after visiting her daughter in Pittsburgh. Her son-in-law gave her a pink orchid, and she wore it on her dress. Because her eyes were weak, she had recently run a stop sign and had lost her license. She had never been stopped for a traffic violation before, and did I, she asked, think it was fair "for them" to take her license away. How, she said, was she now going to get to the grocery. No, I thought it wasn't fair. Old age and death were ordinary; that was the way of life, but it wasn't fair. Context makes not simply the story but the man. Last Tuesday I met one of the campus firebrands coming out of the university bookstore. In his hand was a new book. "Well, Fred," I said, "what do you have? Another text damning us all as racist and sexist?" "No, Sam, not exactly," he said; "I'm having trouble with my boy, Billy. I don't seem able to talk to him, so I bought this," he said, showing me the book, *Conquering Shyness: The Battle Anyone Can Win*.

Custom and knowledge create context and make things ordinary. I don't have a study, and I write in the living room at a card table. Because I have bad disks in my upper back, I wear a neck brace. The house is small and noisy, and in order to enjoy a semblance of quiet, I also wear a Norton Hearing Protector, model 4520P with a noise reduction rating of twenty-three decibels. The protector resembles black and blue ear muffs, linked by a silver band covered in dark plastic. Vicki and the children are used to my head gear. To a stranger I might look odd. Familiarity also breeds understanding. Out of context not only appearances but children's remarks startle. "I wish Mommy was an alligator," Eliza said three weeks ago, "because an alligator can choose if its babies will be girls or boys and I would have two sisters." If I were Eliza and had her brothers, I would also want sisters, and as nice as Vicki is, having an alligator for a wife would be deliciously outrageous. Earlier this spring when Eliza's bath was too hot, I stirred the water to cool it. In the tub was a boat she fashioned out of tin foil, Saranwrap, and popsicle sticks. I didn't notice the boat and in stirring the water swamped it. Eliza was furious. "You bastard," she shouted. I was startled. Five year olds, even peeved ones who have ridden schoolbuses, usually don't call their fathers bastards. Eliza did not know the meaning of the word, and I didn't get angry. Instead I remembered a remark I made to my father when I was young, a phrase I learned in school. "You think you are hot snot," I said, "but you are nothing but cold boogers." Even today the memory makes me cringe in embarrassment. I can't recall what angered me. Father, though, was removing something from the icebox. "Sammy," he said quietly, "you could be right, but that isn't the best way of putting it. A gentleman would say something else." "Eliza, I am sorry I sank your boat," I said, "but please don't use that word. It's not nice. A lady would say something else." I was an only child. Two brothers have toughened Eliza. "All right," she said, looking angrily at me, "you jackass."

Outside the house domestic chat can appear heavy with implications. In a kitchen the table, not conversation, is laden. "Vicki," I said, one morning last week, "I have saved some money. Why don't we take the year off? Maybe we could take the family to Corfu like Gerald Durrell's mother did when her children were young." "Don't be silly," Vicki said, "can't you see I'm busy?" From the toaster she removed a bagel and spread peanut butter on it for Eliza. For Edward she poured a bowl of Crispix and for Francis a bowl of Frosted Mini-Wheats. After the children caught the schoolbus, Vicki went to the grocery and I went to the university bookstore, forgetting Corfu until I saw a case of travel books. "I told Vicki this morning," I said to Suzy, "that we ought to take the year off and live in the Greek isles." "Did she give you an aspirin?" Suzy asked. "She didn't give me anything; she fed the children," I answered, "and then went to Stop and Shop."

Startling plans are rarely part of my familial life. Still, Vicki takes the occasional chance, buying a state lottery ticket every two or three months for a dollar. When she does not win, she is momentarily irritated, usually criticizing the winners as people "who won't know what to do with the money." Extravagant expectation is part of contemporary life. On Saturday Vicki entered four contests in the "Caldor Super Stakes '91." The prizes were a 1991 Chevrolet Lumina van worth $16,500; a $10,000 shopping spree "at your local Caldor"; tickets for a Major League baseball game "for you and 25 friends"; and a movie "per week for 4 for an entire year." Vicki was not going to fill out the coupon for baseball, but because I have never seen a big league game, I asked her to complete it. I am not a gambler and labor not to take chances. I have never had a speeding ticket, and I always pay cash when I purchase something. Occasionally, though, I enter contests, and hope springs outrageous. Although I no longer look at the form for Publishers' Clearinghouse, I will fill out an entry blank on the inside of a Hershey Bar wrapper or from the back of a box of Wheat Chex. In the past Vicki and I have won things. In fifth grade I won seat covers at the Parmer School PTA dinner. Seven years ago I won a case of Coca Cola at a drawing after a five mile road race in Nashville, Tennessee. Just two years ago Vicki won a curling iron at the opening of the Big Wheel store in Willimantic. The iron was worth five dollars, and Vicki sold it for fifty cents in a tag sale.

Little details define. Making me part of place and family, they give me particulars to love. Some people, of course, wish to destroy the context of contemporary life and on its ashes raise their worlds— places, I am afraid, in which power is mentioned more than compassion or duty. Recently an article appeared in a university newsletter in which the author attacked what he called "stereotypes," noting that speech containing stereotypes reflected "a desire *not* to share power." "We'd like to invite you for breakfast, but we don't have grits" was cited as an example. The stripping away of quirk and peculiarity reduces people to abstractions. Abusing an individual does not come easily, and I did not become angry at Eliza as I watched her boat drift toward the drain. Abstractions are a different, easier matter, those *theys*: bad children, bad religions, bad races. After the grits of life are dumped down the disposal and one does not see people eating bagels and buying rings next door to the Piggly Wiggly, then the auction can begin, complete with holding pens, useful mules, whippers in, and cattle cars.

Jeddry, Loppie Groat's mule, was a different sort of mule, having little to do with ideas or auctions and spending most of his time ploughing or working on the highway. Although he was a hard worker, Jeddry was stubborn and some days wouldn't go. "Loppie," Vester McBee said one morning as she made her way to the Hampers, "are you going to let Jeddry do as he pleases? Where's your will power?" "Sister," Loppie answered, his face redder and wetter than the Cumberland River in flood time; "my will power is just fine. What's slowing things up is Jeddry's won't power." Flowing with trend is comfortable. When fashionable thought laps high, won't power takes will. I roam woods and fields, sending snagging roots into detail. Amid the swift current of rote morality, I clutch at dirt. I want to absorb sustenance enough to be outrageous, to be an individual breaking the surface of custom and rippling opinion. I want to know where I live; I want to taste the grits which flavor my town and university. Unfortunately schools teach only the simple languages of mathematics and literature. Rarely does one learn the alphabet of land. In April I spent a night in the Capital Hotel in Little Rock, Arkansas. The following morning I walked along the bank of the Arkansas River. Mockingbirds led me in and out of sycamores and knots of sweet honeysuckle. Paulownia was in bloom, great fans of purple trumpets brassy in the thin light. I had never seen a paulownia before, and I took a handful of flowers back to the hotel. The manager of Ashley's, the hotel restaurant, could not identify the flowers, but the chef, she said, was a "tree expert." "Dogwood," she said when she returned from the kitchen; "he's sure the flowers are from a dogwood, or maybe a magnolia." Trees, the chef clearly did not know; eggs benedict, he did, and after pressing the blossoms flat in a tourist brochure, I ate a hearty breakfast.

Spring was hot and early this year in Storrs. The first week in April saucer and star magnolia bloomed together, and behind the house spicebush blossomed low in the woods like a yellow mist. The flowers on the silver maples by the graveyard were thick with pollen, and when I smelled them, my nose turned orange. Like man, trees have seasons only they are called bark, bud, flower, seed, and leaf, this last enjoying three and sometimes four seasons. Classes ended the second week in May. One morning shortly thereafter I got up at three o'clock and graded examinations. By ten I had finished and was watching bumblebees drifting black down the yellow falls of a golden chain tree. Along the edge of Valentine Meadow black cherries were white, their flowers drooping heavily like pale tired fingers. In the crooks of branches tent caterpillars spun silk sleeves. I chewed the nutlets of sweet fern and sucked May apples. Afterward I washed my hands with sassafras leaves. No matter the temperature, whenever I smelled autumn olive I felt cool and clean, almost as if I had bathed. For the first time I looked at flowers on the horse chestnut. Blossoms rose upward in spires. On each spire white flowers clumped together in groups of four or five like sunbursts. Red dots speckled the petals of the upper flowers in each group while yellow ran across the petals of the lowest bloom. Near the end of May yellowwood slipped into bloom. The flowers hung down in white clusters, some a foot and a half long, thick at the top then trailing off to slim elegance. The clusters resembled diminutive cassocks. Their beauty was priestly, and their perfume smooth and ceremonial. In its almost ecclesiastical formality yellowwood seemed to demand reverence. What evoked awe, if a person can feel awe for a tree, was the tuliptree in the field at the front of the campus, down the slope below Gulley Hall. The trunk was thirteen feet, two and a half inches in circumference. Over it bark ran thick and vallied, making it resemble a massive forehead, furrowed by age and exuding patient wisdom. A magnolia, the tulip-tree is the tallest hardwood in the country. Like leaves of sweet gum, ginkgo, and chestnut, the leaf is individual and recognizable. When looked at from tip to twig, it reminded me of angel's wings made by a short, squat, awkward child in a deep winter snow. Green and blue-veined, the buds resembled old hands pressed tightly together in prayer. Inside, the blossom was yellow. Outside, the petals slipped through color, the base pink, the middle light-green, and the top yellow or orange. The fragrance was creamy with the hint of a tang; sometimes I thought it peppery. In blossom the tree glowed, a green candelabra of yellow cups. The children were still in school, and I walked through May alone, accompanied only by George the dachs-hund. Days were humid, and one afternoon near the end of a nine mile walk, George collapsed in the deep grass under the fence along the road running up the side of Horsebarn Hill. I picked him up and dunked him in a cattle trough, and he recovered. Despite the collapse, George rarely broke my solitude, and away from people I acted oddly. Every day I walked past the tuliptree. Somehow it seemed not simply a tree but part of me, the sight of it vital sap, nourishing joy and bringing vigor to my spring.

Late in May, black locusts in the woods behind the sheep barn bloomed, their perfume cleaning the morning and stilling the mind, making one forget worry and even the sharp spikes on the locusts themselves. I spent days roaming the woods behind the barns. Near the locusts was the old wolf pen, a quarter acre surrounded by a wire fence twelve feet tall and then a wood fence, the slats of which were seven and a half feet tall. Within the enclosure a zoologist once kept wolves. At the south end of the enclosure was a small study with a built-in desk and shelves and three windows, one of which looked into the pen. Much as the enclosure had run to bramble, so remnants of research littered the room: a page torn from a desk calendar and dated November 18, 1979, a rusting gray stool, a cloth glove with blue and yellow stripes around the wrist, and a five-pound can of Tree Tanglefoot "for safeguarding trees and vines against destructive climbing and creeping insects." If spread in a band three inches wide and a sixteenth of an inch thick, Tanglefoot, the label claimed, would protect greenery against cankerworms, tussock and gypsy moth caterpillars, grapebud beetles, and climbing cut worms. Crumpled across the floor and desk were papers; in their creases were mouse droppings. Printed along the right side of each piece of paper were small boxes in which the zoologist charted the doings of the wolves. Down the left ran a list of the activities themselves, among others, tail wag, stalk, lick face, wrestle, jump at, play invitation, bite, and group ceremony.

A dirt road wound along the ridge through the woods. On either side were open spaces, almost glades, in which trees had been cut and grass grew high and thick. At first the spaces puzzled me, and I wondered why the trees had been chopped down. Then the wind changed, bringing the fragrance of death, that heavy greasy smell which makes one close his mouth and breath through his nose. The glades had served as burial pits for farm animals. In the pits used now animals were not buried carefully. A sheep's head protruded from a hole, the skin rotted away, the eye sockets empty, but the teeth in place and the mouth open, gasping and full of flies. Scattered amid the rock and sandy soil were tufts of hair, patches of black, leathery hide, and hunks of bone, a jagged leg bone with a split hoof attached and a pelvis arching like a cathedral. Atop a fresh mound was a small blue and white box, containing, I read, three *Prime* condoms. Beside the box was a used condom. What sort of people, I wondered, made love on a mattress of dirt and over box springs rotten with the bodies of sheep and cattle, flies slipping over them like a loose sheet.

North of the pits, the road spread wide into a thoroughfare resembling main street in a film-maker's cowtown. No gunfighter strode through the dust, however. Instead of dark clumps of saloons and then a block of hardward store, sheriff's office, and livery stable shimmering in the heat, sheds and trash fell off the road back under the trees, as if they, too, had been buried in shallow graves, beam and door jutting out of the ground instead of hoof and horn. To one side of the clearing was a hill of sand for sidewalks in winter. In a shed was a horse-drawn wooden wagon with red wheels and a blue carriage. Each October at the horticultural fair, students put the wagon on the grass near the Ratcliffe Hicks building, and parents pushed children onto the high seat and took pictures of them. Pigeons and starlings nested in a big metal shed with a tin roof. In the shed were a red New Holland baler, A&S hay wagons with tall sides and rubber wheels, and a McCormick lift for loading hay into the loft of a barn. Behind and to one side of the shed were concrete pipes. On the other side was a black mound of tires. In front of the tires were nineteen pink soft-drink machines manufactured by the Vendo Company. Twenty-two inches deep, three feet wide, and six and a half feet tall, the machines once dispensed milk and juice. For fifteen cents one could choose from four drinks: whole or chocolate milk from the university dairy, iced tea, and then fruit punch blended at the creamery from concentrates: grape, orange, lemon, and passion fruit.

Across the road a ridge of trash curved in a hook like a huge scythe. Twenty feet tall at its highest point and running for over a hundred yards, the trash curved gently along the broken spine of a stone wall and around a field green with nettles. Jumbled together were treads for steam tractors; small, black motors; hot water heaters; sterilizers five feet tall and with silver barrels at the top; mattresses, one decorated with orange peonies; a steam shovel, pink roses dangling from the cabin; metal silos, their sides caved in; oil tanks; and from a pickup truck two doors stamped blue and white with the university seal. On the ground near a box of Christmas ornaments was a church program for March 3, 1991. "We are STILL living in Bible times," the minister stated on the third page, "and the Book of Acts continues to be written!" Miracles occurred. *"Malachi was in a coma,"* the bulletin reported, "after God touched him through prayer, he came out of the coma, has left the hospital and has returned to school!" "Kenneth HAD Leukemia! After the HAND of the Lord touched his life his white blood cells are starting to attack the disease. DOCTORS," the bulletin declared, "ARE ASTONISHED!"

A few paces past the trash I turned down the ridge following the cut for the power lines to the pumping stations on the Fenton River. On muggy days dragonflies drifted before me like dark motes, sometimes more than twenty. At the beaver pond, scores of the castoff exoskeletons of dragonflies clung to plants. Once I found a stack of three exoskeletons, the first tight on a cattail, the second clutching the back of the first, and the third grasping the second. In sunlight the dragonflies were colored arrows: white tails, checkered darners, skimmers blue and red, and twelve spotted. In the morning dew, some dragonflies were slow and would occasionally perch on my fingers. Gentle ridges curved across their wings, veins breaking them into small plots resembling rice paddies seen from the slope of a distant mountain. Along the sides of the cut grew alder, hornbeam with its seeds stacks of green pagodas, black cherry, and great bushes of multiflora rose. Binding leaves together with strands of silk, insects nested on trees and plants. A small gray caterpillar rolled the ends of ferns into balls and forming a chamber caulked it with dung. Leaf beetles ate willow leaves. On a rose leaf a snipe fly sunned itself, a gold band behind his eyes and white spots down his sides. The orange and blue caterpillar of the Baltimore butterfly rested on plantain; in the Ogushwitz Meadow caterpillars of the monarch butterfly ate milkweed. Under a leaf the larva of a lady bug chewed a minute green worm, not stopping when I turned the leaf over roughly.

Water ran off the ridge down the center of the cut. Two-thirds of the way down, the cut turned up and rolled over a rise with a road on top. Before the rise the water drained off to the side, making a small marsh. Beyond the road the ground was dry, and birds appeared. Bluebirds sat on wires, and goldfinches hurried through brush. A flock of cedar waxwings hunted high through the trees, and verrys called. An oriole swooped across the cut, its flight seeming to sag halfway like heavy orange clothesline suspended between two poles. At the bottom of the cut was a dry creek and a sandy field gone to sweet fern, black locust, and flowers: birdfoot trefoil, daisy, yellow hawkweed, purple clover, cow and crown vetch, the first blue and the last pink and white. The field was a butterfly garden. Monarchs, yellow swallowtails, and dark spicebush swallowtails wobbled across the road beside the pumping station. From the vetch hung skippers and painted ladies. Some days the air seemed a breeze of butterfly wings: yellow, white, orange, brown, and black. One morning I took a butterfly net to the field, but I didn't use it. Instead I searched for birds' nests in the locust. When the sun rose high and burning I walked along the dirt road to the beaver pond past the police target range and the white trailer with a black pistol painted on the side. The thick, silvery cocoons of Promethea moths hung from spice-bushes. A grackle sat in a low shrub in the shallows of the pond. Warblers hunted around the edge of the pond, and red wing black-birds flew aggressively across the water. At the end of a branch a tree swallow groomed itself, its back a formal blue shading into black and its breast icy white. Along the shore, bullfrogs rumbled. A garter snake unwound and slipped away through the grass. Along the Fenton River laurel bloomed, the flowers spiral crimps unraveling into pink platters, silk stitching woven into the middles. Reflecting up from the water sunlight dappled tree trunks, turning them yellow, then green, then white. Cinnamon ferns hung above a bank color-ing it red and green, softening the current and slowing the pace of the day.

Rarely did I meet people on my walks. Once I talked to a university policeman. On the road near the pumping station he had almost run over a wild turkey. A flock lives in the woods. Despite my wander-ings I have yet to hear or see a turkey. Late one afternoon a gunner shot cans in the Ogushwitz Meadow. He did not wear a shirt and his hair hung down his back in a pony tail. On the ground at his feet was a styrofoam cooler filled with Budweiser beer. His rifle was heavy gauged, and the bullet crackled and whooshed. He drove a battered Chevrolet pickup truck. The truck sat out of doors, and the paint had aged into a dull, soft blue. In the back of the truck against the cab was an eddy of beer cans. On the floor of the cab on the passenger side was another wash of cans. As I recorded the names of plants, so I copied down the truck's license number. The noise made by the rifle irritated me, but then later I noticed the blossoms of cow wheat for the first time and forgot my irritation.

Although I am too old for my character to change, roaming the woods did affect me, making me less conventionally responsible. With burial pits and cow wheat on my mind, I traveled to Conway, Arkansas, for a conference on southern autobiography. My flight was four and a half hours late. On arriving I sent my suitcase to the local Ramada Inn and went straight to the opening banquet. I wore my traveling clothes: khaki trousers, striped shirt, and jogging shoes. "Darn, Sam," Pat Hoy said when I sat down; "I didn't think you would make it and all the work I put into tonight's introduction would have gone to waste. What are you going to talk about anyway?" "Pat," I answered; "the flight was hellish. I am too tired for jokes." Then I told him about something that happened recently to my friend Jay. In the spring Jay lectured at several schools in Virginia. To break his trip he spent two days in Charlottesville with Ann and her husband. When Ann met him at the airport, she said, "Jay, the whole town is looking forward to your talk. Every tree on the campus has sprouted a poster with your picture, and we are expecting at least a thousand people. Can you handle that big an audience?" Jay was flabbergasted. He could not remember agreeing or even being asked to speak at the University of Virginia, and silently he swore he would never take another drink. Nevertheless he said, "I'm ready to go, but what title," he added after a pause, "did you finally decide on for the talk. We discussed several." "Fact into Fiction," Ann said. "That will attract all the high-powered critics in the university." "Good," Jay said. On the trip in from the airport, he tried to organize his thoughts. He had no luck, and when Ann drove through the campus and stopped in front of a red brick building, he knew he would have to wing the lecture. "Come on, Jay; don't dawdle," Ann said as she bound up the steps. "We're late and people are waiting."

Once in the building she hurried down a hall, turned a corner, and opened a door. Jay stood straight, took a deep breath, and walked into an empty room. Behind him a voice said, "April fool."

"That's fine, Sam," Pat said when I finished the story, "but what are you talking about?" "Pat," I repeated, irritation seasoning my tone, "I just got off that damn plane, and I am not in the mood for jokes." The joke had been well-organized, I thought, for during the meal three other people asked about my talk. The keynote address was scheduled for eight o'clock. At ten minutes before eight, I finished a cup of coffee and, standing, said, "I am going to the auditorium and listen to the keynote that I am not giving." As I walked out of the dining room, Judith, a writer whom I had not seen in four years said, "Sam, hello, I am really excited about your talk tonight." Thirty seconds later I was in the car of the vice-president of the University of Central Arkansas racing across town to the Ramada Inn. My suitcase was in the lobby of the motel, and from it, I pulled underwear, suit, shirt, tie, belt, shoes, socks, and a speech which I thought I was to deliver two days later, in short almost everything except a toothbrush. I undressed then dressed while the vice-president sped down back streets, bumping across the Union Pacific railway tracks, treating red traffic lights as if they were yellow, all the while praying a policeman didn't stop him and find me in the car naked. At ten minutes past eight I rushed onto the stage, my tie loose around my neck and shoes in my hands, trees still in them. Pat began his introduction. It was richly flattering, and by the time he finished I was dressed. "Sam," Judith said afterwards, "you really are a showman. Some people actually thought you had forgotten the talk, but I told them the whole performance was staged. I was right, wasn't I?" "To fool you I'd have to get up mighty early," I said; "you are right. Pat and I planned everything but don't tell anyone. This will be our little secret."

Walking shortened my patience as well as my memory. The last week in May I gave the final speech or "benediction" at a peace festival in Storrs. Two thousand school children attended. For class projects they invented "peace" games, board games in which winners overcame the urge to fight and won their ways to peace, not money or land. Several guests attended the festival. From the Soviet Union came a young mother; she did not speak English, but she brought a game created by her nine-year-old daughter. Although uninvited, two local "war activists" appeared and handed out broadsheets urging that the United States withdraw from "the godless, pro-communist, and anti-American United Nations." "By virtue of a secret agreement made at its founding," the broadsheet declared, the "military arm" of the United Nations "would always be controlled by a communist." The men wandered about and were ignored until they discovered the Russian woman and began haranguing her. They did not harangue long. I handed my benediction to a friend, and in the good cause of peace fired a salvo of hearty, salty language. I urged the men to decamp, threatening to thrash them out of regularity into an unexpected bowel movement. They left, and twenty minutes later I gave my speech, preaching the importance of temperance and pacifism. "Jesus," Vicki exclaimed when I told her what happened; "you threatened to beat the shit out of two people at a peace festival? That's outrageous. I suppose you were still wearing the yellow and white striped trousers, the yellow tie, the blue coat, and those black and white winged tipped shoes. And how about those pink rabbit ears?" "Yes, those too," I said, "all four of them." To get the students' attention I wore two sets of Freddy Freihofer's rabbit ears. The ears were eight and a half inches tall, and I wore two sets, one on the front of my head and the other on the back. "No wonder those guys left so quickly," Vicki said; "they were scared poopless. For the first time in their lives they met someone crazier than themselves." "Vicki," I said; "your language is outrageous. A lady would not use such words." With that I turned and went outside. In the front yard by the silverbell were two large bitter boletus mushrooms, the biggest eight inches in diameter. The mushrooms are inedible and make the tongue curl and hide behind the esophagus. What would the grits man say, I wondered, if I telephoned him and said, "We'd like to invite you for breakfast, but we only have bitter boletus." Would he be outraged enough to quote Tennessee Williams or, perhaps, Eliza to me? I doubt it.

9 A Different Summer

*T*his year elementary school ended on the nineteenth of June. Two days later I drove the boys to Maine for seven weeks of camp. At the beginning of July Eliza started day camp. She left the house at nine in the morning and did not return until four in the afternoon. Suddenly days were empty, and without the children to squabble with, Vicki and I scratched against each other, raising welts and tossing rough words about. "I'm going to call my next book," I shouted, slamming the screen door one morning, "*Intercourse with the Enemy, or Marriage in the 1990s*." For a week we bruised each other and turned the summer purple with hurt. Then one morning we cooled. Instead of being chopped into swim and ballet, baseball, piano, doctor and dentist, hours were whole. Moreover they belonged to us. One day Vicki decided to clean the garage, and I planted morning glories and dug a bed for marigolds. Vicki wore a yellow tee-shirt. On the front of the shirt was a sketch of Willimantic, a blue river flowing beneath a silver moon. Along one bank of the river, trees grew in fluffs; above the other bank Willimantic stretched through the horizon, its spires and cupolas resembling a Russian cathedral, bulbous yet jagged. A train ran past the buildings while a footbridge spanned the river, its shadow cutting black fretwork on the surface of the water. Printed around the sketch was the slogan "Romantic Willimantic." The day was clear and green, and when Vicki began singing, I looked up from the marigolds. She was dancing through the garage, her tee-shirt crumpled on the back steps. When she saw me looking, she waved her hands over her head like a ballerina plucking red apples from an imaginary tree. Then skipping out the door, she gathered her bosom in her arms and bent over. For a moment she stared at me, then giggling she opened her arms, her breasts tumbling like water down a quick slope, bouncing in a spray and then settling and eddying soft through the summer morning.

That afternoon I roamed field and wood. I followed a northern waterthrush around Tift Pond. At the edge of the marsh bumblebees burrowed through rotting leaves. I counted twenty-eight bees before a feather from a red-tailed hawk distracted me. The feather was two and one-eighth inches wide and ten and three-quarters inches long. Bars of white alternated with bars of reddish brown, these latter resembling shallow streams choked with mud and clay. Under pines pyrola and spotted wintergreen bloomed. Shafts of white sweet clover and buttons of spotted knapweed blossomed along the South Eagleville Road. Carillons of fuzzy green galls hung under the leaves of the sumac growing behind the high school baseball field. The galls smelled like apples; inside were clumps of cottony fiber and minute yellow insects with white feelers. Japanese beetles covered plants in a fog: boneset, thistle, vervain, rose, blackberry, goldenrod, and autumn olive. Only barberry was left alone, its fruit dangling and swelling into small upright orange vases. To Vicki I brought home shafts of hardhack and boughs of sweet pepperbush, the former blooming yellow and purple down its steeple of flowers and the latter fragrant as gardenias, almost turning the house vanilla.

The next morning I walked down the cut for the power line behind the sheep barns. In the abandoned field at the bottom I picked an armful of bouncing bet. From my walks I usually brought things home: butternuts, fringed sedges, the shell of a wood turtle; and scleroderma citrinum mushrooms, small yellow leathery puffballs, lumpy with purple spores. From a dead pine I removed a hemlock varnish shelf. Attached to the tree by a short stem, the mushroom resembled a fan. While the top of the fan was red, almost lacquered, the underside was corky and white. One morning I brought home a log in which a woodboring beetle was trapped. Having eaten its way through the log, the beetle had pupated. Somehow, though, the adult got stuck, its long antennae waving out the exit hole. That afternoon I picked Virginia meadow beauty, the curved stamens shaped like musical notes, lyrical and yellow above the pink petals. I marked a patch of Jerusalem artichoke, planning to return and dig the roots in the fall. Summer was dry, and I walked up the streambed of the Fenton River, the water running past me into pools. George kept me company on my walks. For a time I watched him carefully, worried that he might stray and get lost in the woods. Then I realized that I wasn't watching him as closely as he watched me. Whenever my weak leg gave way and I slipped, he raced to me in a jangling rush of license and name tag. Rarely did I meet people though I often saw signs of them: beer cans, hunks of styrofoam, shotgun shells, and then, oddly, underwear, almost always boys' or men's jockey briefs, the medium size for thirty-four to thirty-six inch waists, not the kind of underpants or the size worn by my friends. Wandering wood and field both tired and invigorated me, and once or twice after a six mile amble I rushed home, imagining Vicki's tee-shirt blossoming like the morning glories on the trellis by the side door. Of course the shirt wasn't there. In truth I often thought about the shirt. Days passed without Vicki's wearing it, so I asked her where it was. "I think it is in the dirty clothes basket in the basement," she said, a hint of a smile on her face, "why do you ask?" "Oh, no reason," I said, touching her on the shoulder, "I just wondered."

Weekends were restful. Instead of jerking around Storrs in the car, rattling from birthday party to the mall and back, we walked. One Sunday in the drama building we watched a production of *Charlie and the Chocolate Factory* put on by elementary school students, many of whom were Eliza's classmates. Afterward we ambled across campus to an exhibition of insects sponsored by the Museum of Natural History. On July 4, Vicki packed a picnic supper of tuna fish sandwiches, sliced carrots and celery, fudge cake, watermelon, grapes, and potato chips, and we went to the pond near the dog pound. After swimming we ate. Then I stretched out on the grass. Vicki rocked forward and wrapping her arms about her knees, sat like an egg and talked to friends while Eliza hunted along the shore for tadpoles. Later we listened to a folksinger. She played the guitar and sang gentle songs for children, songs with names like "Lazy Bones," "Hairy Harry," "Fishy Doo-Ah," and "I'm Not Too Short." The next night Jay telephoned from Vermont. He had gone to the Rainbow Gathering in the Green Mountains. "Naked people dancing everywhere," he said, "lines of them. The first person I saw was a man in a top-hat and a cutaway coat, and that's all. I haven't seen anything like it since the hippies and the 70s." "I guess not," I said, pausing, then adding, "Did you see anybody wearing a tee-shirt with 'Romantic Willimantic' printed on it?" "What?" Jay said. "Oh, nothing," I answered; "that's just something I've been wondering about." The night was hot, and after talking to Jay, I sat on the front stoop and watched lightning bugs rise from the ground in sparkles. I envied the boys at camp, only starting something that ended for me twenty-five years ago. George crawled into my lap and curled up. I rubbed his ears. The hippies I knew in Vermont owned big, bushy, black or yellow dogs, not small dachshunds. All except Katy, I suddenly recalled. She had a white dog named Miranda. Katy and Miranda washed in a mountain stream and lived on figs and yogurt. Katy and I liked each other, but she would not go out with me. "You are so conventional," she explained, "that you frighten me, and I don't want a life with china and silver, all that sort of thing." As I sat on the stoop, I tried to imagine the me who once lived in New Hampshire. I wasn't successful. George dug a flea out of his ear. Eliza asked me to read "Sleeping Beauty" to her. And, of course, the person Katy saw as conventional others saw differently. On my desk was a letter from Andy. "A reason for writing you of all people," he began, "is that I judged from your remarks on public radio last year that at least your head is screwed on right, something it wasn't the last time I talked with you, thirty odd years ago."

With the boys at camp Vicki and I had time not only for each other but also for spending money. One day, we ate lunch at Everyday Books in Willimantic. We had pita bread stuffed with curried rice and lentils, and for dessert, pie, "sinful chocolate" for Vicki and "ginger custard" for me. We ate slowly, sipping coffee and talking. I mentioned Andy's letter, and Vicki said, "The guy must have slipped. He got things backward. Thirty years ago your head was probably screwed on right, but not now." After lunch Vicki bought me two shirts at Hurley's for $41.25: the first rainbow-striped with a button down collar, made in Hong Kong and normally priced at $24, the other a Hathaway "Regency Oxford," sixty per cent cotton and forty per cent polyester, made in Waterville, Maine, and marked down from $31. From Hurley's we went to Nassiff's where Vicki bought a pair of white Reebok shoes for $54.99. Afterward we crossed Main Street to Office Furniture Warehouse. There I spent $205.16 for computer tables. In December I bought a computer, but without a table to set it on, it languished in boxes in the hall for seven months, gradually making me feel inefficient and undermining my spirits. After buying the tables I felt good, and so we hurried to Holiday Hill and picked up Eliza. The "Great American Circus" was in Willimantic, and at the four o'clock show family admission was twenty dollars. Admission, though, was only part of the expense. We arrived early, and for four dollars Eliza rode a pony then a camel. Cotton candy cost two dollars, and soft drinks and popcorn another nine. At camp that morning, however, Eliza lost two teeth. At twenty-five cents a tooth, they would have cost the tooth fairy fifty cents. Since the teeth were the first Eliza lost, she wanted to keep them, explaining that the tooth fairy could have all the rest. After the fairy's savings were subtracted from expenses for lunch, shoes, shirts, tables, and circus, the day cost $351.89.

"Probably the cost," Vicki said, "of a day on some green island." Neither Vicki nor I ever had an island vacation, and the next morning I began reading travel brochures. Soon I basked in a "watercolor paradise" purple with words, where sands were pink and palm-fringed, sunsets golden, and seas turquoise and shimmering. Candles flickered in dining rooms, and once Eliza was asleep, champagne promised to bubble frosty through the moonlight. Vicki and I decided to go to Bermuda. The night before I booked the holiday, however, Rick called from Nashville. After seventeen months on the market my father's condominium sold. The price was thirty-five percent less than that Father paid for it six years ago, but no longer would I have monthly payments of six hundred and fifty dollars for taxes and fees. Abruptly summer changed. Before me rose waves of furniture, secretaries and sideboards breaking against walls, sofas like reefs colorful in chintz, lush rugs, coves of leggy tables and chairs, and chests tropical with memorabilia.

In twenty days the boys' camp ended after which we planned to spend two weeks in Nova Scotia with Vicki's father, returning to Storrs the twenty-sixth of August, the day before school began. On August 30, the new owner moved into the apartment, and I had to remove the furniture during the next two weeks. Most of the furniture could be entrusted to movers, but Mother's Rose Medallion china was lovely and I had to drive it to Connecticut. Seven years old and shaky after the occasional run to Willimantic, the Plymouth could not endure a round trip to Tennessee, and so I investigated new cars, reading accounts in *Consumer's Reports* and studying charts of dealer costs. Forty-eight hours later I bought a Mazda van over the telephone. "And I will give you," I told the dealer in Nashville after I detailed the options I wanted, "this much and no more." "Mr. Pickering," he answered, "I don't know if we can sell it to you for that." "You have ten minutes to decide," I said, before hanging up; "I will be flying in on Monday and want you to pick me up at the airport. You can recognize me because I will be the only person there wearing a tee-shirt with 'Mister Rogers' Neighborhood' stamped on the front." Eight and a half minutes later the telephone rang. "Mr. Pickering," the dealer said, "what flight did you say you'd be on, and what was that about a Sesame Street shirt?" Never had I been in a van, or a Mazda, but at five o'clock Monday I drove up to Nashville Wine and Spirits in search of boxes. The van is black, and I call it "The Hearse." Vicki does not like the name; she says it is bad "for highway karma."

By the time Vicki and Eliza arrived the next day, the apartment was full of boxes from Wine and Spirits, containers for Wisdom & Water Sherry, Villa Frattina Chardonnay, Smirnov Vodka, Jack Daniels "Tennessee Tea," Orvieto Classico Chianti, and Southern Comfort. Along the chianti boxes vineyards stitched across a hilltop in neat rows. On the Southern Comfort box Spanish moss hung wet from trees and a steamboat sweated down a river. Behind a wooden fence was a planter's house, low and suited for a dank bayou. Supported by seven columns a porch ran the length of the front of the house. Projecting from the sloping roof above were five windows set in gables. The world of the vineyards was light, and a sip of chianti, could, it almost seemed, lift a person into the cool sky. In contrast, weariness blanketed the plantation and anyone who staggered up the six steps to the porch seemed certain to need a fan and rocking chair and for comfort's sake an icy tumbler of something sweet and minty.

I made only one trip to Wine and Spirits. Loaded with liquor boxes, the van, I decided, would look common and turn the long drive to Connecticut tawdry. Even shipping goods in such boxes seemed vulgar, and so most of my boxes came from the H. G. Hill grocery in Belle Meade. A childhood friend ran Hill's, and at nine each morning I loaded the van with produce boxes, containers for grapefruit, lemon, bananas, oranges, and tomatoes: Big Red Tomatoes from Ft. Pierce, Florida; Thomas Tomatoes from Boca Raton; Palmetto Beauty from Palmetto; and from Immokalee, Soweja, Solid Gold, and Exmore's Pride. The best boxes were those containing apples from Washington: Dovex and CMI, and then with a red apple lying on its side at the foot of two blue peaks, Saddle Mountain. On the box of First Fruits of Washington was a big green apple, one leaf light in the air, jaunty like a flying jib. Blowing in a breeze across the front of the apple was a ribbon of white bunting, "Washington" printed on it in blue letters.

Days in Nashville quickly became routine. Each morning I fetched boxes. Twice a day I took Eliza swimming in the apartment pool. Every afternoon I played Crazy Eights with her, and at night I read her fairy tales. Throughout the day Vicki and I packed. Six years ago when Mother and Father sold their house, Mother cleaned out the attic. While two hired men lifted trunks and brought them to her, Mother sat in an armchair at the top of the stairs. After glancing at the contents of the trunks, Mother inevitably raised her right arm, pointed outside, and said, "to the dump." "I threw away generations," she told me, "and you ought to thank me for it." In Nashville I thanked her. Although Vicki and I scoured the apartment after Mother's death, and I returned and cleaned out closets and drawers when Father came to Connecticut, the apartment was cluttered, and we spent moonlit nights, not strolling pink beaches arms full of champagne and each other, but wrapping and taping. The night before the movers came we worked until four in the morning then got up at six to work until their arrival at seven-thirty. Despite invitations from friends, we ate most meals in restaurants. That way we could eat at our convenience, when the Rose Medallion was wrapped or the knife box packed. Moreover in a restaurant we did not have to be entertaining and could slide weary and silent through the evening. Still, despite being tired, I realized that this was my final trip to a Tennessee home, and so I ate familiar food: barbecue and cornbread at the Sportsman's Grill, and a double chocolate soda and a chicken salad sandwich on toast at Vandyland. When my godmother took us to the Belle Meade Club I ordered eggs benedict. One night I drove to the Loveless Motel and ate country ham and red-eye gravy and biscuits sweet with blackberry and peach preserves. I bought watermelons at Hills, and during the two weeks ate three big ones by myself. In the pantry of the apartment I found a gray ironstone jug filled with Mother's watermelon rind pickle. The pickle had turned black, and I emptied the jug into the garbage. Meals were a side dish to packing, but I wanted them to season the trip. Like the pickle most things Southern had aged and lost their savour. Still, I hoped the meals would invigorate my imagination. One day after lunch I stopped by the house in which I grew up. The new owners had knocked down walls and rebuilt rooms. I expected sadness and maybe regret to sweep over me as I wandered the halls. Instead I felt nothing. No change interested me, and memory remained eyeless, imagination and thought crammed into a cardboard box, a rind of paper crumpled thickly about them.

Despite being corrugated with work, days were pitted with plea-sure. Buried under a mound of silver in the sideboard were three bottles of gin Father hid from Mother, a fifth of Fleishmann's and two of Gordons. One Sunday we drove to the Nashville Zoo and spent a morning wandering the hills of Cheatham County. A week earlier a baby giraffe had been born, and it stumbled across the "Afri-can savannah" under its mother's legs. Vicki liked the lemurs best while Eliza and I went through the Reptile House twice. Eliza knows snakes interest me, and she probably went along to please me. More than the boys, she tries to please me. In June the Lebanon School of Dance put on two performances for parents. Each girl in Eliza's class improvised for twenty or so seconds on the stage. I did not attend the first day, and Eliza spun rapidly through her dance. During the sec-ond performance Eliza danced slowly and unendingly. She twirled and bowed, leaped and waved her arms for what seemed hours. The teacher was forced to restart the dance music. I shrank in my seat, closed my eyes, and put my hands over my ears, saying, "Vicki, I can't stand this. Punch me when she finishes." Later I did not mention my discomfort, nay agony, to Eliza. After the performance we hugged her and gave her flowers bought at Stop and Shop. That night before bed Eliza said to Vicki, "I did my best for Daddy. I wanted him to be proud."

My house in Storrs is not large, and in hopes of winnowing the furniture and reaping money enough to pay the movers, I sold some things. The Belle Meade Tower does not allow formal sales, and family friends bought most of what was sold. Selling gave me a chance to laugh and talk to people, and some days I dressed the part of a salesman, wearing hiking shorts bought in Hanover, New Hampshire, in 1973, for a slimmer me; a black short-sleeve shirt with a green and yellow frog on the front celebrating "TOAD SUCK DAZE," an arts and crafts festival in Conway, Arkansas; a red and black silk bathrobe with a tasselled belt attached; and then on my head a Panama hat sold by Cavanaugh which I found in the top of Father's closet. On my feet I wore nothing. Initially I sold things cheaply: an English oak butter tray dating from 1790 for $125, a ten-by-twelve-foot oriental rug for $350, and for $455 six silver plated mint julep cups, an oval, twenty-three-inch silver plated gallery tray, and a print of "The Bounds-Park Oak" by Jacob Strutt. Chairs were a bargain, and I sold wing, barrel, and captain's chairs for $100 apiece. Six old Windsor chairs went for $650. The smallest amount I received was one dollar for an iron skillet, the most, $2000 for Mother's Rosenthal china. A few dealers dropped in. After introducing himself one explored the apartment, pencil and pad in hand, taking notes but refusing to say a word. Only when he left did he speak, saying, "You will hear from me." Later when he telephoned, I was "engaged and unable to speak." A couple introduced themselves, then said, "We really should not be here. We are trying to get out of the business." Later they offered $3365 for a list of items including leather bound books, prints, lap desk, English plant stands, china, shelves of silver, two wine chests or cellarettes, oil paintings, tea boxes, etc. At the end of the list, they noted that their offer expired in twenty-four hours. I telephoned and after thanking them for their generosity and complimenting their taste declined the offer. In truth someone offered me more for one of the wine chests than the dealers offered for the entire list. The wine chest was early American Hepplewhite Mahogany, and one morning I agreed to sell it. That afternoon I changed my mind, telling the prospective buyer "Mother told me not to sell this chest, and I forgot."

Selling is infectious, raising the fervor of the seller more than that of the buyer. I kept account of the money I made, the final tally being $8323. Often, though, I struggled against the urge to sell. At times money seemed almost the equivalent of runs scored in a game. In the hot moment of play all I wanted was a bigger total. Still, the fever did not consume me, and I regret parting with little that I sold. Indeed, some sales gave me pleasure. An old friend bought Father's dresser and put it in her dining room where, surrounded by mirror and table, it gleamed with new life. I gave much away: Haviland china, Italian chandelier, chairs, lamps, prints, linens, and tables. After a drink Father was profuse in his generosity, willing to part with almost anything. Once he gave away an English tricycle Mother's father bought me in New York, this despite my still riding it. In my Aunt Lula's house in north Nashville I found a box of letters written by family members during the Civil War. After a convivial evening father removed them from my room while I was asleep and offered them to a Civil War enthusiast. Another time he tried to give away the pistol which his grandfather and my great-grandfather carried during the war. On these occasions only Mother's sobriety restrained him. Mood not alcohol intoxicated me, for giving possessions away raises my spirits. Later, alas, comes the hangover, the guilty feeling that I have behaved foolishly, maybe even callously in neglecting to consult family before pressing an item upon an acquaintance.

For twenty years Rosie worked for Father and Mother, nursing first Grandmother then Father and Mother themselves. At times Rosie seemed the fiber binding the old bones of the family together. To her I gave beds, chairs, including Father's sitting chair, television, closets of knick-knacks and plates, linen, lamps, a round mahogany coffee table with flower inlays, Mother's dresser and mirror, planters, rugs, nine drawers and sundry cabinets of kitchen equipment including a toaster oven and then five hundred dollars for Steve and her to use on their vacation. Rosie was the last face in a scrapbook of servants who tended me and mine: Lizzie, Pauline, Bertha, Dora, Marie who nursed me when I was a baby, and Peggy with a scar curving above her elbow like a new moon. When another woman made eyes at Harold, Peggy's husband, Peggy fought her with a razor. Wilna died slowly of cancer, weight falling off her like dough from biscuits under a cutter. When she went to the hospital the last time, I was a camp counselor in Maine. The day after I returned from camp I went to the hospital to see her. She was under an oxygen tent. She had not moved in four days, but when she saw me, she sat up and stared. The next morning when I asked to see her again, the nurse said, "Mrs. Hall expired last night." What I left behind was left as much for memory as for Rosie, furniture not flowers piled atop the buried past. In Connecticut we do not have a servant, and the children's childhood is simpler than mine. Never will they know the guilt I sometimes feel; neither will they know the rich love: for Wilna, her bosom as big and as warm as the summer sky, and then for Rosie, who laughed with Miss Katharine at Mr. Sam's foibles and gentled their good nights.

As mine is a life without servants so I do not eat with silver but stainless steel. What I wanted to sell and could not was silver. "You must save it for your children," my cousin Susan told me. "Susan," I said, "how often do you eat with silver?" "Twice a year," she answered, "Christmas and Thanksgiving." A woman wanted to buy a silver-plated roll top dish, but earlier in the day I'd wandered through an antique store. Rolltop dishes, not one of which was as good as mine, ranged in price from $550 to $980. The woman offered $150, but I would not budge from $350. A person selling family possessions should stay out of antique shops. Prices in them are high, and after roaming through one store, I decided not to sell some things. Tea boxes which I thought worth $175 sold for $1250; a lap desk similar to one I thought worth $300 was priced at $2500. "We'll have," I told Vicki, "a fortune in the attic." "Yes," Vicki answered, "the attic's the right place—a fortune in the sky and a silver mine in the basement." Despite the selling and the giving, much remained when the movers came on July 30, eighty-eight items, chests heavier than iron, a secretary stuffed with pictures, two sofas, a dozen tables, a day bed, nine big chairs, an eighteenth-century sideboard, beds, mirrors, and boxes which we will not open for years, in short enough things to furnish a second seven-room house. Unless fire frees them, some grim day hence the children will sit in the living room, cartons towering above them, wondering what to do with cherry and mahogany, Worcester and Spode, pastry servers, butter spreaders, tea caddies, sugar bowls, compotes, and bouillon spoons.

After the movers left, we were tired, and so we stayed in the apartment for three more days, sleeping on mattresses. Even when we finally left on Friday, the second of August, we started slowly, not departing until ten-thirty. Years ago when I traveled back and forth to Virginia with Mother and Father we often left at two in the morning. In truth I was not eager to leave Nashville, and I lingered to avoid the final goodbye. We busied ourselves during the last days tidying up the apartment. For the first time during the trip I paused and poked about. Here and there I found scraps of paper. On the floor of the guest bedroom closet was a scrap of verse. The paper was brittle and gray, and I did not recognize the handwriting. "I place this gift under the Christmas Tree for one who is as sweet as she can be," the verse stated; "I place this gift under this little cedar. For one who to me there is no one sweeter." On a shelf in Father's closet was a letter written by Father to Mother. Postmarked February 20, 1947, the letter was sent special delivery to West Palm Beach, Florida, at a cost of eight cents. That winter I was sickly, and Mother took me south for my health. "Dearest Katharine," Father wrote, "This is a letter of condolence for you having been married to me for 8 years. Anyway I'm certainly glad you have and I don't have to tell you how much I love you." Rosie removed her furniture after we left, and in the front left corner of the mirror over Mother's dresser was a prayer. Printed down a strip of cloth and backed by thin cardboard, the prayer was a bookmark. Although the prayer had stood behind the frame of the mirror for years, I never really looked at it. At the top of the bookmark was a sketch. A small red church stood on a bluff overlooking a tossing sea. In the background a puffy white cloud rose heavenwards. Under the sketch was the prayer itself. "Peace," it began, quoting John, "I leave with you, my peace I give unto you: not as the world giveth, give I unto you. Let not your heart be troubled, neither let it be afraid." I removed the prayer, and when we left Friday morning, I put it in the drawer under the front seat of the Mazda.

At first the trip to Storrs was leisurely. The first night we stopped at Christiansburg, Virginia. The next morning we ate a full breakfast and got on the road at nine-thirty. For Eliza Nashville had been dull. Aside from the day at the zoo, we spent most hours in the apartment. I knew camp would furnish the boys with volumes of tales, and so that Eliza would also have stories to tell, I stopped at Luray, Virginia, and we toured the caverns. After lunch we pushed on along route 81 into Pennsylvania. By seven o'clock I was tired, and so I got off the interstate and drove into Hazelton. All the motels were full, but in Wilkes-Barre, a clerk assured me, rooms were available. The clerk was wrong. Not a room was free. After searching fruitlessly, we stopped in the Burger King before returning to the highway. We looked weary, and after overhearing our conversation, the security guard said to us, "Gosh, I'd put you up in my house for the night, but the wife has just shampooed all the rugs." The man's kind remarks invigorated me almost as much as the coffee and chicken sandwich I had for dinner.

I needed energy. Motels in Scranton were filled, and I settled in for a long night's drive past signs and towns: Ramada, Hampton, and Red Roof inns, Ho Jo, Econo-Lodge, Süsse Chalet, and Best Western. We inquired about rooms in Elmhurst, then Newfoundland, Milford, Port Jervis, and Middletown. In New York a woman stood beside me at a reservation desk and cried. "I've been looking for a room since Albany," she sobbed, "I can't drive any more. Can't anyone help me?" At the Holiday Inn in Danbury, Connecticut, at Exit 8 on Interstate 84, a clerk found a room for us in the new Holiday hotel in Waterbury near Exit 22. At three-fifteen we finally went to bed. Storrs was an hour and a half away. The next morning I drove to Windsor Locks, and Vicki picked up the Plymouth, left at Park, Ride, Fly when she and Eliza flew to Nashville. On the way home we stopped at a farm in Ellington, and Vicki bought peaches, blueberries, beans, corn, tomatoes, zucchini, and yellow squash. Next we picked up George at the kennel in East Willington. He had lost weight and his bark. At noon we were in Storrs. On the kitchen table was a brochure for a resort in Bermuda. In a picture a man and wife lay on their backs in a lagoon, flippers on their feet, masks and snorkels pulled high on their foreheads, the water silvery and fluffy about them, white sand behind stretching up to a blue sky. In another picture a sailboat spun on the horizon, its red keel winking in the lemony sun. "Nashville or Bermuda, the Belle Meade Tower or the Pompano Beach Club," Vicki said, "what's the difference?" "Certainly not money," I said. Our southern vacation had not been cheap. Because we flew with only three days notice airline tickets cost $1013.60. For George's two weeks at the kennel, including "play time," I paid $198.40. Park, Ride, Fly charged $76.97 for keeping the Plymouth. I bought $84 worth of gas for the Mazda and paid $113.63 to motels. Although we ate out most days, groceries in Nashville cost $88.57, my watermelons costing $2.99 a piece. At restaurants our meals ran between $13 and $30. Then, of course, we had incidentals: $7.18 for Ventolin when Eliza's asthma acted up, $5.39 to the zoo for a stuffed snow leopard, a magnum of Moet and Chandon champagne at $53.99, a present for a friend; $51.71 to Hart Hardware for new faucets for the kitchen sink, and then $25 to Robert for installing them and taking down the chandelier in the living room. "Vicki," I said, "I'm not telling you what snorkeling in Tennessee cost. All I will say is that if we toss in the van, Dove Bars, Baskin-Robbins ice cream cones, a key lime pie or two, movers, twine and tape, we could have rented a small island."

Four days later we drove to Maine and picked the boys up at camp. The next night we took the ferry to Yarmouth to spend two weeks at our farm in Beaver River. The family was together again, and in the big dusty house, July sifted out of mind and the summer resembled other summers. Swamp candles glowed yellow in the Quaking Bog; low in the pasture purple orchis flickered. A necklace of pickerel weed hung around the pond below George's Field, blue spikes curving up from leafy green collars. Beside the road running out to the bluff broad-leaf asters blossomed. Above them flat-topped asters shook white in the wind, hover flies clinging to the flowers. From bushes along the stone wall chokecherries jutted out in bold, black clusters while a red squirrel ran over the rocks, its voice a self-important, shrill ringing. Blueberries were thick in the field behind the barn, so thick the ground seemed a carpet of green and blue. Shoots of purple berries started out from shadbushes. In one corner of the field fireweed had gone to seed. Higher than bay and blueberry, the long red pods shimmered and seemed to drift through the sunlight in a pink haze.

A few small things were different this summer. Instead of being baled and stored in lofts hay was rolled and left in the fields. In the past we went to Nova Scotia in June or early July and returned to Connecticut in mid-August. Instead of dripping, supple and yellow, the flowers on the golden chain tree in the side meadow had hardened into seed. The pods hung stiffly from a stalk, resembling a string of misshapen tadpoles, the flesh around the one or two fertile seeds in each pod thick and green, the rest of the pod a dry twist of gray. The leaves of the horse chestnut by the backhouse were ragged and brown around the edges. Instead of rustling smooth and oily when warblers flushed through them, they crinkled, almost rattled. Still, little was really different. The first afternoon Eliza and I walked down toward the bluff to the place where the Woody Bog drained under the road. There beneath a log Eliza found two red-bellied snakes. "This is Daisy," she said holding them close to her chest, "and this other one is Tulip." Last summer Eliza caught Violet.

The next morning was foggy, and I drove to Port Maitland to buy milk. Suddenly the day brightened, and out of the fog strolled the familiar characters of my imagination. Around the corner from the Shore Grocery, Bertha Shifney sat rocking on her front porch. Gracious Chenoweth sat next to her. On Sunday Gracious's new twins, Chosen and People, had been christened. "I hear those babies holler something fierce at night," Bertha said. "Don't that keep the family awake?" "My goodness, no. We hardly hear them," Gracious answered. "Them babies yells so loud they drown each other out." Spring had been drier in Nova Scotia than in Connecticut, and farmers suffered. "The country is in such terrible shape," Judah Saulnier told Otis Blankinchip as they stood on the steps of Bertha's porch, "that the only lucky people is them that don't get born at all." "By gum, you are right," Otis exclaimed, nodding his head, "that's the truth. But how many of them are there? Not one in a hundred," he said, shaking his head and wagging his index finger at the post office across the street, "maybe not even one in a thousand." "Bertha," he said, turning and looking up the steps, "you'd have been better off if you had stayed in Hectanooga. There's been lots of rain up there, and everybody is healthy and happy." "Not healthy," Bertha answered; "Hectanooga is muggy and feverish. If I had stayed there until now, I'd have been dead ten years ago."

"Bertha," Judah said, "did you know that Hornus Roebuck's cousin Peagram drowned in Grand Passage off Brier Island?" "Yes, what a blessing," Bertha said; "he was no good. I heard that Emilda Roebuck was sitting by the fire knitting when the boys rushed in and told her they found the body. 'Don't bother me none,' she said, the needles clacking as steadily as the afternoon train rolling through the flatland between Hebron and Willington, 'can't you see I'm at the end of a row?' 'And that ain't all,' Sheaves Swormstead burst out, 'there was two big green eels curled up in Peagram's belly.' 'What, two eels!' Emilda exclaimed, dropping her knitting. 'Fetch me them eels,' she said, 'and set him again.'" "Lordy, Bertha," Otis said, "ain't that just like Emilda. I used to work on the ferry running out to Westport on Brier Island. Once in a while the water got rough. One day the current was running strong, and we had some tourists from Metagan on board and one of the ladies wanted to know if passengers ever got lost. 'No, ma'am,' I told her, 'sometimes they get drowned, but they don't get lost. They always wash up in a day or two.'" About the time Otis stopped speaking a woe-begotten man with a nose as round as a peach and as purple as a plum walked up the street from the fish factory and stopped beside the fence. "Sister," he said addressing Bertha, "could you lend me five dollars? I'm a preacher heading for the Promised Land and I've been on the way for sixteen years, praise God." "Sixteen years," Bertha said, rocking steadily, "if you ain't got no farther than Port Maitland in sixteen years then you done took the wrong way."

The time in Nashville had passed quickly. Worried that I would not be able to clean the apartment before the boys' camp closed in August, I pushed unobservant through days, rarely even noticing the things I put in boxes. In Nova Scotia days stretched, and I rummaged the hours. As I had the leisure to people Port Maitland and listen to Bertha and Otis's stories, so I had time to explore house and barn. Small things similar to those I swept away in Nashville I now examined in Nova Scotia. In the chest in the Scotch Room I found a yardstick, gritty and almost mahogany with age. Printed on it in black was the advice "Keep This Yard Stick But Buy Your Dry Goods from J. D. DENNIS & CO., 'Best Possible Dollar's Worth for a Dollar.'" Under a pile of red checkered oilcloth in the pantry was a child's plate, four and a half inches in diameter. In the center a boy sat on his mother's lap. Still small, the boy wore a shift and the mother a long dress with puffed sleeves and a ruffled collar. Out a window behind and beyond them a church with a sharp steeple stood on a hill. Stamped above the picture was the phrase "An Only Son"; below was the question, "Will He who stoops to care for little sparrows falling down despise an infant's prayer." Around the edge of the plate ran a border of splotchy flowers, blobs of blue, green, and red. In the backhouse I found a four-ounce bottle of Mrs. Stewart's Liquid Bluing for White Clothing, manufactured by Lutherford and Company in Winnipeg. A picture of Mrs. Stewart appeared on the label. She wore a pudding-shaped black cap, sober rectangular wire glasses, and a black dress topped by a modest lace collar. Her mouth curved down in a scowl, and she seemed a competent washerwoman, not simply the sort of person who starched clothes but the sort who lived a starched, ironed life. In the loft in the barn I found a curved draw knife with vase-shaped, beech handles. While the knife measured seventeen inches from handle to handle, the blade itself was ten inches long and two inches wide. Pressed into the blade was the name of the maker: James Cam. In the nineteenth century several shipbuilders lived in Beaver River, and the knife had probably been used in smoothing spars.

In past summers I explored the house and outbuildings carefully. Realizing that the chance of finding interesting things was small, I rummaged more thoroughly than ever this year. Selling the apartment snapped my tie to Nashville. No longer was childhood bound to the main of my life. Years had worn a passage between it and the present. To reach that past I would have to be a tourist and take a ferry. Instead of difference I sought sameness in Nova Scotia. Instead of breaking with the past, I wanted continuance, and so I roamed house and field as I had done before. Under the spruce around the woody bog mushrooms bloomed. With orange gills pushing their caps up into wrinkled funnels, Jack O'Lanterns blossomed in rough fairy rings. Amanitas thrived: the blusher, more brown than pink; yellow patches, the bright cap warty and the stem yellow at the bottom fading upward to white, and American Caesar's mushroom, luminous caps thrusting through the green moss and resembling big orange acorns. Clumps of Russula nigrans covered the forest floor. New, they resembled potatoes carelessly dumped out of a sack, but, soon they rotted, blackening and crinkling like thick burned paper. In leaf litter grew entoloma salmoneum, fragile and orange; nearby amid moss was entoloma strictipes, the moist brown cap rippled and almost dancing. Pasted over their white stems and gills the caps of red russulas burned. In their bright heat the russulas appeared hard and dry; in contrast slippery Jacks were slimy and the caps of thick boletus seemed damp sponges, the yellow stems turning blue when broken and seeming to run to water. The wood was a garden, cinnamon cortinarius to my left, a lactarius to my right, the brown stem topped by a dark circle, the gills white above, and the top of the cap ochre. The garden, though, was fanged. Hypomyces thrust stubby from the moss, almost as if some long-buried pagan deity was awakening for a rude season of lust. Venomous amanitas lurked throughout the wood: the cleft-foot, fly agaric, and then by itself, demure and shyly green, the death cap. I spent days searching for mushrooms, knocking fern and bush aside, my eyes on the ground. Once I walked into a hornets' nest and was stung on the left cheek and right hand. The side of my face puffed like moss over a mushroom. The stings did not slow my roaming, however. Every summer I beat paths through brush and shrub, and I had long expected to be stung.

Father and Mother were buried in Carthage, Tennessee, seven miles off Interstate 40, the first highway I drove traveling from Nashville to Storrs. I did not stop in Carthage on the way back to Connecticut. Because we left Nashville late in the morning our schedule was so tight, I told Vicki, that we did not have time to visit the graveyard. Of course I frittered away most of the next day at Luray Caverns. Strangely enough after wandering about Nova Scotia for a while I returned to Carthage, not to a bare hill of tombstones but to an imaginative and sentimental place quick with story. Quintus Tyler, I learned, enjoyed only a short retirement from teaching at the Male and Female Select School. Not many people wanted his job, and those who did were not qualified. The school board interviewed an acquaintance of Beevie Povey, one of the Finches from Bezaleel. Judge Rutherford heard that the woman didn't, as he put it, "hold truth in particularly high esteem." "Well," Beevie said when the Judge asked her about the woman, "if she tells you the truth you can believe every last word of it. But when she gets to lying you best not put no confidence in her at all." Slubey Garts recommended Proverbs Goforth, a deacon at the Tabernacle of Love, and the board interviewed him. When Judge Rutherford brought up geography and asked Proverbs whether he thought the world was round or flat, Proverbs was silent for a moment. Then he began to nod, his head working up and down like a handle on a pump, almost as if he were pulling a reply deep from within Battery Hill. "It don't make no matter to me," he declared, "I can teach both systems."

My leaving Nashville did not effect life in Carthage. Hoben Donkin brought home another stray cat. The cat was going to have a litter, and Clulee ordered Hoben to drown it in Dunphy's Pond or else lose it in the woods behind Liberty. Hoben obeyed the order, and getting up early one foggy morning, he set out for Liberty, the cat tucked under his left arm. He was gone all day, so long that Clulee almost called Sheriff Baugham. But then at eight o'clock the cat strolled in through the kitchen door, Hoben staggering behind, clots of burrs as thick as sourdough bread clinging to his trousers. "I got lost," he said, after drinking a glass of ice water, "I never would have found my way back except I followed the cat home." In spring Vester McBee's grandmother MaudyMay came down with the croup. MaudyMay was ninety-four and had never been sick or ever seen a doctor in her life. Worried about her grandmother, Vester asked Doctor Sollows to drive up to Gladis and give her grandmother a thorough examination. The next day Vester herself visited MaudyMay. "It was mighty nice of the new preacher to come and see me," MaudyMay said. "Why granny, that won't no preacher," Vester said; "that was Doctor Sollows from down to Carthage." "Oh, a doctor," MaudyMay said, "well that explains it. I thought he acted kind of familiar, for a preacher."

Vicki and I did all the things we normally do in Nova Scotia, and the two weeks did not seem different from our usual two months. At the Farmers' Market in Yarmouth, Vicki bought beets, Swiss chard, peas, carrots, broccoli, cauliflower, a mincemeat pie, and both rhubarb and strawberry preserves. I bought tomato soup cake and pickled quail's eggs for a picnic under the tall bluffs between Salmon River and Cape St. Mary. After shopping we ate fish chowder at the "Quick 'n Tasty." Next we bought rolls and war cake at Edna's. That afternoon we climbed the rocks at Cape Forchu. Francis explored a narrow ledge. I could not bear to watch, and so after warning him to be careful, I examined wildflowers. Painted ladies fluttered around seaside goldenrod. Blue flag had gone to seed, the green pods swollen and resembling sofas in a garish Florida room. Roses had become hedges heavy with red hips. Behind the beach clover flowed over the ground in pools: white, purple, and yellow. Sheltered from the wind I found dried umbrellas of cow parsnip. From the stems thirty-six tines curved smoothly upward into stars.

The next morning I watched warblers hunt through the trees around the side meadow: redstarts, black-throated greens, black and whites, myrtles, and yellows. After breakfast I picked blackberries in the patch behind the willows at the corner of Ma's Property. Then I walked to Beaver River. A great blue heron stalked through the reeds behind the beach. In the afternoon I picked blueberries in the field behind the barn. Later I sat atop the bluff and watched a black-bellied plover hunting across the beach at low tide. The plover's feet pulled him in quick rushes over the sand to buried worms. At times the bird stood still and looking out to sea resembled an old man, a sad octogenarian watching the water roll silver and heavy, his thin legs frail sticks to be tossed and swallowed by time.

The day we returned to Storrs I mowed the grass and got stung five times by yellow jackets. The next morning before the school bus arrived Edward played catch with George. Edward threw the ball into bushes, and when he went to retrieve it was stung seven times. I knocked hornets off his clothes in the kitchen and one tumbled to the floor then fluttered up and stung Eliza. I told George to get in his bed. He obeyed, but soon he starting shaking. I picked him up. On his stomach were two hornets. When Vicki saw the hornets, she went upstairs and took off the "Romantic Willimantic" tee-shirt and put on a long-sleeve shirt, to protect herself, she explained, from being stung. That afternoon I got a haircut. The sign for Roffler's "Products for Hair and Skin Care" was still above George's chair, but on the wall was a price list, listing along with prices for the ROTC Haircut, "Ladies Cut and Blow $12" and "Perm with Cut, $46 and up." "Women have had their cut for years at George's," Vicki said when I told her about the list of prices. "You have never noticed before. Nothing has changed except summer is over, and school has started."

9 Sweet Auburn

Cows sifted down Bean Hill in clumps. Geese gleaned in the marsh behind the dairy. Above the new red barn a crow pushed north toward the Old Turnpike. High in the blue sky, clouds were soft and mouldy. Occasionally one frayed in the wind, its edges slipping through silver before trailing off into gray. A flock of pigeons swept over the box-elder along the top of Horsebarn Hill. For a moment they paused, coasting, then they swooped down toward the marsh, each spinning as if frightened by a hawk. Under the barb wire fence George followed a groundhog run, his tail switching like laughter. At the top of the hill Eliza flew a kite, Vicki kneeling beside her and helping play out the string. Eliza got the kite at McDonald's. On the front pasted against an orange background was the Hamburglar, a grinning thief in a black mask. The Hamburglar's arms ran along the struts of the kite, and as light shined through the plastic behind him orange glowed around him. The color softened the kite's quick falls turning them into gentle curves, almost smiles. For a while I stood watching Eliza fly the kite and listening to George rustling through the tall grass. But then I reached into my trousers and took out a letter. Earlier that afternoon I picked up my mail at the English department. Most of the mail I threw away, but this letter I kept, stuffing it into the back pocket of my jeans. Sitting on the ground to help Eliza assemble the kite wrinkled the letter and so before reading it again I smoothed it out. "I am pleased to inform you," the letter began, "that your name has been placed in nomination for the presidency of Auburn University."

My father enjoyed poetry. In college he memorized much verse, and as he grew older he often recited bits and pieces, particularly after a drink or two. One of his favorite poems was Oliver Goldsmith's "The Deserted Village." "Sweet Auburn, loveliest village of the plain," Father began, holding his glass before his face and looking through it back to youth, "where health and plenty cheared the labouring swain . . . Sweet smiling village, loveliest of the lawn, Thy sports are fled, and all thy treasures withdrawn." Storrs, I thought, as I stared across the green fields to the wood beyond, was my Auburn. Unlike Goldsmith's village, depopulated and ruined by greed, Storrs was not deserted. My little house, though, had grown quieter. At eight and ten, the boys had started living in worlds about which I knew little and into which I did not fit. From camp in Maine they wrote letters about friends I would not meet: Bear, Sleeping Beauty, Pine Man, Sticks, and Cookie. They described card games of which I had not heard: Uno, Cheater, and Bart Simpson. Although loving, the letters saddened me. At six Eliza was still my baby, calling whenever I neglected to kiss her goodnight and in the morning blowing strings of kisses to me when I left the house. Still, she too would soon have an exclusive world. First grade was but a month away, and next summer, she wanted to go away to camp. A cloud passed over my mind, shadowing mood and chilling thought. With the children deserting my domestic village, perhaps the time had come for me to take a new position, one that would clutter days and fill empty hours.

The following week the boys' camp ended, and Vicki, the children, and I went to Nova Scotia for a fortnight. I did not answer the letter before leaving Storrs. Fifteen years ago I visited a friend in Auburn. All I recalled was that one night we drove to a restaurant outside town and ate catfish and hush puppies for dinner. What I remembered clearly, however, was the bus station in Montgomery. I rode the bus from Nashville to Montgomery. Before leaving Nashville I drank a pot of tea, and when the trip ended in Montgomery, I went to the lavatory. I was there only a few moments when someone rushed in. Before I could arrange myself, he thrust a hand between me and the wall. In it were several shiny pieces of glass. "I found these diamonds on the street," he said, "and I'll sell them to you for twenty dollars." "No," I said, backing off to the side and adjusting things. "How about ten dollars," he said. I did not buy the diamonds, and by the time he reduced the price to five dollars, I was out the door.

In Nova Scotia I pondered the letter. Legality binds college presidents as thread a spool. Aside from erecting buildings and starting new programs presidents can do little. Dismantling even the most decayed intellectual mausoleum is beyond a president's power. With luck, a person could, I decided, become a voice for the good, the true, and the beautiful, and maybe decorum, perhaps even intelligence, but all one could do was talk. For my part I knew I could mouth the appropriate tired phrases: quest for excellence, foundations of knowledge, mission to the community, service in the name of humanity. Without deeds, though, to give them body, words poison, not the listeners who often confuse sound with substance but speakers themselves. Forever observing audiences mistake word for accomplishment, a speaker can easily lose self-respect, seeing himself but an actor, a word-twister, manipulating people. Coming to think life but a stage on which players strut for nothing higher than personal advantage, he may eventually harden out of vital feeling into dead cynicism.

In the letter the secretary to Auburn's board of trustees wrote that the "Search Advisory Committee" intended "to maintain total confidentiality regarding all candidates until final interviews." To me confidentiality seemed a small virtue. At worst a candidate could only be rejected, a matter of no significance. Still, the emphasis placed upon secrecy led me to doubt myself. Perhaps secrecy was important, and only a person not suited for such a post would think otherwise. Whatever the case, I mentioned the letter to a couple of friends before going to Nova Scotia. "I hear you have been selected as president of Auburn," Suzy said when I saw her on my return. "Does this mean we are going to lose you?" "Not likely," I answered. In the mail was a letter from a friend in Oregon. I had not heard from him in four years. "Auburn?" he began, "What a kick in the butt! Just tell them you used to play center for the Crimson Tide and they won't care how many times you were knocked in the head—the job will be yours."

Secrecy I finally concluded was important to the person who took himself seriously and who wanted other people to take him seriously, too—just the sort to appeal to trustees "in whose hands," as an old platitude might have put it, "responsibility for the well-being of the institution rests in an almost sacred trust." Would that I took myself seriously. I do not. Recently a radio station in Baltimore interviewed me. "I read an article," the announcer said, "in which a writer stated that you were arguably the finest essayist in the country." "Well," I broke in before the announcer finished, "all I can say is that the man would have to argue long and hard before he convinced me of that." As for others taking me seriously, they are few and far, far distant. Friends in the English department write mocking letters whenever my books appear, letters which I enjoy. "We have brought," the staff of the New York Public Library supposedly wrote after the publication of *Let It Ride*, "and sometimes after almost unpardonable delays, paid for several copies each of your almost innumerable collections of personal essays that, we all feel, present to the American people a portrait of themselves unrivaled in the works of any other essayist at any other time in history. We yield to no one, however fierce be the struggle, in our admiration for those essays. Few of us, and those few mostly the unwed, have neglected to read your essays to our children and bedridden loved ones, thereby inspiring many of them to take up their beds and walk, or even run, haltingly."

In truth this letter was almost too subtle for my taste. My sense of humor is broad and not presidential. For the past month I have told friends about the deadly Foo bird. Three anthropologists, it seems, wandered up the Amazon to explore an ancient Indian temple. Natives guided the anthropologists through the jungle. Once they reached the temple, however, the natives refused to go farther explaining that the dreaded Foo bird nested inside. When the anthropologists asked what made the Foo bird dangerous, the natives wagged their bottoms then ran away. For a while the anthropologists were nonplussed, but being intrepid explorers they girded their loins, climbed the steps, and entered the temple. The corridors in the temple were dank, and long hairy vines twisted like snakes between the broken stones. Initially the anthropologists listened carefully for chirps and tweets, but when they heard nothing they relaxed and, cataloguing the Foo bird as superstition, began to search for arrowheads and the remnants of stone clubs. Suddenly a shadow swam out of the darkness and swooping down pooped on the head of one of the anthropologists. Immediately the anthropologist began brushing the droppings out of his hair, using for a brush an ancient jawbone he found on the floor of the temple. A goodly number of teeth remained in the jawbone, and soon the anthropologist brushed the last bit of poop off his head, whereupon he groaned and keeled over dead. The death of their colleague upset the remaining anthro-pologists, but having come all the way to the Amazon, they were de-termined to complete their research. For the next several days things went well, but then just after they gathered a final pelvic bone from the rubble of the temple for their collections, a Foo bird appeared and flying past sprayed poop over one of the anthropologists. Be-side the temple was a stone pool. From various platforms around the temple small aqueducts drained into the pool. These once gushed with the blood of young virgins. At the time of the temple's heyday, civilization was in its larval stage, and the elders and priests bathed in the pool, convinced that such a dip washed their sins away and guaranteed them a rich diet of grubs, howler monkeys, and okra in the afterlife. That notwithstanding, only water and green frogs now filled the pool, and the second anthropologist stripped off his clothes and jumping into the pool washed himself thoroughly with Ivory soap. The soap did a good job, but, alas, as soon as the anthropolo-gist wiped away the last nub of poop, he threw up his hands and sinking under the surface, blew a big red bubble and slipped to death in the moss below. The last anthropologist walked to the edge of the pool and looking down saw his comrade on the bottom. For a moment he thought about giving his friend a good Christian burial, but suddenly another Foo bird dived out of the trees and pooped on his head. He reached up to brush off the droppings, but then he stopped, remembering what happened to his friends when they cleaned themselves. Instead, he shrugged and gathering his bones, stones, slides, and film, began the long trek back to New Haven. On his return he lived normally, as normally as anyone could with a pile of Foo poop on his head. Gradually, though, the Foo dropping eroded. After ten years only a lump remained. After fifteen years just a small end. After twenty years only a speck was visible, and looking at it one morning in the mirror while he was shaving, the anthro-pologist became impatient, and muttering "to hell with it," flicked the speck off with his tooth brush. Immediately he staggered back-ward and toppled over into the bathtub. Before his head hit the drain he was dead. "He should have known," the undertaker said, hoisting him out of the tub, "any fool knows, 'If the Foo shits, wear it.'"

Two days after returning to Connecticut from Nova Scotia, I ap-plied for the presidency of Auburn. I am not sure why I did. Ambition may have gotten the better of common sense. Whatever the reason, though, I suspected I was not suited for the position. The letter I wrote reflected mixed feelings, at one moment being humorous, the next platitudinous. "If things get to the interview stage," I requested, "let me know a month in advance. I munched through pastures this summer and," I explained, "must do a little contour work on the middle forty before I talk to people." I also wrote that my family was happy in Storrs. With that I should have stopped but I continued, shamefully sappy and sycophantic, adding, that "if I thought I had a chance to do something important for Southern education, by gosh I'd jump at the opportunity." In the next week I hopped instead of jumped. During the past two years I have roamed the country lecturing about education. Audiences have enjoyed what I said, and the success of the talks lay behind the nomination to Auburn. Almost in response to the letter of application, I decided to stop traveling. I turned down requests for speeches, and big fees, in Ohio and New Jersey, accepting invitations only from within my community, agreeing: to welcome freshmen to Eastern Connecticut State University, to sign a book of essays at the campus bookstore, to be interviewed on the local radio station at 6:30 one Thursday morning, and to read descriptions of Horsebarn Hill at a fund raiser for the Greenway, conservation trails running alongside rivers throughout eastern Connecticut. At the town fair I joined the Natchaug Ornithological Society and donated money to the Soup Kitchen in Willimantic. Not only did I wedge myself into community but I became more outspoken. If news of my nomination flew to Oregon second day air, perhaps Trailways would carry my remarks to Alabama. When asked what I thought about upcoming elections for Town Council, I said I had renounced politics, at least until "this nation follows the shining example of our liberal brethren in the Soviet Union and lets our captive peoples go." Some tribes, I added, should be thrust from us. Louisiana could be ceded to some progressive Central American country, Guatemala, I suggested, for the government in Guatemala City was almost as bribable as the junta in Baton Rouge.

For a month my attitude toward the nomination remained inconsistent. The football stadium is the largest structure on the Auburn campus, tiers of seats rising high over the field, the whole resembling a bomb crater. For years I have criticized big athletic programs, believing they trivialized learning and corrupted universities. Nevertheless the afternoon of the town fair I went to the Connecticut–Furman football game. Edward and Eliza accompanied me. Three years ago the whole family went to a game. The day was hot, and midway through the first quarter Francis rolled off his seat and stretched out in the shade at our feet. By the end of the quarter he was in tears because of both heat and boredom. Shortly after the beginning of the second quarter, he, Vicki, and Eliza went home. Edward refused to go, and so I sat through four long, hot quarters with him. Vicki and Francis did not attend the Furman game. However they sat on the slope beneath the parking lot built for basketball games and watched sky divers parachute into the stadium before the kickoff. Afterwards they ate lunch at Jonathan's, the snack bar on campus and then went to the Benton Art Museum. Edward and Eliza ate hot dogs and drank Coca Cola with me on the forty-third row. At halftime I walked Eliza home while Edward ate another hot dog and munched his way through a box of popcorn. Afterward he drank a second large Coke. When Vicki and Francis came home, I returned to the game. Later, as Edward and I walked along Hillside, I thought about football. I enjoyed the afternoon—Edward's and Eliza's company, more than the game—but the game was still fun, albeit trivial. Too trivial, I temporized that night in bed, to become a matter of principle and prevent me from accepting a college presidency.

By Monday the sophistic fit passed, and when I looked again at the picture of the Auburn campus, the stadium reminded me of a giant pock market, a scar beyond intellectual surgery. I felt relieved, a bit like the way Googoo Hooberry, a character in my essays, felt when he recovered from the mumps. "How are you doing, Googoo," Hoben Donkin asked when he met Googoo in Read's Drugstore. "Oh, Hoben," Googoo answered, "I was better, but now I'm getting over it." My literary acquaintances are simple, and my friendship for them will not impress trustees searching for someone "wrapped in the mantle of lifelong learning." I'm particularly fond of widows, though in my essays they have small capacity for affection, especially for husbands. Clevanna Farquarson was eating pickled pigs' feet when Hoben Donkin ran into the house to tell her that Royce her husband was dead. "The worst thing has happened," Hoben burst out, "Royce fell into the headsaw up at the sawmill and got killed deader than a doornail." When Clevanna did not respond but continued gnawing, Hoben said, "Seems to me you ought to be a little upset. It ain't everyday that a woman's husband gets sliced and planed like a two-by-four." "Hoben," Clevanna answered, reaching for the last foot on the plate and picking a hunk of fat out of her teeth, "just you wait until I finish this here pig's trotter, and then you'll hear hollering what is hollering."

Alive and on the hoof, Royce wasn't worth much. He drank, dipped snuff, and ran around with every loose piece of lattice in Smith County. "Good always comes to them who suffer and wait," Clevanna was fond of saying, and at his death Royce balanced the ledger, turning Clevanna's losses into gain. With an eye to the main financial chance, Clevanna took out an insurance policy on Royce, and when the saw at the mill fell like the Sword of Damocles, she became almost wealthy. "Lordy," Hoben exclaimed, when he heard about the insurance, "a body has to get up awful early to beat you out of anything, Clevanna." "Huh," Clevanna said, looking Hoben in the eye, "they don't have no time in Tennessee as early as what I get up." Clevanna's remark was too subtle for Hoben, and not knowing how to respond, he looked at his watch and said, "Gracious me, it's one-thirty. I had no idea it was so late." "So it is," Clevanna answered, glancing at the clock on the wall; "it's always one-thirty here at this time of day." Time was on Clevanna's mind. Reckoning that she wasted good years on Royce, she determined to marry again, and soon. A month after collecting the insurance, she began courting Loppie Groat's cousin, Newbern. Although Newbern was not one of Smith County's most eligible males, he was handsome, owned a team of red mules, and did not drink or take snuff. Even better he was a little slow, and Clevanna thought she could collar and haul him to the altar quickly. She succeeded, although Newbern did not have a romantic constitution. One night not long before they married, they sat spooning on the bench outside Read's Drugstore. "Just look how blue the sky is," Clevanna said, squeezing Newbern's hand. "Mighty blue and high too," Newbern answered. "And the stars," Clevanna continued, her voice a hoarse whisper, "aren't they numerous?" "Yes, indeed," Newbern answered, "and ain't there lots of them."

I resemble Newbern. High observation is beyond me, and my thought naturally runs to the low ground. Whenever Auburn came to mind I did not think about large matters of policy; instead I dreamed of little things: planting iris in a garden, blue and yellow ones like those Grandma Pickering grew in Carthage, or dove hunting—well, not so much hunting, for as a boy I was a terrible shot and have not hunted in twenty-five years, but instead squatting at the edge of a corn field, shotgun broken open across my knees, furrows clayey in front of me, a breeze rippling trees along a bank in the distance, below a small river twisting sleepily through bends, the water curling around snags in slow, red circles. Some football Saturday when the bomb crater was filled I would slip away from Auburn with the children, and we'd wander the field searching for arrowheads. We'd talk about nearby towns with Indian names, sounding them out, letting them roll over our tongues like seed: Opelika, Tallassee, Wetumpka, Letohatchee, and Sylacauga. On the way home we'd stop for ice cream at Eufaula or Hatchechubbee. That night I would not know who won the game, but I'd have a sense of place.

When Marty changed the oil in my new Mazda van, he noticed that the left front headlight was filled with water. "If you don't replace the light," he said, "every time you drive you will have to take dramamine to keep from getting seasick." Last week I took the van to Manchester to have the light repaired and a roof rack put on top. I arrived when the dealership opened at six-thirty in the morning. The manager told me the work would take two hours, and I walked up Center Street to The Whole Donut and for $1.49 bought a glazed chocolate doughnut and a medium-sized cup of coffee. I spent the two hours at The Whole Donut. The shop was busy, and people flowed through in quick currents, only the old and the homeless eddying into nooks. On the front door a sign stated, "No Shoes, No Shirt, No Service." Below and to the right was another sign, reading "Open 24 Hours"; next to it was an advertisement for Camel cigarettes, on the front of which was sketched a jaunty orange camel, a cigarette drooping from the left corner of his mouth and sunglasses resting on a nose as long and as round a grinder. The store sold cigarettes; hanging on the wall over the counter was a rectangular box with shelves resembling a rack for storing cooking spices. Instead, though, of containing small jars of curry powder, celery seed, oregano, caraway, and thyme, the rack was stuffed with packs of Winston, Doral, Vantage, Salem, and Camel. Although some of the people in booths smoked, no one bought cigarettes while I was in the store. For that matter no one ordered a "Morning Magic Breakfast Sandwich," the choices being ham, egg, and cheese; sausage, egg, and cheese; bacon, egg, and cheese, or egg and cheese, served, the advertisement stated, "on Your Choice of Croissant, Bagel, or Roll." Neither did anyone buy the thirty-two-ounce soda for ninety-nine cents "plus tax" and receive as a souvenir a large plastic cup with the insignia of the New York Yankees baseball team stamped on the front. Fall and football had arrived. A thick man wore a blue jacket with UCONN Football stamped on it while students wore shirts proclaiming loyalties to the Chicago Bears, New England Patriots, Green Bay Packers, and Indianapolis Colts.

Although Doug ordered coffee with "three and a half sugars and beaucoup milk," I did not hear much that was said. Behind me in a booth a man told an acquaintance that he'd drunk so much the night before that he could not remember where he parked his car. When he awakened, he recounted, he thought he was in jail. "I've always hated her," a large woman exclaimed to a small man sitting across from her. Before seven-thirty, most customers were workmen, batches of keys clipped to belt loops, boots laced only through the fourth eye, the tops splayed open and looking soggy. Most wore blue trousers and blue shirts, their names, Mike or Whitey, appearing above an upper pocket, dark letters printed on a white platter-shaped background. One or two wore windbreakers advertising companies for which they worked: NEW Home Sewing Machine or Northeast Utilities. Occasionally a mailman or bus driver bustled in. At seven-thirty costumes changed; blue shirts and workpants became blue sport coats, slacks, and blouses as secretaries and managers picked up doughnuts for morning coffee breaks. Throughout the morning old people drifted in; sometimes one looked at the wall clock impatiently, pretending that time mattered and that schedule bound him to responsibility. Old men lingered expectantly over their coffees, seeming to hope someone would talk to them and fill the gaping minutes. When they left, however, they usually rushed out, as if they had indulged themselves and malingered through appointments. After eight o'clock, four women who lived hard appeared, their faces yellowish, hair caked, eyelids swollen and dry, eyes watery, and shaking hands clumpy and arthritic. The women sat apart from the other customers, rarely speaking or looking up from their coffees.

When I left The Whole Donut I felt depressed. Trash removal was that morning. Beside driveways and in the gutter along Center Street trash cans overflowed and plastic bags split, the oily, black smell of ripening waste misty along the road. On the sidewalk outside Lloyd's Auto Parts was a rusty handle from a child's wagon. Somebody, I thought, might trip over the handle, so I stuck it into a garbage can. When I turned around, a man in Lloyd's smiled and waved at me. I noticed a white sign with big red letters in the window of Flo's Cake Decorating Supplies. "Hope: Always Possible," the sign declared, advertising a lecture at the local library. "Right," I thought. Suddenly I noticed flowers pushing through cracks at the curb and growing in dirt next to the sidewalk: Queen Anne's lace, butter and eggs, goldenrod, and Asiatic dayflower, the blue and yellow blossoms glowing in the early morning sunshine.

Vicki is happy in Storrs and does not approve of my applying for the job at Auburn. I tried to reassure her, asking if she could name a single grant or job for which I had applied successfully. "That's just it," she exclaimed, "you deserve most of the things you have applied for, yet you have not gotten one. Now you apply for something which doesn't suit you and for which you aren't qualified. Logic damns you to a presidency." Vicki is polite and quietly intelligent, yet she will on occasion use unpresidential language. Last fall the children took swimming lessons. At sign-up in the spring the director of recreation noticed that Eliza was five years old. According to the rules, the director told Vicki, Eliza could not take lessons with Francis and Edward on Monday, Wednesday, and Friday nights. Instead her lessons would be on Tuesday and Thursday. When Vicki explained that Eliza swam with the boys in the fall, the director listened unsympathetically. Rules were made, he said, for the good of the children and had to be enforced. The prospect of five nights of swimming tried Vicki's patience. She threw Eliza's registration on to the director's desk and, standing, shouted, "This really pisses me off." She then stalked out the door. I met Vicki in the courtyard behind town hall, and she told me what happened. "Don't worry," I said in my best presidential manner, "I'll take care of this." "There has been," I said walking into the director's office, "a slight mistake. For some reason when my wife registered our daughter Eliza for swimming just now, she got the year of Eliza's birth wrong. Eliza was born in 1984, not 1985." "Oh," the director said, relief in his voice, "that makes her six years old." "Yes," I smiled. "Well, Mr. Pickering," he said, "we'll just switch her into the same class as her brothers." "Thank you," I said, leaving the office and beaming like a tomato.

Despite the lapse at town hall Vicki behaves more decorously than I. Rarely do I behave in a presidential manner. Eliza and Edward play on the same soccer team. Edward is a star scoring and stripping opponents of the ball while Eliza is a starlet. Instead of running about the field she prefers to play goalie. In the goalie's black shirt and pink gloves, she dances about and sings songs and, in truth, stops most shots. Last week when Edward missed a game to attend a birthday party, Vicki planned a late supper, forgetting that Eliza still had a game. When I reminded her, it was too late to make dinner, so I drove to Paul's and ordered a pizza, a large one, pepperoni on one half, olives on the other, and since Edward was out of the house, mushrooms over everything. Beneath the radio in the van is a tape player. Never before have I owned a car with a tape player, and I was curious about its operation. The pizza took fifteen minutes to prepare, so I walked next door to the Disc and bought my first tape, 12 Hits from The Best of Chuck Berry, songs such as "Roll Over Beethoven," "Maybelline," and "Johnny B. Goode." Forty minutes later Eliza and I were reeling and rocking around Hillside Circle, windows down and music blaring. How many college presidents, I wondered, hammer along the road with Chuck Berry howling, and six-year-old daughters bouncing on the seats behind them, shouting, "Go, baby, go."

Last fall Googoo Hooberry and Loppie Groat went opossum hunting in the woods behind Bible Hill. That night a storm blew in from west Tennessee. Rain washed through the hills, spilling boulders down gulches. Thunder smashed, and lightning broke trees, turning the forest blue with smoke. Googoo and Loppie were so frightened they became lost and after wandering aimlessly for four hours spent the night under a ledge. The next morning Googoo clambered over the ledge, hiked to the top of a bluff, and climbed a tree to find out where they were. For ten minutes he scanned the horizon. Finally he got his bearings. "Great God, Loppie," he shouted, "we ain't here at all. We're six miles east of here." For most of September I wasn't in my Connecticut village. On the last weekend of the month, though, I returned home to a walk through Schoolhouse Brook woods followed by the Lion's Club cookout. Tulip-poplar, birch, and maple had lost leaves, spotting the ground yellow. Pine drops were red, and most ferns had faded out of green and begun to shrivel and turn brown. When the wind blew, acorns slapped through the branches, bounced on the ground, and ran across the path. Eliza gathered a bag of oak apple galls for show and tell at school. Edward caught one of the summer's last garter snakes, and Francis collected mushrooms: smooth chanterelles, white cheese polydores, pear-shaped puffballs, and his favorite, the spotted cort, dappled with purple and white. That night Loppie reported that Clevanna's marriage was not working out well and she had begun to dip snuff. One Friday she took the train to Nashville and spent the weekend there by herself. Loppie blamed the trouble on money, saying that if Clevanna were poor she could not buy snuff, much less imagine a trip to Nashville. Still, he admitted, Newbern wasn't exciting. Just last Thursday, Loppie accompanied Clevanna and Newbern to Abner Turrentine's funeral. After the burial the three of them strolled through the graveyard, reading tombstones and talking about friends who were dead. Newbern was almost garrulous, albeit not entertaining. Curiously the dates of people's deaths affected him more than the inscriptions over graves. "Oh, Lord, that's awful," he exclaimed after reading on a stone that Wilbur Hutchins died in 1832; "I can't bear to think about it." On seeing a stone with 1894 carved on it, he shook his head and said, "That's terrible, just terrible." He paused before a marker with 1916 on it and scowled, but didn't speak. Finally, though, he stopped before a tombstone and smiled. "Nineteen thirty-three—that ain't bad," he said; "a fellow might could live with that."

9 Fall

*F*or two weeks Vicki weeded the attic and raked closets, stuffing toys into boxes in the hall and building a compost heap of clothes in the basement. Then for four days she washed and folded. Finally, the tag sale arrived. On October 5, I got up early and lined one side of the driveway with bookshelves. On them Vicki stacked clothes: children's shirts and sweaters priced fifty and seventy-five cents apiece and trousers from fifty cents to two dollars. Furnishing the other side of the drive was the stuff of two rooms: rugs, lamps, chairs, tables, and two playpens. Against the garage door were toys, a parking lot crammed with metal cars and trucks and then four boxes of plastic toys: a one-cent box, a five, a ten, and finally a twenty-five-cent box. A rack of Vicki's dresses hung in the garage. Worn in the crisp spring before babies, the clothes were light and flowing, and whenever anyone touched the rack, they swished back and forth like the quick rippling step of a young woman. "Priced to sell," Vicki said, a change purse shaped like a hunk of watermelon strapped to her middle, "bargains galore." She was right; things disappeared quickly. Vicki furnished plastic bags, and mothers bought seasons of clothes. To a grandmother she sold our baby carriage for twelve dollars and then for ten dollars the high chair that once cost a hundred dollars. A slender girl in a red car bought six of Vicki's dresses. She didn't want a clothes bag. Folding the dresses over her arm she switched down the drive and out of sight. "She'll learn," Vicki said. "What will she learn," I said. "That she'll need dresses with pockets," Vicki answered, "bulky pockets." "Yes," I thought, pockets big enough for family and throbbing fear, big enough for the ache of guttering through the attic and selling one's youth and the childhood of one's children: the red sweater with the yellow engine pulling a green train across the front, and the pink dress, balloons like lollipops lifting a teddy bear up through a blue sky toward orange clouds.

By noon almost everything had sold, even the clothes rack and book cases. What remained Vicki packed into boxes for WAIM, Windham Area Interfaith Ministries. After subtracting nine dollars for tag sale signs and an advertisement in the local newspaper, Vicki made $304.35. Unfortunately during the morning I noticed Mark Roberts, a tree surgeon, working across the street. At the edge of our dell stood a big sugar maple. Just above the ground the tree split, resembling the wings of a gull in flight. While one wing hung over the brush pile in the woods, the other swept over Mrs. Carter's driveway and, blowing against her upstairs bedroom, made her nervous. For two hundred and twenty-five dollars Mark removed the tree, reducing the day's profits to $79.35, enough for four family dinners at Tony's Pizza in Willimantic and afterward trips down Main Street to Mr. Donut.

Along with the success of the tag sale, we celebrated the end of summer and the beginning of fall: Eliza's last dose of amoxycillin, twenty-one days of pills prescribed for Lyme disease. The medicine had not sapped Eliza's energy. Beginning in September and running throughout October, she and Edward played soccer in a town league. Local businesses donated tee-shirts, and Edward and Eliza wore numbers 34 and 35 on the team sponsored by Mansfield Supply. The shirts were pink with white lettering, colors appealing to Eliza. Three nights a week Mansfield Supply played Realty World, Marty's Service Center, Keeper Corp., the Eagleville Fire Department, or Brody, Prue & Parlato. The children played for fun, not victory, and whenever Mansfield Supply dominated another team Coach Bohn shifted his best players from offense to defense. In the last game parents played their children, and lost. Afterward the Bohns treated everyone to pizza and presented awards to the children: Jeremy, Lori, Arlo, James, Devin, Eric, Neeva, Eliza, and Edward. While Edward was "The Greatest Breakaway Threat," Eliza was "Most Courageous," battling after the ball, and leaving third graders tumbled behind her. Not once during October did Edward call her "a regular chubby Egyptian dweeb from Pluto." Instead she was "rock," and "the girl of steel."

Only in fall are athletics part of my life. The homecoming parade for the football team is small, but I never miss it. Led by the university band in white puttees, blue suits, and balaclava helmets, the parade winds pass the gymnasium then turns down Gilbert Road and wanders through the campus, ending opposite the library. This year the day was yellow and mild. On the field next to the library families cooked lunch. Beside grills smoking with hot dogs and hamburgers stood card tables, oil cloth across the tops and stacked with mustard, ketchup, paper plates, plastic spoons and forks, fat bags of potato chips, and bowls of creamy onion dip. Underneath the tables were tubs filled with ice and cans of soda, mostly Coca Cola and Pepsi, but a few Dr. Peppers. At one end of the field students sold pumpkins, and around the edges of the field footballs and frisbees soared and fell like leaves in the wind. Students on floats tossed candy to spectators, and along the parade route parents clustered in groups and talked while children hovered at curb's edge, filling their pockets with bubblegum, caramels, and hard gold candies. The people watching the parade were an informal blue jean and khaki crowd, wearing sweaters and light jackets, running shoes and Blucher moccasins. Grandparents pushed strollers and baby carriages; young long-haired mothers carried infants in back packs, seeming old-fashioned. Indeed the parade and day were familial and old-fashioned. A green turtle cartwheeled through the air; a gorilla beat his breast, and Little Red Riding Hood chased the Wolf. A clown rode by in a motorized bathtub, a red umbrella mounted over the faucet. A two-legged blond Holstein followed a milkmaid carrying a shepherd's crook. Dressed in woodsy, brown uniforms, the Nathan Hale Ancient Fife and Drum band from Coventry marched past, stopping occasionally for the rifle corps to fire into the air. The rifles made much smoke, but not so much as Al's M.G. Every year Al drives in the parade. Usually he follows the Shriners. This year the Sphinx Temple sent both the Motor Pool and the Cycle Unit, the first riding in go-carts and the second mounted on small red Kawasaki motorcycles, all except the leader who drove a black Harley-Davidson. Not far behind the Shriners was the student "Shopping Car Unit." Dressed as Moors they pushed shopping carts borrowed from the A & P and decorated with blue and white crepe paper. At commands from their leader, a tall boy wearing Mickey Mouse ears, the unit raised the fronts of the carts, spun them in a circle, and turning about wove through each other forming a figure eight. A Dalmatian sat in the front seat of the big red university fire truck. An orange and black dragon danced along the sidewalk. A policewoman rode a brown Morgan horse, the animal not affected by the Gaelic Highland Pipe Band just behind, playing "Yankee Doodle Dandy" on their bagpipes. Several cars got caught in the parade, and I saw Boris in his new Volvo stationwagon, baby seats high on the back seat and bumper sticker reading "School's Open Drive Carefully." Anyone who wants to join the parade can do so. Next year I plan to wear my green wig and red cape, and putting George in the basket, ride my bicycle. Edward and Eliza, and maybe Vicki, will be embarrassed, but Francis and I will like it.

Most of fall's doings are not seasonal. Instead they continue the foolishness of the year. Still, fall changes some things, giving daily matters a supple, leathery texture, making them resemble leaves from white and red oaks, those brown leaves which blow across the forest floor and gather along paths, adding body and stability to the gray, open woods. In September a book of my essays was published. In October reviews began to appear. The *Hartford Courant* called me "a state hysterical landmark." A critic in Birmingham wondered why my books were "not familiar to others" who shared his "interest in southern writers." In an editorial entitled "The Literate Corner," the *Willimantic Chronicle* mentioned ten writers in the "Quiet Corner" of Connecticut. I was the last mentioned. The next morning Josh dropped by my office. Josh lives outside the comfort zone. "Don't be disappointed," he said, putting the editorial on my desk, my name circled in red ink. "In that better paper to come, the ass shall be first, and the first shall be last." Neither Josh nor the jibe lingered long. That afternoon I was guest on a radio talk show broadcast from Baltimore. The host talked to me, after which callers telephoned to ask questions. Phil made the first call. He called from his car phone, saying he had read all my books and "had to talk" to me. "A roll," I said that night to Vicki, "I'm on a roll, a big mother of a roll." Waiting for me in the office the next day was a letter marked "PRIVATE AND CONFIDENTIAL." With "Offices in the Principal Cities of the World," LeBoeuf and Lamb, "Consultants in Executive Search," informed me that I had been nominated for the presidency of a university in Kentucky. I knew little about the school, so I telephoned the man who wrote to me. "This is Sam Pickering," I said to the secretary; "I would like to speak to Mr. Dobbs please. He wrote me about the presidency of a university." There was a pause, then Mr. Dobbs picked up the telephone. "Hey, Sam, baby," he said, "what can I do for you." "Obviously," Vicki said that night, "he was a friend of Phil, and it's all part of the roll."

Since the tag sale Vicki herself had been rolling along. She resented her profits turning to sawdust and once or twice steamed over me. "Sometimes," Eliza said recently, "I like it when you and Mommy fight. It gives me something to watch." Through a dinner party early in November ran a creek of wine. During dessert Vicki picked up her glass and peering through it, looked at me and said, "We should make love for four straight hours." "What," I said, a hunk of chocolate cake quivering on my fork. "Four hours. At fifteen minutes a whack," she continued looking off into the distance to check her calculations, "one hour would equal four times, or a week's worth. Four hours would take care of four weeks, a month of 'that' over and done with in an afternoon." Vicki's idea stopped conversation for a moment then the wives around the table began to nod. At first the men were silent, but after glancing at their mates became garrulous. "More wine," Charles said. "Me, too," said Elbert raising his glass; "you know I'm not much of a basketball fan, but what about this year's Huskies? Some team, eh?" "You bet," Pat said; "and I'd like a drop more wine myself." The homecoming football game occurs once a year; the game between men and women has no off-season or off-age. In mid-November a new boy entered Edward's third grade class. "He has played spin the bottle, Daddy," Edward told me. "He has?" I answered; "I played that in the sixth grade." "You did?" Edward exclaimed, wrinkling his face in disgust, "Why? What's the fun? It's gross."

Instead of explaining the pleasures of the game, I read. For years I have read to the children for an hour each day, twisting out of sticky questions and, in truth, having much fun. This fall I read L. Frank Baum's books, six of which "Grandmother Jones" gave to Vicki's father when he was a boy in Columbus, Ohio: *The Marvelous Land of Oz, Ozma of Oz, The Emerald City of Oz, The Tin Woodman of Oz, Glinda of Oz,* and *The Patchwork Girl of Oz.* Before I read Baum's books, Edward was writing *Magical Mysteries,* a collection of short stories including "Oddball Owl," "The Moon Rock," and "The Ten-Armed Starfish." After I began the Oz books, he put the mysteries aside and started work on a novel, *Big Indian Joe of Oz*. In the first chapter Indian Joe visited Moneytown. Coins from around the world lived in Moneytown. Having inherited wealth, the coins did not work, and the sides with heads on them spent their days gossiping. From Moneytown Indian Joe travelled to Pencilville. Unlike the coins who asked endless questions, the pencils were too busy writing to notice Joe, much less talk to him. Mine is a bookish house, and comfortable with tales, the children play with words. One night in November I judged a password contest for which the children fashioned secret phrases. Third prize went to Eliza for "How will you wake up for school, my dear." Francis captured both first and second with "Ruby wants a fat baby" and "Always remember to wash your fruit." "Great careers lie ahead for them in advertising," Josh said later, "Or if you prefer, in 'word management.'"

Occasionally I think I am in the word management business. By the end of September I doubt my teaching. If words are used not to illuminate but to obscure, not to explain but to win, why do I stress clarity? Three weeks ago I bought stock in a company that manufactures chemicals. "No, not chemicals," the broker said, "we now say ethical pharmaceuticals." One morning during an examination given for a graduate degree my mind drifted. Outside the classroom wind blew, and as the bare limbs of oak trees pushed and shoved, seeming to scratch the sky, I thought about teaching. On the first day of class some teachers ask students what they expect to gain from a course, after which the teachers draw up "contracts" detailing not only the content and objectives of the course but also the students' responsibilities. Why, I wondered, don't teachers ever ask, "What do you hope will not happen in this class?" Instead of platitudes, the question might reap an honest answer. Rarely, of course, does honesty go down well. Usually it rises to the educational gorge, smacking not of spice or fun, but of bile. Shortly after the examination I went to the Middle School for a conference with Francis's teachers. Francis's grades were good, and all was conventional until a teacher said, in passing, "and he is getting better at working with others." "What," I exclaimed, "I hope not. Arrogance runs in my family, and until now I thought Francis inherited a saving dose of it. Nothing would upset me more than seeing him at ease amid the undistinguished herd." "Well done," Josh said after I described the conference to him, "now to solidify your reputation why don't you wear a costume to the Early American Potluck Supper next week? You could be a Puritan if you wore black and carried a banner saying 'Beware Fornication.' Or if that's too strong why don't you glue a gooseberry to your forehead and go as a Native American Berry."

Josh talks to me more in fall than in any other season. By winter I am too busy for conversation. The children's doings tire me and so fill the hours that I rarely think about teaching. Instead of being irritated by platitude I am thankful for it, ready to embrace anything that fosters routine. Of course, much of fall is seasonal, or routine. In October Vicki puts chrysanthemums on the front porch, this year pots busy with white, yellow, and purple blossoms. In fall relatives who have remained distant over the hot, green summer pull close, almost as if they believe family can sustain them through the gathering cold. "Our life is as exciting as ever," my cousin Katherine wrote from Nashville, "I have been to three funerals this week, and it's only Thursday. I guess when you are my age there's not a whole heap left." What is left is a mausoleum packed with tales about death and dying. Loppie Groat weeded the cemetery in Carthage last week because, as he explained to Turlow Gutheridge, he "wanted to make it more inviting." When Vester McBee had stomach problems after eating some ancient country ham, Dr. Sollows prescribed a laxative, instructing her to take it twice a day. "Drink it with milk and Hershey's chocolate," he said, "and then keep a close watch and see what passes." Four days later Vester met Dr. Sollows outside Read's Drugstore and told him she felt "considerably better." "That's mighty fine," the doctor said, "and did anything out of the ordinary pass?" "No, I kept my eyes peeled," Vester answered, "and the only things that passed were two loads of hay, a barrow of coal, the ice wagon, Loppie Groat's mule Jeddry, Isom Legg, Clevanna Farquarson, and then Slubey Garts and that no account deacon of his, Proverbs Goforth." Not long after he passed Vester's house, Isom Legg got sick. The medicines Dr. Sollows prescribed didn't help, and although he'd never even been to Sunday school, Isom suddenly became interested in religion. "What do you think about this here deathbed repentance?" he asked Dr. Sollows one morning. "I don't know much about it," Dr. Sollows answered, "but it's probably better than nothing." "Well, if I ain't feeling better tomorrow," Isom exclaimed, "I'll be damned if I don't try it."

On the same day Katherine's letter arrived, United Parcel delivered a box of chestnuts from Aunt Elizabeth in Richmond. Brown and waxy, the chestnuts grew on a tree in Aunt Elizabeth's yard. Vicki put the box on the floor by the door to the pantry closet, intending to roast the nuts on the weekend. The next day Vicki noticed greasy splotches on the kitchen floor and at dinner accused me of dropping raisins on the linoleum and then stepping on them and tracking the grease around the room. What Vicki said was plausible. I eat raisins by the handful, so I apologized and promised that I would be tidier in the future. The next morning at breakfast, however, Vicki discovered six pudgy white worms humping across the kitchen floor. Not raisins but crushed worms caused the grease spots, and before leaving for class, I dumped the chestnuts on the compost pile in the backyard. Indian summer was upon us, and some nuts sprouted. Soon seedlings were fifteen inches high, and I wondered if they would survive the first heavy frost. They didn't, and I buried them under a hill of leaves. Although cold cut the chestnuts down like a scythe, it did not level the crawling creation, at least not the portion inhabiting the house. In the second week in November a cloud of small moths blew into the kitchen. Like dusty snowflakes they fluttered above table and sink, drawing attention then curiosity. Their home was the top shelf of the pantry, and snug amid folds of napkins and paper towels, tinfoil, waxpaper, and sandwich bags were scores of minute yellow cocoons. The worms dined well. Joining the brown rice, oats, sesame seeds, yellow and green peas, dried yeast, barley, and powdered soy sauce of Nature's Burger was a new ingredient, one adding body and vitality to the "meatless burger mix." The worms were hardy trenchermen, and although they took gustatory pleasure in all corners of the pantry, they leaned heavily on the staff of life, gathering in clans to banquet on buckwheat groats, basmati rice, tabouli salad mix, wheat bran, hulless barley, and oriental noodles, in the case of this last not differentiating between beef, shrimp, and chicken flavors but preferring them all equally.

The duties of fall are various. The Friday before Halloween I took George to the veterinarian for his yearly shots: distemper, hepatitis, rabies, Lyme disease, parovirus, parainfluenza, and leptospirosis. As the tag sale marked the beginning, so Halloween marked the midpoint of fall. The night before Halloween we went to the Haunted House at Echo Grange in Mansfield Center. Just beyond the entrance Eliza started crying, and I carried her the rest of the way. While we crawled through a tunnel, she clung to my stomach, arms clutching my neck, legs wrapped around my middle, resembling Ulysses clinging to the sheep's belly and escaping the Cyclops. The next night Eliza was in good spirits. Halloween gives us the chance to visit neighbors and so despite sleet and a cold rain, we walked the neighborhood. We dug through trunks for costumes. I found a red cape from Saudi Arabia, and wearing a mask was the devil. After putting on a green wig topped off with flashing skulls, Vicki wrapped herself in a tablecloth bought ten years ago in Damascus and became an enchantress. Edward wore the jacket to one of my old suits, a necktie, and one of Father's hats, and for the second year running was a businessman, not, though, a gorilla businessman as last year but just an "insane" businessman. For her part Eliza put on a silver ballet dress, cut and pasted a golden moon for her hair, and was the Evening Star while Francis turned himself into a wizard, wearing a white beard, long green rubber fingers, two pairs of glasses, galoshes, a white Egyptian robe, and around his neck a blue glass chain from Greece, guaranteed to ward off the evil eye.

As the year shredded into humus, Vicki planted and gathered. "I got him," she said walking into my study the Monday after Halloween, "come see." "What?" I said. "The puppy," she said, "the one at the pet store that no one bought. I couldn't bear the thought of his being alone." For the last three weeks of October whenever Vicki went to the mall, she looked at a black and brown dachshund in the pet store. When Edward went with her to the mall to buy ice skates and saw the puppy, he named it Henry. On Vicki's mentioning Henry to me, I told her not to buy him. Pet store puppies, I said, came from dog factories. Raised in pen and cage, they were unstable and difficult to train. "Not like the fice," I said, pointing to George, only a part of which was dachshund, the rest being, we decided, "scratching, digging, smelling country dog."

Round and fat from lack of exercise, Henry resembled a saddle of veal. I bedded Henry down with George and afterward opened a bottle of California chardonay. Buttery, even a little fruity, I hoped the wine would make me see Henry through garnished eyes, if not make him slip smoothly over the palate. Alas, Henry needed not only parsley and celery, but sweet thyme, aromatic bay, and a gallon of Four Paws Stain and Odor Remover to make him appealing. At seven, ten, two, and then at five-thirty the next morning I cleaned the kitchen floor. After two days Vicki longed for chestnuts and clean white worms. After a week she washed her hands not only of Henry's accidents but of Henry himself. "Why did you let me get this dog?" she burst out one night as I sipped a "Fumé Blanc" from Washington. "A strong husband would have told his wife to keep out of the pet store." "If you ever write about this dog," she said ten days later, "don't pussyfoot around. Tell the mangy truth. Our lives are nothing but poop. Some night I am going to chop up a hunk and dump it on that veal you are always simpering on about." Not only was Henry undisciplined in doings private, but he had the manners of a pantry worm and bolted his food. Last spring I read Jack London's novels to the children, and after watching Henry churn through a meal, Edward said, "Daddy, why don't we rename the dogs. George could be White Fang and Henry, Call of the Kitchen."

Eventually Henry did better, but there were days when he almost broke me. "At fifty," I thought, sitting at the kitchen table one morning at four o'clock, "my life only amounts to one wife, two dogs, and three children." After all the sowing I had stored little away to stave off the cold ahead. To be sure a handful of books lurked in the root cellar, but they were at best straw, something the children could spread over an afternoon to warm a barren hour. Despite seeding the dell with bulbs and grafting story to the silverbell in the yard, the house wasn't mine. For years a dean of the business school lived here, and often when I describe where I live, people nod knowingly and say, "Oh, yes, the Ackerman place." Fall is a contemplative time. As the woods open and one can see beyond the brambles at the edge of fields, so people look inward. A stone wall of intentions slumps gray across the years while memory lies tumbled, no longer vigorous with leaf, but a log, green with moss and host to mushrooms, bits of recollection twisted and fantastic. Or so I thought early in the morning, Henry in my lap wagging his tail, paper towels and Four Paws on the table in front of me, and on the floor the trash can overturned, an apple core beneath the ice box and, resembling my sleep, wax paper gnawed and torn. Later, my gloom lifted. At eight o'clock I was in woods below the sheep barns. Henry tumbled happily after George, and beeches rose blue in the sunlight. A stream chattered down a slope; beside it grew winterberry, its switches red with fruit.

Throughout the fall I roamed field and wood. Not only did walking help me cope with Henry, but it soothed, turning petty annoyances into the stuff of joy. Walking even tempered my frustration with school. Instead of dwelling on failure I thought about success. Instead of chaffing at flaw and platitude, I smiled, remembering some of the educational doings in Carthage. Proverbs Goforth sent his second son, First Corinthians, to the Male and Female Select School. The son inherited his father's mind and was not a good student. When Quintus Tyler asked the class why days were longer in summer than winter, First Corinthians raised his hand. "That's an easy one," he said. "When something gets hot, it expands and that makes the day longer. When something gets cold, it shrinks, and that's why days are shorter in winter." That fall First Corinthians finished at the bottom of his class. "Son," his father said, looking at the report card, "why are you so low in the class?" "Pa, it don't make no matter whether I'm at the top or the bottom," First Corinthians said, stretching and yawning. "They teaches just the same at both ends." Although education did not take with the son, it raised a welt on the father. When Quintus started teaching the names of the planets to students, Proverbs got upset and, dragging Slubey Garts along with him, went to see Asa Lungerford the principal. "We're for education and don't hold none with censorship," Proverbs began. "We want Mr. Tyler to teach the stars and moons to the children, but we are progressive Christians here in Smith County, and it's time to get rid of them old-fashioned heathen names. I've got myself a list of good Bible names," Proverbs continued, pulling a scrap of paper from the right front pocket of his trousers, "Venus could become Bessie; Mars, Nathan Bedford Forrest; the Big Dipper, Enos Mayfield's Inn over in South Carthage, and the North Star, Nashville."

When I began walking, morning glories bloomed on the trellis beside the back door. By the end of November they had wilted, the vines drying into knots of twine and the leaves hanging down in brown bunches like tobacco in a barn. In early October goldenrod bloomed low around the edge of the cornfield above Valentine Meadow. In scrub grass small blue asters clustered in fingers, and mustard and spotted knapweed blossomed beside the road. Thistles drooped, the blossoms gone to seed, but amid the tatters an occasional flower puffed purple and glowing. While a mocking bird preened on a bramble, sparrows skittered by, dipping and bouncing like skiers over moguls, the yellow strips on their brows streaming back across their heads creating the impression of speed and daring. Canada geese gleaned in the field, their black heads rising above the pitch of the land and resembling stalks left when the corn was cut for silage. Above the creek, leaves on a walnut were brown and yellow. Chunks of green nuts hung heavy, and pulling the branches down made the tree forlorn. Dogwood smouldered through color, the leaves close to the trunk still green, the rest a black, almost cindered pink. Seed capsules of winged euonymous had popped, the orange seeds dangling, the pods above rolled into dark red scrolls. Bittersweet twisted through all the trees, its seed capsules unopened. In November, pods would split into three parts, each part resembling the back of a yellow beetle. Bittersweet held its leaves longer than most trees, and in November the vines stood out, seeming to wash down from the sky splattering the forest yellow.

In the brush behind the storage sheds in the woods was an old steam shovel. After the leaves fell, pushing the brush aside was easy, and I climbed into the cab. Once red, the shovel had rusted through orange into brown. The clutch was manufactured by the Twin Disc Company in Racine, Wisconsin, while the Buda Company in Harvey, Illinois, made the engine. Something there is that compels a man to pull levers. Near the front of the cab nine stuck up through the floor like ribs. Sitting in the driver's seat, I slammed them back and forth, shifting myself out of sagging middle-age back to hard youth. Across the clearing from the shovel was a big metal shed filled with bales of hay. I hauled myself up through the hay, and standing above the rafters touched the roof. Forty years ago on my grandfather's farm in Virginia I turned our barn into a castle. Shifting bales of hay I built turrets and walkways, dug a moat, and then tunnelling through to the middle of the loft constructed a dungeon with secret entrances.

I chew through summer and on walks stuff myself with berries: black and red raspberries, service, straw, huckle, blue, and blackberries. Although the berries stick to the ribs and I rarely eat lunch after a long morning walk, they don't cling to mind. Amid the distractions of a summer day, berries fold into the background, becoming one brush stroke among many on a painting luminous with leaf and flower. On fall's spare, open canvas berries bunch prominent. Not soft with summer's promise, many are gritty. Instead of fermenting sweet with good feeling, they bite and awaken. By the abandoned wolf pen grew a black cherry, its bark thick and gray, its fruit bitter. On the borders of fields buckets of summer and fox grapes hung purple through sumac and hornbeam. Grainy with seeds the grapes were tart, and despite imagining eating so many that the juice ran winy down my chin, I managed to eat only half a bunch at a time. Mould grew on the grapes and worms burrowed through them. Although I roamed fall, I was not able to wander far from cleanser and tile. If Nature's grapes had been as meatless as Nature's Burger in the A&P, I would have chewed them by the carafe. Many berries were inedible: blue privet, black maple leaf viburnum, and the white berries of red osier dogwood which turned sticky and soapy when crushed. Others smacked of the kitchen: nannyberries of raisins, and elderberry, staghorn sumac, and double file viburnum of cupboards rich with jars, white wax thick at the tops and jellies beneath catching the light and turning it back blue and red.

Spicebush turned yellow around marshes and under ridges in dells shaped like the center of palms, the heels rising rocky above and creeks running through them in creases. Only on solitary trees which had lost their leaves did I find berries. The cool yellow leaves full on other bushes must have attracted birds, probably thrushes. On the tongue the red almost waxed berry broke sunny and clean, but then the taste lingered, turning brown and drawing the mouth. In contrast barberries seemed bland at first but then the flavor gathered strength, flowing green and lemony. My favorite berry was the silverberry. Red and flecked with silver, the berries clustered around limbs, turning trees into springs, spraying up from the ground then tumbling out and over in crimson rainbows. I picked six quarts of silverberries. Aside from Francis who ate five berries one morning, and this only after I ate the berries for breakfast for six days and suffered no ill effects, no one else in the family sampled the berries. Rarely does the family taste foods I find on walks. Not long after picking silverberries I dug Jerusalem artichokes. After I scrubbed then sliced them, Vicki fried them in olive oil and served them to me for dinner. She cooked enough for the whole family, but I was the only one who tasted the artichokes. I liked them at first, but then as the children dumped their helpings on my plate, making assorted grunting sounds, the artichokes lost appeal and flavor. Still, I did not want the family to think me squeamish. The next day I asked Vicki to cook another batch for dinner. I ate it, but that was all. That night I buried the rest of the artichokes in the compost pile.

One afternoon Albert Hennard sat in Enos Mayfield's Inn writing a list of names in a tablet. The list was long and covered three pages. "What's that?" Ben Meadows asked. Tall and with hands square as four-by-fours, Ben farmed a rocky hilltop between Many and Less. Ben was not in a good mood. Drought had killed his corn; a plague of worms had fallen on his tobacco, and just the day before his best mule, Lion, turned up crippled by spavins. "It's a list of men I can lick," Albert answered. "Hellfire," Ben said, picking up the tablet, "you've put down my name." "That's right," Albert said. "I'll be damned if you can whip me," Ben said, pulling off his town jacket and rolling up his sleeves. "Are you sure about that?" Albert said, his eyes getting big. "I'm goddamned sure, you pissant," Ben answered. "Well, if you're sure," Albert said, "I'll just mark your name off the list." Much as talking to Ben changed Albert's list, so walking through the woods made me see mushrooms differently. Sitting at the kitchen table in the dark morning, I imagined them twisted and repulsive. In the bright day as children clambered over rocks following George and Henry, mushrooms appeared wondrous, if not lovely. From the sides of stumps, chicken of the woods fanned out in yellow and orange clumps. The meat of the mushroom was white and edible, and in my mind I heaped asparagus and wild rice on the plate beside it, a curry sauce running creamy over it. Life has taught me restraint, however, and no matter the hankering I do not eat wild mushrooms. Instead of rolling pear-shaped puffballs across the tongue, I turned turkeytail through the hands, marveling at the velvet texture, colors running in ripples, purple and red, brown, gray, orange, and green. Circles of amethyst tallowgill pushed leaf litter aside, and phyllotopsis nidulans clung orange to logs, its sides curving in on themselves and spinning the mushroom into ruffles. Birch polydore oozed gleaming through bark; gray hunks of hoof fungus hung like steps down the sides of beech trees, and clumpy semi-circles of phellinus nigricans stuck to trunks, the upper surface zones of misty color, the underside soft and cinnamony. A fairy ring of hardwood waxcaps rose white amid oak and hickory leaves. Resembling capitals on columns the gills ran fluted down the stalks, raising the edges of the caps and turning them into broad saucers. The ring was nine and a half feet in diameter, and its appearance was so sudden that it seemed the magical stuff of old wife and tale, not spore and hyphae. All seasons, of course, cast spells, and for the person who looks, enchantments brew everywhere.

Some people don't like magic. In October the beaver dam behind the police firing range was bulldozed. The pond drained into the Fenton River, sweeping away not only the beaver but summer's king-fishers and blue herons. On the ridge above the pond lived a herd of deer. Often I heard them clattering through the brush or saw their white tails bobbing. Occasionally a buck glided across my trail, making me want to leap. Deer soar too high, and I am more at ease among small, earthbound animals. One morning I caught a mole above ground. I brought him home and after showing him to the children freed him in the backyard. In the graduate center Harlow asked me if I knew whom to call to get rid of a bat. "Me," I said. I caught the bat in a wastecan and turned him loose under the white pines on the ridge behind the basketball parking lot. Birds fluttered the fall. Chickadees and titmice rattled through scrub; red-tailed hawks spun above meadow and river, and juncos hopped through stalks at the edge of corn fields, the white feathers in their tails scissoring. One high cold afternoon in a field above Unnamed Pond a peregrine falcon downed a pigeon and sitting on a hump of earth shredded the carcass, ripping feathers off and tossing them aside with an efficient yet almost reckless speed.

Impressions of fall stuck to memory like beggar-ticks to trousers. Brushing the seeds off I wondered where I picked them up. Many impressions were fragmentary, random bits of days: a tree frog green and yellow on a leaf of milkweed, the afternoon sun turning silver as it shined through bushy seed heads of phragmites, empty seed pods of winter cress white along a road, or the nests of tent caterpillars battered and shaggy with droppings. On a rock I found a dead white-faced hornet. High above in a beech was the nest, a giant gray top, the wood pulp on the outside swirled and almost spinning the nest through the trees. Stuck to damp wood under the bark of rotten logs were slugs, not orange like those who wander grass in summer but gray and speckled. Near Unnamed Pond sensitive fern dried, and turning brown fell inward into circles, the stalks of spore capsules beaded and suddenly visible. Nearby bittersweet nightshade wound through brambles, its leaves purple-green lances resembling the heads of vipers and the brambles themselves fanged, the berries seeming red drops of venom.

High above everything trees burned, the candelabra of fall flickering in the breeze of days. The cut for the power line ran trimmed down the ridge behind the sheep barn. At woods' edge staghorn sumac smouldered blackish red, the leaflets of the long pinnate leaves sweeping out then trailing down combed, pulling the eye away from the tangle of log and brush just behind. Over the lip of the ridge witchhazel bloomed, both leaves and papery shredded flowers yellow. Almost lost beneath the color were batteries of brown seed pods. In the field by the power station brambles tangled in thickets, their canes no longer purple or red but pale blue. Near the firing range leaves of big-toothed aspen clapped in the wind while gray birch and quaking aspen throbbed, awash in the undertow of season. The leaves of the big-toothed aspen were yellow and orange, and the edges were scalloped, almost as if someone nibbled at them with a tip of a spoon. In brush above the remnants of the beaver pond seed pods of sweet pepperbush stuck up in scratchy spikes; in October some leaves remained green and only splattered with brown. Later the green faded into yellow, and when crushed, the leaves smelled like pepper, the brown splatters flaking and resembling tea.

Down the ridge behind the barns grew beech and yellow birch. When the light slapped low through the woods, the birch gleamed, its small cones suddenly visible. Often I chewed twigs, and when I drank birch beer at the Lebanon Antique Show I forgot where I was for a moment, association seeding the long green and flat open field with rock and ledge, bush and tree: scrubby chestnuts, the trunks splitting near the ground, but the long leaves finely cut and yellowing, and then beech, the trunks blue amid the buying and selling and the leaves mellow, thinly orange in the clean, empty light. I saw few people on my walks, and these were usually alone or accompanied only by a dog. At six one morning as I wandered around Tift Pond looking at paper birch, I met a Japanese man chipping a golf ball through the woods. He used an eight iron and on his left hand wore a white golf glove with raised red and blue stripes crossing the palm and running over the back of his hand. The day before I found a golf ball near the soccer field. I forgot to put it into the golf basket in the garage, and it was still in the pocket of my jacket. I gave the ball to the man. He couldn't speak English, but he bowed and smiled, after which he chipped both balls off into the deep rough of leaf litter and disappeared.

On Saturdays after early walks, Vicki, the children, and I drove around eastern Connecticut looking at trees and then, after the leaves fell, at streams breaking white through small valleys. We stopped often, one day to look at a large cottonwood. Yellow and gray, the leaves resembled broad spades. The bark of the tree was deeply cut and furrowed. Silverberries grew nearby, and I ate a handful. No one else ate any, so I promised to stop at the yogurt shop on the way home. Our trip was roundabout. We bought three pumpkins at Crooke Orchards. The bags of apples looked good, but our pantry already rolled with empires, Spartans, and Macouns, so I didn't buy any. After putting the pumpkins behind the back seat, we turned toward Storrs. Still, we stopped two more times, picking up a case of wine at the Ashford Spirit Shop and then driving to the Enchanted Bakery in Tolland. The bakery was closed, but the owner was inside. She recognized me and let me in, and I bought five chocolate crois-sants. Although sweet, the croissants did not push the promise of yogurt out of the children's minds, and when we got back to Storrs, they held me to my word and bought sundaes, Eliza's and Edward's covered with M & M's and Reese's Peanut Butter Cups, but Francis's awash in blueberries and raspberries, and almost healthy.

The red leaves of white ash were the first leaves I noticed on paths in the woods. Soon, though, the paths became carpets of color. I remembered the Greek tragedy I read in college and wondered whether I should walk on the leaves. Only a person blinded by pride could tread on such beauty. No matter how I brushed words I could not color pages as the maples painted the ground. Red and sugar maples did not simply age red and yellow but resembling ramekins were aromatic with baking color: orange, slightly soured and winy; corky and charred browns; and misty purples savoury with the memory of love. In curtains leaves swirled down the Fenton River. Wrinkling at snags and gathering against banks, they turned into bright sills, sunny with blowing chintz. The leaves were almost too florid, and in November when paths became smoky with oak I felt more comfortable. Instead of shimmering through color and almost out of form into instability, oak leaves wore like thick hide. Rain did not wash them out of texture, and on damp days they crinkled underfoot, resilient with hard substance.

On walks I picked up many leaves: a white oak leaf as big as the silver platter on which Vicki serves the Thanksgiving turkey; yellow sassafras leaves resembling mittens, and then leaves from tulip-poplars. These last I often chewed. The tulip-poplar belongs to the magnolia family. Although bitter on the tongue, the leaves were sweet to association, reminding me of my grandfather's farm in Virginia. In another season, one long since drained of chlorophyll and wasted in recollection, magnolia cones were bombs to throw at friends. The blossoms themselves sat in low dishes in the middle of the dining room table, and although my hands were often gritty and my feet bare, the table was white and formal with fragrance. Walks often led to memory. In October the woods were yellow with hickory: butternut, mockernut, and shagbark. Although shagbarks lost their leaves first, they never seemed completely bare. The strips of bark jutting out from trunks preserved the trees' identity and gave them presence. Several shagbarks grew in our front yard in Tennessee. Their nuts fell early, and when I mowed grass, the blade of the mower spun them about, ground, and then heaved them at me, bouncing hunks off my shins and launching slivers at my face. Gray squirrels ate the nuts, and sitting in branches chewed them, dropping a woody rain into gutters. Time changes perception. What was once a nuisance was now a sentimental link to childhood days, glowing in imagination like the trees gold against the blue October sky.

Most conifers remain green throughout the year. Consequently they seem almost beyond season and don't attract me so much as do deciduous trees. Still, I wandered pines, examining needles and bringing home dry cones, the long open cones of white pine and the squat prickly cones of pitch pine. Hemlocks were thick along the

Fenton River, and the air beneath them was quiet and cold. Above Schoolhouse Brook white cedar grew in shaggy, snagging groves, blocking the light and keeping me to the path just as they did in summer. I was content to stay on the paths, for nearby tamarack shed needles. A soft orange sifted down through the treetops, and stopping to look up, I noticed red and brown flowing through the tamarack's loose bark. Although wandering fall was satisfying, toward the end of November I began to imagine other times and other places. One afternoon as we walked beside the cedars near the brook, Vicki said, "Last night I dreamed I had an affair with Mikhail Gorbachev." "Huh," I said. "The power attracted me," Vicki said, "and he was gentle." "What did you have?" I said. I had not been listening to Vicki, for I was far from fall and family. I was in the Dodecanese: Rhodes, Kos, Kalymnos, the island did not matter. Spring had arrived. Bougainvillea whirled red over a white wall. By a dry pitted rock, grape hyacinth bloomed. On a bluff above the sea, ladies' fingers pointed toward the sky. Jasmine was sweet on the air. And I? I wore sandals and shorts and a floppy white hat, a red cow poppy wilting in the hatband. I sat alone at a table, looking out over the sea, waves breaking blue against a gray bluff to my right. In my left hand was a battered copy of Byron's poem *Childe Harold*. Before me on the table were a loaf of bread, a bowl of black olives, and a bottle of retsina, half-empty and pale yellow in the sunlight.

That afternoon a telephone call brought me back to season. Public radio asked me to judge a Thanksgiving essay contest. Listeners were instructed to write three pages describing what they were thankful for, the best two pieces to be read on "Weekend Edition." I agreed to judge the contest, and on Tuesday Federal Express dropped a fat parcel of essays off at the house. On Thursday UPS brought a second packet; the following Monday Airborne Express delivered the third and last batch of essays. Altogether I received eighty-two essays. They came from almost every state, from big cities and small towns: Atlanta, Milwaukee, Denver, Memphis, Detroit, Columbus, Boston, and then Hebron and Sharon, Ironwood, Stone Creek, Sisters, Big Fork, Gunlock, Cockeysville, Ashfield, and Toftë—names with which to baste imagination. The essays did not come alone. Tumbled among them was a copy of the *Gifted Children Newsletter*, "For Parents of Children with Great Promise." The American Indian

Center in Baltimore announced the "4th Annual Native American Cultural Arts Festival." A public relations firm in New York sent a flyer announcing a musical review based on the works of Edward Gorey, the cartoonist and illustrator. "Dear Opinion Maker," the flyer began, "What's more gothic than 'The Addams Family,' bleaker than 'Bleak House,' and more fun than balling in a graveyard?" "Oh, no," I said aloud, crumpling the flyer and tossing it into the waste can before picking up an essay. At the top of the first page was a quotation from Emily Dickinson, "If I can stop one heart from breaking, I shall not live in vain." "Yes," I thought, "yes, indeed."

The essays were rich with the real stuffing of life. People were thankful for "small treaures," as a woman from Minnesota put it, crickets, sweet smelling woods, lady bugs, sunny mornings, hot Swedish bread, seeds in the toolshed, otters, woodsmoke, and someone to mow the grass. Thankful that his wife laughed at his "corny stories," a man from Missouri told a tale. A countryman had an accident while ploughing and crushed his right leg so badly it had to be amputated. When he got out of the hospital, the man paid a carpenter to make him a wooden leg and soon he was able "to get around pretty well." Some years later the man visited an old friend in St. Louis. A cousin of his friend's wife was also visiting. The woman wasn't intelligent, and when she saw the man's wooden leg, she asked, "where did you get that leg." "Ma'am," the countryman said; "it's a family heirloom. My daddy wore it proudly, and so did his daddy before him, and when I die, I'm leaving it to my oldest boy, Tommy Lloyd."

Many essayists looked forward not simply to Thanksgiving but to the winter beyond; to scraping ice off the windshield with a library card, "to the time when the pond freezes and becomes bumpy with snow." Thankful for "the sheltering skies" of this country, others pitied peoples less fortunate: families in Iraq picking up the scraps of their lives, beggars in Calcutta picking up scraps. Shouldn't we Americans, they asked, do more to help the world, "weave webs of caring which will stretch," they wrote, beyond "this nation's borders," "bend our backs to shoulder more of life's burden." Those writers who served others seemed especially joyful: the man who volunteered in a hospice and women who worked in soup kitchens. Last year, one of the women wrote, "little children in our neighborhood dressed up as Indians. Too poor for real costumes they made Indian suits out of grocery bags."

Amid the thunderclaps of life, writers heard bells and found seams of gold. Sadness did not break but strengthened as people smiled through tears, remembering husbands, wives, children, fathers, and mothers. "Friends dropped loads of firewood in the yard after he died," a woman wrote from Vermont. "All the casseroles," a woman wrote from Georgia, "tasted like ashes, but, oh, how thankful I was for them." "Come spring," a man declared, "I know daffodils will bloom outside this black kitchen window." In her gentle dying, another man recounted, "my wife turned me into a poet." When the dead went to heaven, they didn't just "toot on trumpets," they started vegetarian restaurants and, "in anticipation of my arrival and the resurrection of the body," a woman from South Carolina wrote, "ordered a shelf of x-rated movies." Like a fugue, family turned through the essays. One man sent a picture of his newly adopted daughter from Honduras. A woman drew a picture of her son from Korea; in his right hand he held a baseball bat; in his left he cradled a football. At forty and with "too much education to land a man," a woman married. A year later she had a baby. "Miracles," she said, "happen." A man with a new daughter-in-law agreed. The changes rung upon family were many and complex. The sister with the "nerve disorder," the retarded brother, the nephew who refused to work had made "life difficult but all in all," a man wrote from Oregon, "I'm thankful for them." In the essays family sometimes pressed hard on people, and while one woman was thankful to be "alone and free," another said she was glad "no one wants to make love to me tonight."

Many letters came from old people, almost all thankful to be old. Who but the old, a man asked, has ever hauled water from a spring or pulled the feathers out of a turkey? "The first Thanksgiving I recall," a woman wrote from Maine, "was eighty-eight years ago. I was six years old. The Tarbells drove over in their sleigh and brought their daughter Nellie who was my age. We went sliding, and I had no mittens. Nellie had a quarter and wanted to buy me some. We walked down Center Street, and all the stores were closed except Patterson's Restaurant. They did not have mittens, but they had long sticks of gum in a square glass jar and Nellie bought some." Awareness of mortality enriched many essays and seemingly many lives. "One day

I suddenly realized that you could get out of bed in the morning, get dressed, go to work, and not live to get home at night," a man wrote from Indiana; "that day my life began." People accepted heavy portions of disease and sadness. The man with cancer and the woman whose husband left her after thirty-eight years of marriage thought life "full and beautiful" and were "thankful for the past wonderful year." Poor for the first time in his life, a man sold his car and walking "discovered beauty I passed by unseeing a thousand times." "I'm thankful," a woman wrote from Iowa, "that the tornado which blew the roof off the barn left the house intact." People suffered strokes and blindness then gave thanks for the capacity to accept what life brought.

"I am thankful to be able to write this essay," a woman wrote from Maryland, "maybe it will inspire someone to appreciate life. Life is precious and we should be thankful for what we have, be it a lot or little." I selected two winners and sent their essays to Weekend Edition. I wanted to hear the writers read their essays, but the Sunday on which the essays were read, I roamed the Fenton River and losing track of time missed the broadcast. Like beech leaves enduring the November rains and clinging to trees deep into winter, the essays stuck to mind. They made me appreciate life more, and sappy as it sounds, made me want to be better. I am not religious, but on Thanksgiving morning I hunted through the attic and found my old prayer book. Robert Shaw, the minister at St. George's Church in Nashville, gave it to me after my confirmation "on Whitsuntide, the 24th of May, 1953." I turned through the order for Morning Prayer, and that afternoon when Vicki served the turkey, I told the children to bow their heads, and I said a blessing. "Almighty God, Father of all mercies, we, thine unworthy servants, do give thee most humble and hearty thanks for all thy goodness and loving kindness to us, and to all men," I began, quoting the General Thanksgiving, to which I added, "We thank you for what we have and for what we don't have. We thank you for the seasons, in particular this fall. But above all we thank you for decent people, people who walk in holiness and goodness, the brightness of their deeds shining about them and lighting the way for the rest of us." Then I said a loud "Amen" and turning toward Vicki held out my plate for turkey. "Daddy," Eliza said looking at me, a perturbed expression on her face, "What about

George?" "And Henry," Francis added, "he's almost housebroken." "Oh," I said, putting the plate down. "Bow your heads again, and shut your eyes," I began, "and Lord thank you also for George, and for Henry who is almost housebroken. And Lord, while we are chatting about such things, I'd appreciate it if you'd take Henry in hand. I'm awful tired of cleaning you-know-what off the kitchen floor."

5 Reading Martin Chuzzlewit

"*Martin Chuzzlewit*," I answered. "It's a wonderful Christmas book. A chapter after dinner will warm the night and push cold news out of mind, making you feel good about the bruised world, maybe even making you believe in Santa Claus again." I had not expected the question, and when the host of the radio program asked me to recommend a book to read over the holidays I paused. On the bottom shelf of my bedside table was a copy of *Martin Chuzzlewit*. At Cambridge then later at Princeton I studied Dickens's novels, reading most of them four times. *Martin Chuzzlewit* was one of my favorites, and three years ago I bought a paperback copy intending to start rereading it that very evening. Something, however—gutters or the children, maybe just life—sapped my energy and *Chuzzlewit* remained unopened and gathering dust, eventually becoming part of a monument to intention, the base of a heavy column of unread books.

What was good for listeners, I thought after the radio show, was probably good for me, and that afternoon I pulled *Martin Chuzzlewit* from the shelf, proud of doing so without tumbling the stack of books. Alas, three years is a long time in the life of the eyes of a middle-aged man. Reading brought not simply story but page to life. After a few minutes words and sentences began to splash about, letters flailing upward in gouts, then falling and breaking, running off the margin in nonsensical driblets. I placed the book back on the bedside table and went to the university library. There I found a copy printed in big type with great white spaces between the letters. The spaces were so large that my eyes did not hurry forward, cramming them with broken words and headaches. Instead I had room to blink and stretch. Sentences rolled slowly, and I turned through the holiday, days and paragraphs bound together by the little narratives of life, the stuff of happiness and laughter.

At noon the next day Vicki and the children and I went to the Horse Barn for the Christmas sale. Shortly after we arrived, twelve "elves" left the barn to fetch Santa Claus. The elves rode Morgan horses and wore white stocking caps and red trousers and sweaters. On the road outside the barn horses and riders formed a line. Then with a shout they cantered off, bridles jangling with bells. As they wound about the hill, damp muffled the bells and the elves seemed to vanish, only the impression of horses sticking to mind, the line thrust together like a stream pushed down a hard channel, the muscles of the horses rippling then turning like rolling stones, wet and gleaming, the white snow behind a still frame.

The elves found Santa Claus in a two-wheeled cross country cart behind the Ratcliffe Hicks Building. Guiding him as surely as Dasher and Dancer, Donner and Blitzen, they led him to the barn. Alighting at the riding rink he lifted a bag from the cart, and shaking hands and shouting, "Merry Christmas," handed out red and white striped candy canes. Afterward he climbed into a sleigh, and taking children in his lap asked them what they wanted for Christmas. "I want to lose this front tooth," Eliza said, opening her mouth and twisting her tooth with the thumb and index finger of her left hand. "I promise you," Santa said, bending over and peering into her mouth, "that you will lose your tooth." Santa was true to his word. Not only did Eliza lose the tooth before Christmas, but on New Year's Eve she lost the one next to it.

Silver stars and loops of red ribbon hung from the rafters of the barn, and fresh sawdust had been spread. Horses stood in some stalls, ready to be petted and rubbed. Students converted other stalls into stores and warm nooks for children: a manger with dolls and two ewes from the Sheep Barn, and then "The Children's Farm" with a brown lop-eared rabbit in a cage, a green turtle in a bucket, a young Holstein tied to a bale of hay, and an assortment of metal trucks and earth-movers, dandy for shifting sawdust. In the next stall students sold coffee, apple cider, tea, and hot chocolate for fifty cents. Brownies and popcorn balls cost twenty-five cents while doughnuts were fifty cents. Baklava and chili were the most expensive treats, each costing a dollar. Over the public address system, Christmas songs played—"Away in a Manger" just when Edward rubbed the sheep. At one end of the barn stood a tall, white spruce decorated with glass bulbs and long red and gold ribbons on which was printed "New England Morgan Horse Show 50th Anniversary, 1939–1989." At a table across the room pots of cyclamens from the greenhouse sold for five dollars. For fifteen dollars volunteers made wreaths out of hemlock, spruce, and dried flowers, among these last black-eyed Susans, the seed heads of poppies painted red, empty milkweed pods, and shafts of evening primrose sprayed silver and blue.

Surrounding the tree was a wreath of tables sagging with ornaments for sale: small red sleighs, bearded elves, and wooden horses, some leaping, others confined to rockers. Almost hidden by boxes of bulbs was a stack of blue tee-shirts, white cows grazing across the fronts, not on clover but over a nourishing soil of letters reading "UCONN DAIRY CLUB." People lingered around the tables, not so much, I thought, selecting ornaments carefully but instead turning through the past, remembering seasons long gone, bulbs swept into dustpans, and families vanished into snapshots and tattered letters. I looked at a white sleigh. "Too little," I thought, "not like the one Grandfather gave us for the table in Tennessee." Each Christmas Mother rolled cotton down the center of our dining room table. Around the edges she raised a hedge of holly. Through the middle of the cotton slid Santa in his sleigh, pulled at first by eight reindeer, then by six. The last year Mother put the sleigh on the table she found only three reindeer in the attic, and the sleigh was battered, a runner broken and its white paint chipped. The first year Santa rode down the table, he brought a bag of presents, small boxes wrapped in shiny paper then four colored balls attached to white sticks and supposed to resemble balloons filled with helium. By the last winter in Tennessee the presents and all but one balloon had been lost. In their place Mother stuck chocolate truffles and plastic mistletoe.

I didn't buy the sleigh because it was small. If I had really wanted something big, I could have bought a horse. Eleven were for sale, seven mares, Rollercoaster Babe, Ikura, Pepper, Ms. Aviance, Dixie, Weatherwell Sundance, and Weatherwell Finalle, and then four geldings, Luke, Spuds, Texas, and Ruskins Debate. Foaled in 1984 Luke was a thoroughbred, 16.1 hands high. Priced at fifteen hundred dol-

lars, he, the description stated, "enjoys dressage, hunt and jumping, but needs that *one* rider to enjoy it with." Priced the same as
Luke, Rollercoaster Babe was a quarter horse. Riding English or
western, she loved trails and would, the description declared, "be a
great Christmas present for any child." The most expensive horse was
Weatherwell Finalle, a Morgan mare priced at twenty-five hundred
dollars. Born in 1988 she was young and had not been in training
long. Nevertheless, the description said, she was "very intelligent
and eager to please," beside having the "ability to be a top notch
show horse." At five hundred dollars Dixie was the cheapest horse,
a grade mare foaled in 1973. Having played polo "for years" and
"given many a good ride," Dixie wasn't the stuff of shows. Still, she
was friendly, and Eliza and I were scratching her forelock when Vicki
found us. "It's time to cut the tree," she said, "tell Santa good-bye."
Each December we drive to Hye Acres tree farm on the Middle Turnpike and chop a spruce. Mrs. Talmedge gives the children cookies
after which we roam the hillside, selecting first one then another
tree. This year the blue spruce glowed, seeming glazed with sky, and
for a moment we toyed with the idea of an artistic tree hung with
icicles. Christmas, though, is for family, not art, and soon we found
a fat white spruce, just the meaty thing for the boxes of ornaments
in the attic.

December is nutcracker month. Vicki puts tall wooden nutcrackers, bearded soldiers dressed in red and blue, atop the piano and
dowry chest in the living room, and we take the children to the ballet. After fitting the tree into the stand so it would not topple, we
changed clothes and hurried down Hillside to Jorgenson Auditorium for the Pennsylvania Ballet's production of *The Nutcracker*. Two
nights later Eliza was a bonbon. Her ballet school met in the church
on the green at Lebanon and for parents performed parts of *The
Nutcracker*. The night was windy, and as we drove to Lebanon snow
gusted through the headlights. The children danced in the recreation
hall. A Christmas tree stood in a corner; beside it an American flag
flowed down a yellow pole. Wreaths hung in windows; on the walls
were signs saying "Faith Gives." Stapled to a bulletin board was a
big square of blue drawing paper. On it was pasted the white trunk
of a paper tree, the lower branches lifting upward and resembling
arms raised in supplication. Attached to the branches were bits of

gold and silver foil shaped like tulip-poplar leaves. Printed beneath the tree were two lines written by the English poet Gerard Manley Hopkins: "The world is charged with the grandeur of God. It will flame out, like shining from shook foil." For the person who cut out the tree, as for the parents in the room, that grandeur was familial. On each piece of foil was a child's name: Sarah, Scot, Amanda, Jabez, Nicole, Katie, and Ashley.

As my little girl danced shining across the room, I became melancholy, wondering what lay ahead of her, and I longed for Hopkins's certainty that the Holy Ghost broods "with warm breast and with ah! bright wings" over our "bent world." While freshness sparkled dewlike through the eyes of the children, we parents were a wilted lot, tired but not tired enough to escape worry. How deep would the snow be when the dance ended, I thought, dreading the drive home. Wearing jeans and corduroys, thick sweaters, parkas, and heavy boots, the parents were nondescript. Only when our children danced did we bloom. "Sugar, you were wonderful, my little Christmas tree," I said, pulling Eliza close and forgetting about the snow as we turned to leave the hall. The two weeks immediately before Christmas were a fruitcake of event, nutty and slightly intoxicating. The Friends of the Windham Free Library asked me to read from my new book of essays, and one Sunday, Vicki, the children, and I went to the Baker-Weir house in Windham Center. Sprawling down a hillside the house had been the home of J. Alden Weir, the impressionist painter. While the children explored the long halls upstairs, I read in the parlor, a cup of eggnog behind me on the mantle, a fire burning and warming my calves, and the house itself smelling vaguely like a swimming pool, the owner having washed the walls with chlorine to kill mould. The next night we went to Northwest School for the Christmas Festival. Classes sang and danced, Edward's voice clear and strong in "Zumba, Zumba" and Eliza turning through the "Chinese Ribbon Dance," spinning a long yellow ribbon in a circle and waving at us with her free hand.

The week before Christmas I drove to Buckland Hills Mall near Manchester. Never before had I gone to a mall alone, and I was excited. I filled the van with gas at Marty's and bought the third and last "volume" of Citgo's "24 Karat Classic Rock 'n' Roll." On the tape were "Poison Ivy" and "Whole Lotta Shakin' Going On."

I slapped the tape into the player, turned the sound up high, and rocking down the road was, for a moment, a teenager again, watching Jerry Lee Lewis bang a piano in the Fair Grounds in Nashville. At the end of the show police formed a wedge around Lewis and pushed through the crowd, many of whom tried to tear strips from his clothes. Although I was far from the stage, the wedge came straight at me. I tried to get out of the way, but a boy in a leather jacket slammed into me, and I fell. A man tottered above me, and as he dropped to his knees, I scrambled aside. "That was my last rock and roll show," I said aloud, suddenly noticing that I was driving too fast. I slowed and turned the sound down. Still, I was a little itchy when I arrived at the mall, and to settle down I nibbled some lotion, not the Calamine recommended by the Coasters but a "Belgian chocolate chocolate" ice cream cone.

Few people were in the mall, and most of them were women. Buying makes me flirtatious, and riding down the escalator, boxes under my arms, I grinned at women riding up, loaded with shopping bags. They always smiled back; two even winked, almost as if purchasing gifts created a secret life or at least made one imagine a hidden life, an hour tangled with ribbons and sweet red surprises. Affection was not the only appetite stirred by shopping, and I munched through the morning, downing on top of the ice cream two cups of coffee from Gloria Jean's Coffee Bean, one being her regular blend, the other a coconut concoction; a large Coca Cola, a bowl of potato salad, a corn beef sandwich heavy with "the works," and then as I drove home, a chocolate croissant. I saw two former students in the mall. In Cacique Laura sold me a pink terry cloth bathrobe for Vicki. Outside Brentanos I met Bethany. "I'm looking for something for my sister-in-law," she said, "and I don't know what to get." "Maybe I can help," I said, "is your sister-in-law married?" "Yes," Bethany said, "to my brother." "Well," I said, "that does make it difficult."

As I strode in and out of stores, I felt confident and assured. Beside the robe I found several other presents for Vicki: "Gardenia" cologne from Crabtree and Evelyn, from The Limited a red and yellow sweater with blue beads stitched across the front and back, a pound of "Macadamia bark" from Munson's, and then at Brookstone, two presents, a "multi-purpose" kitchen knife and an electrified "cup warmer." Only once did I falter, and that was in buying a tee-shirt for Edward with "Washington Redskins" stamped on the front. Before I left home Vicki wrote a description of the shirt for me and told me where to buy it. Unfortunately I left the description on my desk, and once in the mall I could not decide in which of three athletic stores I was supposed to shop. As a result I bought Edward tee-shirts at two different stores. Vicki liked them though, and we gave both to Edward for Christmas. Aside from the bathrobe, Vicki's presents were not successful. The cologne disappeared down the sink in the bathroom. Although I examined the front of the sweater carefully, I neglected the back where the beads had come unstitched. Vicki, I learned, does not like Macadamia nuts, so I ate the bark myself. When Vicki returned the knife and cup warmer to Brookstone, she told the saleswoman "my husband gave them to me for Christmas." "Boy, he's a romantic one," the woman replied as she recorded the exchange, "Full of surprises."

In *Martin Chuzzlewit* young Martin traveled to America. Instead of a new world, he found an old one, patchy with scamps and scoundrels: Colonel Diver, Jefferson Brick, Hannibal Chollop, Esau Slodge, Elijah Pogram, Generals Choke and Fladdock, Mrs. Hominy, Zephania Scadder, and Mr. LaFayette Kettle. I read the names aloud and as I did, I laughed, recalling characters in my essays. Instead of Eden where Martin bought land, getting fleeced in the process, my characters lived in South Carthage, or Russia, as it was called by the inhabitants of Carthage itself, just across the river. When the census taker visited Molly Travis or Ethel May Blodgett— it could have been either—he counted fourteen children playing in the yard. "Ma'am," he explained when Molly came to the door, wiping her hands on a dishrag, "I'm the census-taker, and I'd like to talk to your husband. You folks sure have a nice mess of kids." For a while Molly hemmed and hawed, twisting the rag in her hands, but eventually she confessed she wasn't married. "I'm just a poor woman what takes in washing and ironing," she said; "I ain't got no husband. I just have to get my children the best way I can." The patriarch of the Blodgetts, old Sawyer Blodgett, was probably the father of two or three of Molly's children. Not only was Sawyer an active man about town, but he was progressive. Even though he was almost deaf he got one of the first telephones in South Carthage. One day after repeating himself several times Hoben Donkin shouted into the telephone in exasperation, "Sawyer, have you lost your hearing?" "Certainly not," the answer came back, "I can hear you all right until you begin to talk, and then I can't tell a word you say."

Sawyer drank. When flush with money, he went to Enos Mayfield's Inn. When times were poor, he bought moonshine. Aware of Sawyer's standing in the community, Proverbs Goforth decided to convert him. If he could convince the old man to climb aboard the temperance wagon, then, Proverbs thought, Russia might mend its shiftless ways. One Sunday after church Proverbs visited Sawyer. After refusing a drink, he asked Sawyer how old he was. "Eighty-seven," Sawyer answered, spitting a loose hunk of tobacco into a blue Maxwell House coffee can beside his chair. "Damnation," Proverbs answered after watching the tobacco slap against the side of the can then slip heavily under the surface of a dark pool, "just think if you hadn't drunk all that whiskey you'd probably be a hundred by now, maybe even older."

Despite Proverbs's urgings Sawyer didn't stop drinking, or aging. On his ninety-fourth birthday the *Carthage Courier* sent young Billy Dobbs to interview him. "Mr. Blodgett, I'll bet you've seen a lot of changes in your time," Billy said, beaming at the old man. "Yep," Sawyer answered, rocking forward on the porch and spitting a wad of tobacco over the railing into a lilac, "yep, and I've been again 'em all." Sawyer cared for winter even less than change, and on cold nights, he informed Billy, he wrapped his false teeth in underwear before putting them on the bureau. Otherwise, he explained, they became chilled and starting to chatter woke him up. Sawyer talked a lot about teeth, in part because the weekend before Billy's visit his daughter Bettie Claire took him to Nashville to buy a new set. Several dentists had offices on Church Street. Competition was fierce, even biting, and the bicuspid brethren exhibited their handiwork in windows facing the street. After stopping outside one office on the sidewalk, Sawyer took his daughter by the arm, and pulling her near, pointed to a window, saying, "Bettie Claire I'd like that set of teeth, right there." Bettie Claire had just read an etiquette book, popular, so the jacket said, in Cincinnati and Baltimore. "Hush," she said, looking around in embarrassment, "Pa, don't you know it's bad manners to pick your teeth on the street."

Martin Chuzzlewit was only one of several books I read during the holidays. To the children I read four of Frank Baum's Oz books: *The Magic of Oz*, *The Road to Oz*, *Tik-Tok of Oz*, and finally *Dorothy and the Wizard in Oz*. I also read a collection of Ralph Waldo Emerson's essays and two volumes of Hal Borland's descriptions of rural life in northwestern Connecticut. For a seasonal book I read *Whiteout*, an account of fashionable doings in Aspen, the ski resort in Colorado. The book amused me, but the author spent much time writing about people whom I had never heard of, celebrities whom he assumed were familiar family-room names. Although the celebrities led intriguing lives, they were uninteresting people, in contrast to my literary friends, most of whom lead sedate, conventional lives but who themselves are wonderfully entertaining and interesting. Finally I read the *Journals* of John Cheever, the writer. Cheever seemed to envision himself almost as a mysterious house or mansion. While his public life was led downstairs in parlor and dining room, Cheever implied that his real life was private, the matter of journal, attic, and closet. Although most people have a private shelf somewhere in the house of personality, they live in one-story ranches without attics and closed off wings. How flattering to the ego it must be to see one's self as a man with secrets. I suspect Cheever enjoyed writing his journal almost as much as I did wandering the mall. Still, I have only been once to a mall by myself, and I don't keep a journal. "Sam," my friend Josh said the other day, "there has to be more to you than appears in your essays. When are you going to come out of the closet?" "Closet," I exclaimed, "the closets at home are stuffed with the children's toys and all the presents I gave Vicki that she doesn't want. Once," I continued, "I did come out of the living room, but I didn't get any farther than the kitchen."

Many nights I walked more than I read, and instead of accompanying Dickens to America, I wandered wood and field with George and Henry. Some nights the wind felt like iron; other nights the cold was slack, hanging damp and sluggish like a soiled towel on a line. Then instead of pulling my coat tight and jamming my chin under the front collar, I expanded and, slowing my pace, looked at the stars and followed planes swimming and winking high through the air. When the temperature fell suddenly, white pines snapped, the sound cracking the quiet. Dark hillsides resembled splatterware, splotched with snow and shadow. Shelves of ice curved out from the banks of the Fenton River, resembling hunks of bracket fungus, thick and white in the moonlight. One night after an early evening snow I found two sets of footprints in the woods, a dog's and then those of his master, a man wearing big boots with heavy corded soles. I wanted the woods for myself, and for a moment the prints pressed my thoughts down, much as the man's feet had crushed the light flakes. Soon, though, I remembered something Vicki said in the kitchen before dinner, and my thoughts loosened and began to drift. In the newspaper that afternoon I read an article which described the popularity of pornographic videos. "Something must be wrong with me," I said, "I've never seen a pornographic movie, and I guess I never will. I don't have the nerve to rent one." "I'd watch one," Vicki said, stirring the pasta, "but you just wouldn't leave it at that."

I roamed both night and day. At noon sunlight fell flat through the marsh west of Tift Pond, and the slow creek turned black, snow and ice narrowing the channel and burying color under shadow. In the quiet above Barrow's Pond ropes of water twisted down the hill, jerking forward over stones, pooling under roots, and then slipping through blades of ice, ringing softly like chimes. The granite rocks that hardened hills in summer softened them in winter. When the trees became stalks, the rocks flowered, moss and lichens suddenly blooming green to the eye. Scrub beeches held leaves longer than other trees. Curled into small funnels the leaves gleamed silver in the sun on dry days; on wet days they seemed orange and pink. Near Tift Pond needles of red pine dangled in clusters, sticking to low branches like feathers. Under deciduous trees candlesticks of ground cedar burned through the snow, their tips bright orange. Open fields resembled burlap, the grasses shredded and the remnants of asters, goldenrod, boneset, and Joe Pye weed snagging and fibrous. Low trails froze, the earth rising icy while rocks remained stationary, creating the impression they had been dropped, forcing mud out from under them. Along the Fenton River a few waxy green leaves clung to greenbriar; catkins drooped from speckled alder, the twigs that held them gray and sometimes purple in the light. On red maple, buds clustered in scarlet hunks, in the late afternoon turning black against the sky and making the trees ominous.

I saw few people and animals on my walks although the occasional stroll seemed all dog, tails and bottoms forever switching through

my sight. Once when the children accompanied me, George twisted
down a hole on the sharp slope of a ridge. He was out of sight for
what seemed a long time, and when barking suddenly rang deep
under the hill, Eliza screamed and Edward started crying. Every day
I saw gray squirrels and the tracks and droppings of deer. Beneath
the willows at the edge of Unnamed Pond was a muskrat lodge, a
heap of frozen cattail and reed resembling a weedy trashpile of lawn
trimmings. On walks I found much litter, and sometimes I thought
man marked the world, not with book and monument but only
with trash. Above Kessel Creek was the debris of a cookout: Budweiser, Keystone, and Busch beer cans; sixteen-ounce paper cups
with "Miller Beer" and "Made the American Way" printed on them
in red, and then a blue and white "Coleman Snow-Lite Cooler," on
the front of which was a bumper sticker reading "Catch the Spirit—
The United Methodist Church." Students probably left the litter, for
around the charred remnants of a fire were four empty packages of
Marlboro cigarettes, the brand most popular with students. When I
saw the packages I sighed in disappointment and frustration. If the
never-ending warnings against smoking made so little impression,
what could I expect to accomplish in a one-semester course? I started
to walk away, but then I stopped. Stuffed under a root was an empty
package of Camels, on the front the familiar rusty camel, behind
him two orange pyramids and three palm trees. On the back was the
walled city of spires and prayer towers, a place of romance or so I
thought as a child. Forty years ago I had not heard of cancer or em-
physema. When I held Father's packages I dreamed, imagining stony
crumbling citadels, a dust of black birds above the walls; tiles purple
and red, writing flowing across them like perfume; and then gardens
curious with dates and peacocks, fountains with bronze lions in the
center spewing water high, golden in the yellow sun.

The days before Christmas slipped past so quickly that Christmas
itself arrived in a rush. For a moment tension lowered heavy. "I hate
our children," Vicki exclaimed after breakfast on Christmas Eve. That
night she stayed up late, wrapping presents and waking me at 3:48
in the morning to read a letter from Santa Claus. "Thanks for the
yummy snack for my 'boys' and me! Great as always," Santa wrote,
describing the cookies and carrots the children put on the hearth for
him and his reindeer. "I gave your two little critters a treat each, see-

ing as they weren't too sure of me and I didn't want them to bark," he continued, referring to George and Henry. "Enjoy your gifts. You're good boys and girls—and A MERRY CHRISTMAS TO ALL!" The tension vanished, and Christmas was happy and relaxed. That night I telephoned relatives: Sherry and Aunt Elizabeth in Virginia, Uncle Coleman in Texas, Cousin Katherine in Tennessee, and Aunt Lucille in Florida. "Did you get what you wanted?" I asked Aunt Lucille. "No," she exclaimed; "ninety-two is old enough, and I asked for a pair of white wings. I am ready to dipsy doodle around the golden streets." For Christmas Vicki gave me videos, not pornography but the Audubon Society's Birds of America, and after talking to Aunt Lucille I watched volume four, hoping that by spring I would be able to distinguish one warbler from another.

Much as I did not want the holiday to end, so I did not want to finish *Martin Chuzzlewit*. After Christmas I read even more slowly, drifting quietly through pages and time to New Year's Eve. For dinner on New Year's Eve Vicki cooked buckwheat pancakes, and after putting the children to bed, we watched a movie, *What About Bob*, a comedy about a goofy patient driving his psychiatrist nuts. At midnight I peeled a tangelo and opened a box of Pepperidge Farm cookies, eating two Tahitis while Vicki ate a Milano. Dickens's good humor seeped through the following days. As young Martin traveled home from America toward a calm, happy ending, so little disturbed me. Backing the Plymouth out of the garage I turned too soon and smashed the left front fender. When I paid the repair bill, $347.25, I smiled. Despite being an outspoken critic of big-time college athletics, one night I watched the University of Connecticut play basketball on television, though to be truthful I often switched channels. One station showed a movie featuring a man with a mechanical hand. Whenever villains threatened him, he summoned the hand, pressing a button on a dial. Immediately the trunk lid of his car raised up, a box opened, and the hand became airborne, flying out to throttle malefactors. The second week in January Vicki and I drove to the Eaglebrook School in Deerfield, Massachusetts. This past summer Francis built a bookcase at camp. Fifty-two inches tall and forty-four wide, the bookcase was too big for a car loaded with parents and children. Carter MacDonald, head of shop at camp, was an old friend, and he volunteered to take the bookcase to Eaglebrook where he taught. Later, he said, "you can pick it up at your convenience." Memory is selective, and I conveniently forgot the bookcase until Francis put it on his Christmas list. When we arrived at Eaglebrook, Carter introduced me to his class.

The students had good manners, and the holiday darkened, as once again I wondered if my children would be better off in private school. "Not that we could afford the tuition," I said to Vicki driving home; "still, a touch of class wouldn't be bad, would it?" Feeling disgruntled and somehow dissatisfied with myself, I read rapidly that night, not savouring the gentle goodness of Dickens's conclusion but instead rolling the novel to the end. Christmas was over. Santa Claus had dropped from conversation; the ornaments were boxed and back in the attic, and the tree was wilting on the brushpile in the backyard. Instead of reading my way out of the vain world, I thought about earning money, maybe school tuition. Still, before starting to work, I decided to reread *Pickwick Papers*, "sometime soon." That Sunday my latest collection of essays was reviewed in the *New York Times*. The review was eight hundred and two words long. Although generous, the writer said little about the essays. Instead he discussed my being the source of the Keating character in *Dead Poets Society*. Thirty years ago I taught Tom Schulman who wrote the screenplay, and pieces of me and that class appeared in the film. Still, fictional characters are fictional, and whenever interviewed about the movie, I had explained that Keating was a blend of teachers, certainly one containing memories of me but a blend nevertheless. Despite the disclaimers, however, reporters insisted upon hanging Keating around my neck. To have bridled would have appeared silly and self-important, and so I wore the film, making the best out of it, seeing it not as an albatross, as literary friends inevitably said thinking of Coleridge's Ancient Mariner, but as a pheasant, piquant and even nourishing. Over time, though, the bird grew rank and I began to think it more buzzard than pheasant. I winced on reading the headline above the review, "Robin Williams and Then Some." In discussing the film, Williams said he modeled his performance on the antics of one of his secondary school teachers. Three years ago the man lost his job, and when accounts appeared in newspapers across the country, I received mail. Strangers declared *my* firing "underlined the bankruptcy of contemporary education," and old friends commiserated, wondering if there was anything they "could do to help." That fall when the head of the English department visited the registrar to discuss enrollments, the assistant registrar said, "who is going to teach Sam Pickering's courses, now that he has been fired?"

During the next week I began to think more highly of the review. I received four letters, only one from a relative. Two of the four letters were even from out of state, Florida and New Hampshire. Two old friends sent cards, one a belated Christmas card on the front of which was a picture of his family: himself, his wife and two boys, these last dressed in just the right clothes for private school. On the back my friend wrote, "Read a review of your book in the *Times*. Maybe I'll read it, looks interesting." Four members of the English department gave me copies of the review, and three people telephoned, one from Massachusetts. On Friday afternoon I found a message in my box in the English department. "TV Show, Inside Edition, West Coast, Please Call," the message said, providing a name and an eight-hundred number. "Holy cow," I said to myself. "Big guy, this is it. Those fellows read the review in *Times*, and they want you." A program which advertised itself as a television magazine, *Inside Edition* featured stories on celebrities, the sort of tarty people who hang out in Aspen. *Inside Edition* was the kind of show I flicked quickly past, hunting for films about mechanical hands. Still, its audience was huge, and an appearance on the show would, I thought as I dialed the number, sweep my book right up on the best seller list.

The person who telephoned was at lunch. The secretary took my home number, assuring me my call would be returned later that afternoon. I walked home, papering the walls of my imagination with royalty checks. I decided I could live with *Dead Poets Society* a little longer, buzzard or not. *Inside Edition* would probably ask to film my classes. I would grant them permission, I thought, if they met two conditions. First, the show would have to say nice things about the University of Connecticut, and more importantly, the program had to publicize my writing. At home I lay down and waited for the telephone to ring. What a pity, I thought, that my interview would take place in Connecticut. Maybe I should insist, I pondered, on being flown to California. If "they" objected, perhaps I'd refuse to appear on the show. At four-thirty the telephone rang. So that I would not appear too eager, I let it ring three times before answering. "Oh, Mr. Pickering," a voice bubbled, "this is great. I have tried so hard to get you." "Oh, dear," I responded smirking into the receiver, "you've got me—the one and only—what can I do for you?" "Mr. Pickering," the voice said, "we are doing a show on Robin Williams, and I understand you taught him." That night I began reading *Pickwick Papers*.

9 No More Study

*F*or a decade I had a study at the university. Each morning I went there to write. This spring, I relinquished the study. I've changed. Distraction now appeals to me, and when I write I want a dog in my lap and children raucous through the house. Before turning the study over to a younger person eager to be alone with ideas, I cleaned the room. Clutter was everywhere. Across the top of the desk washed a wave of paper clips; pencil nubs; manilla envelopes; yellow sheets of paper, stains crinkling across them like dried creekbeds; rubber bands, hard and sticky as old pasta; a pair of scissors, and then two four-ounce plastic bottles of CVS "all purpose glue," the price tags still attached and reading seventy-three cents. A red "hot pot" stood on the desk, an extension cord looping around a white porcelain cup then trailing over the floor to a wall plug across the room. Beside the pot a yellow metal tea kettle sat on brown cardboard. Stuffed into a blue and black can, once containing four ounces of Twining's Russian Caravan, was a fistful of tea bags, Bigelow's "English Tea-time." From a golden teapot a stream of tea fell across the front of the wrapper into a gold cup. Beside the can lay a box of herbal tea, Celestial Seasonings Sleepytime, ingredients blooming down the side of the container: chamomile and passion flowers, lemon grass, scullcap, rosebuds, hops, spearmint, tilia and raspberry leaves, orange blossoms, and hawthorne berries. On the floor under the desk was an empty jar that once held nine ounces of Ann Page's "Stuffed Spanish Olives." How the jar got into the study I couldn't recall.

Behind my chair were five boxes and three bags. White with "UCONN Co-op" stamped on them in blue, two of the bags were plastic. The other was paper. Printed in green across the front was "Jonathan's," the name of the university snack bar, and then the statement "This bag is made with 100% recycled paper." Inside were two small packets of sugar, distributed, I read, by Pocohontas in Richmond, Virginia. "Our best to you," Pocohontas declared on the back of the packet, "every day!" Four of the boxes were rough cardboard, the largest having been sent to Vicki by L. L. Bean in February, 1986, probably containing items put on sale in the new year. Made from waxed cardboard the smallest box was six inches wide, five inches deep, and three and a half tall. From "The Flower Basket" at 110 Nassau Street in Princeton, New Jersey, the box once held a corsage, judging from its size most likely an orchid or gardenia. Where the box came from was another mystery. Rarely do I buy Vicki flowers, and when I do, they are always potted plants, hyacinths and begonias.

The drawers of the desk were almost empty. Beside more paper clips and pencil nubs the top drawer only contained a class list from a short story course I taught to forty-three students in 1985 and a blue examination booklet, half of its first page torn out and the rest of the pages blank. In the upper left-side drawer lay a copy of the magazine *New Hampshire Profiles*, the issue for October, 1978. On the cover a leaf from a sugar maple hung, caught between blue twigs like a canvas on an easel. Light shined from below and behind, thinning the leaf and turning it pale. Beneath the magazine was the White Flower Farm Catalogue for spring, 1989. On its cover a bank of double red rugosa roses boiled into bloom, rising upward out of a well of rough, veined, green leaves. I counted the blossoms three times. I don't see red clearly, especially on a green background, and each time I counted the number of blossoms increased, starting at thirty-eight and growing to forty, then to forty-three. In the second drawer on the left side of the desk was another catalogue, this one blooming with books rather than flowers, exotic books, not the stuff of a small town library. The compilers of the catalogue annotated the volumes listed. Of a poetry chapbook entitled *I Went To Italy and Ate Chocolate*, they commented succinctly, "He did." *Rat Jelly* was not the sweet it appeared. It was, the compilers wrote, another collection of poems, "by a writer who pushes the unexpected toward the reader delicately, almost imperceptibly." Some titles startled. *The Great Stone Tit* was "a penetrating study of contemporary tit fixations," depicting "denuded desert beauties in fold-out sequences that allow for mythical, mammorial implications." Although I paused over this comment and for a moment drummed my fingers across the top of the desk, the only book I might have bought, had the catalogue been current, was *Trick or Treat*, "a photo sequence in which a man is transformed into a candy bar and consumed by an insatiable streetwalker." In the same drawer was a small pocket-sized *New Testament with Psalms and Proverbs* distributed by the Gideon Society. The text was the King James version, and I spent the goodly part of an afternoon wandering Revelation and Corinthians. The book, the Gideons declared, contained "light to direct you, food to support you, and comfort to cheer you." It was, they assured readers, "the traveller's map, the pilgrim's staff, the soldier's sword, and the Christian's charter." Herein Paradise was "restored, Heaven opened, and the gates of hell disclosed."

The contents of the drawers seemed sweepings, tailings left behind at the end of a life, sometimes puzzling or touching, but more often than not, just dead slag: a flyer from Little Caesar's Pizza advertising two medium pizzas with "Extra! Pepperoni" and "Extra! Cheese" for $9.98, or from Texas a postcard mailed in 1984, on the front of which sat one of Kate Greenaway's little girls wrapped in ribbons and puffs and resembling a muffin. On the back of the card somebody I once knew thanked me "for all your help and encouragement." In an envelope was the calling card of Larry Davis, Deputy Sheriff in Des Moines, Iowa, with an office located in Room 204 of the Polk County Courthouse. I have never been in Iowa or had doings with the sheriff's office in Polk County, much less met Officer Davis. On the photograph of a young man resting on his haunches under trees heavy with oranges was the inscription, "For Proffessor Sam's family with warm regards from the former Jasem." A decade ago, before Vicki and I had children, I taught in Latakia, Syria. As I held the picture I looked through the yellow oranges and saw an energetic teacher standing in the front of a narrow, dusty classroom, students stretching gray back through the room, row after row. Smiling, cajoling, the teacher labored to pull answers from the class and to instill hope and confidence. Although I liked that teacher, he was not the person now holding the photograph. At best he was truly "the former."

The contents of the drawers were diverse, and my mood shifted as I rummaged the desk. In the big lower right-hand drawer were

several pages from old newspapers, six from the front section of the
Nashville Tennessean of May 26, 1928, and then four inside pages
from the *Nashville Banner* of July 10, 1928. I could not remember taking the papers to the study. The pages were wrinkled and
looked as if they had been used as packing, perhaps around china.
In 1928 the *Tennessean* was twenty pages long and cost three cents,
"On Trains Five Cents." Because of fog and northwest winds, the
dirigible *Italia*, the headline stated, had not been heard from since
its "victorious flight over the North Pole," forty-seven hours earlier.
Under the command of General Nobile, the ship, the article speculated, was probably headed for Siberia or Nova Zemlya. Even if
the vessel were forced down, a correspondent reported, the crew
had large stores of gasoline to supply heat and food enough for a
month, this last consisting "principally of pemmican and chocolate."
Bank robberies were also news. From Dighton, Kansas, came the
report that airplanes had joined four hundred men, searching for
"the four desperadoes" who robbed a bank in Lamar, Colorado, killing two bank officers then a doctor whom they "lured away" from
his home to dress the wounds of one of their number wounded in
a gunfight "25 miles south of Oakley, Kansas." After "a mad flight
over the Western Kansas prairies," the killers were reported near
Modoc, Kansas. "Armed with a machine gun," the murderers, it was
thought, "would fight to the last to prevent being taken." "In the
belief that the desperadoes were attempting to escape into Colorado
or Wyoming," Sheriff George J. Carroll of Cheyenne "organized a
squad of expert riflemen." From Calhoun, Georgia, came word that
"500 Possemen" had run four payroll bandits to ground in a swamp
six miles outside Rome. Having stolen "a large covered sedan" from
officials of a stove foundry, the robbers raced through Calhoun at
"not less than sixty miles an hour," "firing many shots" and injuring
the Chief of Police John Crow when he tried to stop them. When
the robbers reached the bank of the Coosawattee River, however,
their luck foundered. The ferry was on the opposite shore, so they
were forced to abandon their car, steal a small boat, row across "the
stream," and flee on foot into the swamp.

Although the robbers were cornered, capture was not certain, at
least not if one heeded the wisdom contained in a filler on page five.
"I see by the paper that policemen are going to be vaccinated," a man

stated. "What for," a friend replied, "they never catch anything." The fillers in the papers were better than the anecdotes about "celebrities" that pepper today's news. "Fat people die earlier," one filler stated, "the plan of nature apparently being to eliminate a man when he has his share." Fashions, of course, change, and to joke about girth now is not simply in bad taste but it proves one to be insensitive, even a bigot. That aside, however, many fillers focused on men and women. "Well, she was wild," Joe answered, "but I've got her so tame now she'll eat right out of my purse." Doings between the sexes interested folks in 1928 almost as much as they do today. On the front page the *Tennessean* noted that "Mme. Ida Chernoff, the international known apostle of beauty and charm" completed the fifth and final lecture in a series held at the War Memorial Building. Over a thousand women heard her declare, "Every man in the world should think he is the boss of his home. It is pitiful when a man is allowed to lose his self-respect because of a bossy type of a wife. But down underneath the surface of that home the woman should be the real boss."

Despite Mme Chernoff's assertion or perhaps in oblique support of it, on page two of the paper, the NEHI Bottling Company ran a half-page, two-column advertisement for its "Knee-High Contest." "GIRLS!" the advertisement began; "Cash in on your 'Understanding.'" To discover "who has the 'shapeliest' legs in Nashville and the surrounding territory," NEHI offered one hundred dollars in cash and "other prizes." Female residents of Davidson, Wilson, Smith, DeKalb, Cannon, Rutherford, Warren, Coffee, Franklin, Moore, Bedford, Williamson, Hickman, Humphries, Dickson, and Cheatham counties could enter. Seven finalists would be selected, each of whose "photo" would appear in the Rotogravure Section of the Sunday *Tennessean*. "*Come Prepared to be Photographed*," the advertisement concluded, directing contestants to "apply" at the Tennessean's Art Studio on May 29, 3 P.M. "*Postively nothing objectionable to any lady will*," the paper emphasized, "*be permitted*."

Although I read the political columns, what interested me more were notices. Many described religious matters: the meeting of the Carroll Country chapter of the Women's Christian Temperance Union in McKenzie, Tennessee; the success of a tent meeting led by the Reverend Edward Hazelwood, "the railroad evangelist"; and Bishop H. M. DuBose of the Episcopal Church saying he would "endeavour to keep 'Alcohol Smith' out of the presidential chair." At the Tulip Street Methodist Church "members of the Byrd Murray Men's Bible class" kept track of how many chapters of the bible they read from June 3 to July 1. Several members "read the Bible through twice" and "others read a number of additional chapters after reading the entire book." J. W. Rogers read 2,659 chapters and as a prize "was presented with a copy of 'The Christ of Indian Road,'" while D. K. Conditt read 2,512 chapters and won a New Testament. Medical matters also consumed much space. On the editorial page of the *Tennessean* a medical correspondent responded to a reader who asked if syphilis could be cured by medicine prescribed by a doctor, writing, "It doesn't matter whether the medicine is prescribed by a doctor or by a popcorn vendor. I know of no medicine which may be fairly called a cure for syphilis." In contrast to the correspondent's doubt about medications, Cora Mayberry of Sageeyah, Oklahoma, was certain that Thedford's Black-Draught cured "constipation, indigestion, and bilousness." Under bold type declaring "Miss Cobb's Record Has Been Shattered," the *Banner* stated that although Miss Margaret Cobb was in her tenth week of unconsciousness at St. Thomas Hospital following an automobile wreck she did not, "as it has been reported here," hold "the record." That belonged to Miss Helen Buschmann, who had been unconscious for one hundred and seventy days and was "in Lake County Memorial Hospital at Painesville, Ohio." On a less morbid note, the *Banner* also reported that Gene Tunney's bruised ear had healed and would "not afford Thomas Heeney a choice target when the two heavyweights met on July 26." Tunney's training partners, the paper recounted, "took pot shots at the injured member in six rounds of sparing yesterday, but the cut did not reopen, although it may blossom forth into a regulation cauliflower in time."

I spent a morning reading advertisements. At the B & W cafeteria supper cost fifteen cents, and a person could choose between "Baked Fresh Pork Ham with Apple Sauce" or "Short Ribs of Beef with Brown Potatoes." Every Wednesday at the Little Gem Cafe Mrs. Musa M. Stanton served fried chicken "with other meats and vegetables" for thirty cents. At H. G. Hill Stores Tropic Nut Oleo cost nineteen cents a pound while Grandma's Wonder Flour, plain or self-rising, cost $1.38 for a twenty-four pound bag. Fresh corn was five cents an ear, and three pounds of snap beans cost a quarter. For a penny more one could buy a dozen "No. 1 Country" fresh eggs. Milk-fed hens were thirty cents a pound, and sugar-cured hams twenty-two cents. Strawberries had not come in, but soon they would be for sale, as the *Tennessean* carried a notice saying "1,000 Strawberry Pickers Wanted at Once. Report: 307 Cedar Street." In advertisements for automobiles names interested me more than prices: Oakland, Essex, Maxwell, Moon, Nash, Hudson, Studebaker, Packard, Overland, and Hupmobile. All sorts of advertisements caught my eye. While the Lord Hatchery sold red and rock chicks for twelve and a half cents apiece, Jersey giants cost twenty cents. At G. P. Rose on Eighth Avenue "young Cuban parrots" sold for ten dollars. At Tyree Springs, near Cottontown, Tennessee, one could rent a cottage from thirty to sixty dollars and "for the rest of the season" could enjoy shady grounds and "splendid sulphur and freestone waters." At Castner-Knott's, women's summer dresses cost $16.75. Made from Georgette, Crepe de Chine, Chiffon Dots, Chiffon Prints, and Solid Georgettes, they came in white, black, navy, poppy, French beige, and aquamarine. Linen golf knickers were $1.95. "Every boy who can wear sizes 6 to 14 will appreciate having a pair of linen knickers just like dad's," Castner-Knott's declared, adding "there are sport stripes and checks." At Phillips and Buttorff refrigerators were on sale, $26.75 for a three-door, white-enamelled, side-icer capable of holding seventy-five pounds of ice. With a water cooler on top, the same refrigerator cost thirty-six dollars. About seven miles from Crofton, Kentucky, I read, Sheriff Stuart Lackey seized more than five hundred gallons of mash, "two gallons of poor quality whiskey," and a one-hundred-and-fifty-gallon still, connected by a pump to a stream. Printed on the side of the still was "Owned and Operated by M. E. Keel, Crofton, Kentucky." Father knew a number of country sheriffs, and once or twice in the 1950s when they broke up a still and confiscated good whiskey, they sent Father a jar. After decanting it into an ordinary bottle, Father served it as a liqueur and conversation piece. For me the papers were moonshine, and knowing that I would return to them day after day, tippling down the columns and never get on with cleaning the office, I stuffed them into the box from L. L. Bean and started uprooting the loose eight-and-a-half by eleven-inch white paper that grew like plantain in weedy clusters throughout the room.

I dug up a pile of paper nine and a quarter inches tall: manuscripts of reviews, talks, articles, even of a book. One speech was eighteen pages long, another, twenty-two. I could not recall the occasion of either talk although both began with specific references, the first starting "When Christina asked me to speak," the other beginning "Karen's confidence in me is misplaced." I made the talks in 1982 or '83 because I mentioned Francis often, listing nicknames I gave him when he was an infant: Captain Fatness, Doctor Jowls, The Emperor You Can't Sleep At Night, Mr. P., and The Radish. Aside from the nicknames, which I had forgotten, little in the talks interested me. I said that although I disliked writing I enjoyed seeing my essays in print, adding that I was rarely ashamed of what I wrote. Shame now seems beside the point. By the time an essay appears in print I have forgotten it, so much so that it seems written by someone else and has little to do with me. Also in the pile were several unpublished essays, descriptions of a day at a writer's conference, of yardwork, and of the road from Amman, Jordan, to Damascus, Syria. Although I had pillaged this last piece, hacking off branches and grafting them to the stumps of other essays, I enjoyed rereading it. In it was a letter from Joseph, the oldest of nine children and a Palestinian who once lived in the Ba'qa refugee camp outside Amman. I taught Joseph at the University of Jordan. After graduation he emigrated to Abu Dhabi in order to earn money to send to his younger brothers. "It is very difficult to establish strong relationships with others," he wrote. "Every body is interested with his own affairs. There is no time for going or coming. Life here is a ceaseless struggle for money. Money is everything in this country. May God curse money." "The population," he continued, "is mostly young. The young are willing to immigrate to this country. You can see more than fifteen nations in Abu Dhabi. There are a few young ladies, not like Jordan. You can not see women with bikinis on the beach. In hotels, on the other hand, you can see whatever you like."

Among the essays was a piece about adults' reading to children. Out of contrariness I criticized the idea that children benefitted from adults' "sharing" books, and lives, with them. After noting that many

countries probably wished that the United States had never com-
municated with them and offered to share, I noted that the foundation of a good marriage could be raised upon silence just as well
as upon wordy blocks of communication. "What wife," I asked,
"tells her husband everything she thinks? What would happen if
she did? While manners, decorum, and ceremony make communal
life possible," I continued, "they presuppose restraint and order—
silence or at least a formal communication built upon silences. Why
should children," I opined, "who have fewer words with which to
express thoughts than adults, be urged to share, not simply literature but their lives with people whose concerns are vastly different?"
What I thought commonsensical, a reader thought inflammatory,
and when the journal to which I submitted the essay rejected it, the
editor mailed the copy back without erasing the reader's marginalia.
I was, the reader declared, "mean, and small-minded, the sort of person who should never be a parent." "Greatness of soul," Montaigne
wrote and I quoted in a review found in the study, "is not so much
pushing upward and forward as knowing how to set oneself in order
and circumscribe oneself. It regards as great whatever is adequate,
and shows its elevation by liking moderate things better than eminent ones." Although embracing one's small-mindedness does not
generally lead to greatness of soul, it was, at the very least, I thought,
characteristic of that person who enjoys moderate things more than
eminent ones. In any case the longest unpublished essay I discovered
described the first trip Vicki and I took together to Nova Scotia. We
went in 1981, the summer after Francis's birth. I drove our nine year
old Pontiac, valued at $670 by the Town of Mansfield. The paint had
faded, and the car had begun turning white around the edges, resembling, I thought at the time, an aged opossum. On the front seat next
to me were a paper sack full of apples and a yellow "carri-cradle baby
seat." On the floor to my right was a plastic diaper bag decorated on
the outside with raccoons and lions. Stuffed inside were two quilted
diaper pads, fourteen Pampers, a tube of Desitin for diaper rash, two
rubber pads, and eight cloth diapers. On the back seat on the right
sat Vicki. Jammed between her knees and the front seat was a thirty-
six by twenty-four-inch mattress for a portable crib. To Vicki's left
was a new Strollee car seat. It cost $44.50. In it sat Francis. Three

months earlier he had cost $2111.31, I wrote, and "then some for the obstetrician." That sum, I suddenly remembered, was four hundred dollars. Would that I could recall more. Sadly, names like Pampers and Desitin have dropped from mind. If Vicki and I had had five or six children, perhaps I would remember more. Maybe I would not have given up the study.

After reading the essay, I carried the papers into the hall and dumped them into a blue plastic barrel to be recycled. Left in the study were books and notecards, not many books, however, only three shelves full. After reading books I usually give them to friends, graduate students, or the Mansfield Library for its winter sale. Rarely do I read books twice, and those I do are novels found in every library and which I read too quickly in school thirty years ago. The books in the study were various. Some were review copies, newly published. Others I plucked from home, so that the children would have more space for toys. In many of these I wrote my address inside the front cover. The address changed, and as I examined the books, I traced my life, from my parents' house, 4402 Iroquois Avenue in Nashville, Tennessee, to college dormitories at Sewanee, first Hoffman 13 then Tuckaway 121. Next came Cambridge, 28 Station Road, followed by a year in St. Catherine's College. From Cambridge I went to Princeton, first room 14A and then 163 in the Graduate College. Finally I taught at Dartmouth, having an office in 204 in Sanborn House. As well as addresses, the books marked changing interests. On the shelves were Milton's *Paradise Lost*, a book I taught twice a year for five years at Dartmouth, and for a course at the University of Connecticut, Moliere's plays *The Learned Ladies* and *The School for Wives*. Also on the shelf was the copy of *Walden* assigned in the American literature class taught to sophomores at Montgomery Bell Academy in Nashville in 1965. I taught only the first five chapters, the ones John Keating quoted in *Dead Poets Society*. "I went to the woods because I wished to live deliberately, to front only the essential facts of life," I read, "and see if I could not learn what it had to teach, and not, when I came to die, discover that I had not lived." Odd, I thought, recalling that when I read that passage to students at MBA I had never really been to the woods. Only in my forties did I learn the names of trees and wildflowers. Only then did I begin to suck "the marrow" out of life, drawing sustenance and contentment from leaf and vine, from the pitch of hill, the roll of cloud, and the bright stripes of birdsong rising sunny in the morning.

Among the books were remnants of subjects which once appealed to me: two studies of poetry written by soldiers during the First World War, then Francis Brett Young's memoir *Marching on Tanga*, an account of fighting in East Africa in 1916 and redolent with names once magical in my imagination, Kilimanjaro, Zanzibar, Mombasa, and Dar-Es-Salaam. Although Joseph's letter from Abu Dhabi made me smile, I lost interest in the mideast years ago, and among the books on the shelves were Kathleen Kenyon's study of archaeology in the "Holy Land" and *Glubb Pasha*, Sir John Glubb's account of soldiering with the Arabs, culminating with his taking command of the Arab Legion in 1939. Also on the shelves were several "airplane books," volumes I read while traveling: Edward Abbey's *Beyond the Wall*, for a flight between Denver and Hartford with a stop in Nashville, and then Mikhail Sholokhov's *And Quiet Flows the Don*, a description of the hard, red world of the Don Cossacks during the Russian Revolution, read on two trips to Atlanta or maybe during one trip to Atlanta and another to St. Louis. Despite literary intentions I had not read and knew I would never read some books: Stendhal's *The Red and the Black*, the epic *Gilgamesh*, Geoffrey of Monmouth's *The History of the Kings of Britain*, and *The Glorious Adventure*, an account of Richard Halliburton's wanderings in footsteps of Ulysses. As a child Halliburton's books thrilled me, and I imagined swimming the Hellispont in his wake. When I was a young teacher in New Hampshire and found *The Glorious Adventure* in a box of books sold to benefit Bryn Mawr College, I bought it, intending to read it immediately. I never got beyond the first page. Something in *Paradise Lost* or perhaps age itself got in the way. No longer did I want to swim naked in the Blue Grotto and heap flowers on Rupert Brooke's grave on Skyros. To be sure I dreamed of, and still occasionally imagine, green seas peppered with black islands under a blue sky. Still, I don't yearn to follow paths trod by others, Richard Halliburton or even Ulysses. Body changes faster than mind. I am not the boy, the youth, or the man I once was. Instead of imagining myself atop craggy Olympus, I wander the Ogushwitz Meadow, my Vale of Tempe, haunted in the summer not by nymphs with green eyes and red hair but by butterflies and warblers, muskrat and beaver. Also on the shelves were novels I could no longer read, not because I had outgrown the stories but because the print was now too small for my eyes: George Meredith's *The Egoist* and Sir Walter Scott's *Heart of Midlothian* among a score of others. From the study I took home only one volume, that being a book I owned since Valentine's Day, 1951, *Snakes of the World* by Raymond L. Ditmars. One morning after a cloying semester of munching eighteenth-century children's books, I took Ditmars to the study in hopes of balancing my reading, and prose, with a venomous diet of bushmaster, puff adder, mamba, and fer-de-lance.

After I donated the books to the Mansfield Library, only note-cards remained in the study, three thousand two hundred and eighty-six notecards, the stuff of two volumes and a decade of articles on education and literature. Measuring five by eight inches, the cards had eighteen lines both front and back. I typed notes on a few, but on most I wrote by hand, generally with a number-two pencil, though occasionally I used ballpoint pens containing blue or black ink. Counting the cards took fifty-three minutes, an average count of sixty-two cards a minute. I was careful, and the count was accurate. Dry and slippery because of graphite, the cards were difficult to hold, and so that I would have purchase and not be forced to keep licking my thumb and index finger, in the process swallowing an alphabet of letters, I filled the yellow tea kettle with warm water and set it on a stool to my right. Every thirty or forty cards I plunged my right hand into the kettle. Sometimes I stuck in my left hand, most probably because counting was boring and seemed to dry the room as well as my hands. Once or twice I thought about dumping the kettle over my head. If I had done so, however, I would probably have lost track of the count, something I did not want to happen. Indeed I kept a running score just in case my mind drifted, and after finishing a handful of cards I was careful to record the total: 166, 300, 401, 568, 664, 812, on and on until I reached 3,286.

After counting the cards, I browsed through them. The reader who condemned my essay on reading to children, thinking I trivial-ized the effects of books, would have found support amid the cards. "Literature," the Eclectic Society stated in 1798, was "the great en-gine acting upon Society." "At the awful but glorious day of judgment, when all things shall be made known," a writer declared in the *Evangelical Magazine* (1801), pondering the influence of a religious tract, "how will he that drew the bow at a venture rejoice with him that received the blessed golden arrow dipt in the blood of Jesus!" "I leave you to judge," the *Universal Spectator* stated in 1730, "what an excellent housewife a Damsel is likely to make, who has read the *Persian Tales* till she fancies herself a Sultana." Writers believed that childhood education, of which reading was thought an important part, shaped the future adult. "Now," Hezekiah Woodward wrote in 1649, "we look to the preventing of evils, which, while they are but in the seed, may be crushed, as it were, in the egge, before there comes forth a flying Serpent or Cockatrice." In 1622 Henry Peacham said much the same thing, albeit more gently. "As the Spring is the onely fitting seede time for graine, setting and planting in the Garden and Orchard," he wrote, "So youth, the *Aprill* of mans life, is the most naturall and convenient season to scatter the Seeds of knowledge upon the ground of the mind."

What drew my attention on the cards was not what but how something was said. Words interest me more than content. Indeed the essay on reading to children was, for me at least, simply an exercise in which I tried to twist platitude back upon itself. On the cards I found criticism of my love of words. "Words being but the Image of Matter, to be wholly given up to the Study of these," John Ray wrote in 1691, "What is it but Pygmalions Phrenzy, to fall in Love with a Picture or Image." "Fair words," *The Child's New Play-Thing* warned in 1743, "butter no Parsnips." Maybe not, I thought, but so what— bowls of parsnips and words were so sweet they could be served without butter. In my fondness for words I resembled Pruy Savoury, a child so "gluttonous" that, the author of *The Juvenile Story-Teller* (1805) declared, her nose "was ever in the cupboard, and her finger as constantly in the sugar-bowl." One day Mrs. Savoury, Pruy's mother, gave a dinner party to which she invited a company picked for "elegance of manners and propriety of behaviour." Beforehand she prepared a magnificent dessert, "consisting of a variety of the choicest sweetmeats, and of fruits of the richest flavour to the taste, and of the greatest beauty to the eye." When she finished the dessert, the butler put it into his pantry. Unfortunately he forgot to lock the pantry door, and "this occasioned a temptation to Miss Pruy which her voracity could not surmount. Here went her fingers into one dish, pop went they straight into another, ice-creams, currant-jellies, cheese-cakes, gooseberry tarts, all went hickeldy-pickeldy into the devouring tomb of her stomach, and left behind them such havoc and devastation as have never been witnessed since the creation of confectioner's shops."

For her gluttony, Pruy received a whipping. Under a covered dish Mrs. Savoury served "the remains of the dessert" with the addition of a birch-rod stuck in amid the remnants of "the niceties, like a large bunch of celery." After the guests viewed the "shameful devastation," Mrs. Savoury grabbed Pruy in one hand and seizing the rod in the other led her "into an adjoining apartment" where she "trimmed her till the blood ran down in streams" and the "rod lay in fragments." For one who slaps adjectives and adverbs on pages with almost as much relish as Pruy popped tarts and jellies into her mouth, Mrs. Savoury's punishment seems harsh. Sweet words, the cards revealed, saved the Kingdom of Lilliput from Gog and Magog in 1795. "Utter strangers to the Arts and Sciences," the two giants resembled cannibals and "devoured all the little People they met with." In attacking Lilliput, however, they, unlike Pruy, bit off more than they could chew. The "Gothic Heroes" underestimated the strength of Lilliput's army. Under the command of King Tom Thumb, the Alphabetical Infantry, the Royal Regiment of the Primer, the Orthographical Grenadiers, and the Intrepid Sons of Syntax routed the giants' forces. Prodded by horn and spelling book, primer and grammar, Ignorance, Superstition, Conceit, and Cruelty turned tail and vanished into the dark night.

Words without deeds may indeed be "Pygmalions Phrenzy." Still, Pigmalion carved rock into life, and words sometimes soften stony hearts. In 1794 the *Arminian Magazine* printed a letter from John Berridge to Charles Simeon in which Berridge advised Simeon, later to become a leading evangelical minister, on the art of itinerant preaching. "When you open your Commission," Berridge wrote, "begin with ripping up the Audience, and Moses will lend you a Carving Knife, which may be often whetted at his Grind-Stone. Lay open the universal sinfulness of nature, the darkness of the mind, the frowardness of the tempers,—the earthliness and sensuality of the affections: Speak of the evil of sin in its Nature, its rebellion against God as our Benefactor, and contempt of his authority and Love:—Declare the evil of Sin in its effects, bringing all our sickness, pains, and sorrows, all the evils we feel, and all the evils we fear:—All inundations, fires, famines, pestilences, brawls, quarrels, fightings, Wars,—with Death these present sorrows,—and Hell to receive all that die in sin." "When you Hearers have been well harrowed," Berridge advised, "and the clumps begin to fall, (which is seen by their hanging down the head) then bring out your *Christ*, and bring him out from the heart, thro' the lips, and tasting of his Grace while you publish it."

Consistency is a small virtue, beyond the capacity of anyone who ages. Certainly I am incapable of it. For John Wesley man came to the "Knowledge" of God by "Reasoning upon the Works of the Visible Creation," that "mighty Volume wherein God hath declared himself." Behind my long walks lies more than fondness for the green names of field and slope. Although unable to will myself into belief, I want to think the natural world a door through which one can glimpse meaning. "Every field is like an open book; every painted flower hath a lesson written on its leaves," Anna Barbauld declared in her *Hymns in Prose for Children* (1781); "every murmuring brook hath a tongue; a voice is in every whispering wind." Anna Barbauld was religious, and behind Nature she envisioned God. "We cannot see God, for he is invisible," she wrote, "but we can see his works, and worship his footsteps in the green sod." Slowly I read the hymns. They seemed an invitation to spring, not simply to the spring of a year but a spring of the spirit, a place where words bloomed, not to call attention to themselves but as an act of adoration. "Come, let us go forth into the field," Mrs. Barbauld wrote; "let us listen to the warbling of the birds, and sport ourselves upon the new grass. The winter is over and gone, the birds come out upon the trees, the crimson blossoms of the peach and nectarine are seen, and the green leaves sprout. The hedges are bordered with tufts of primroses, and yellow cowslips that hang down their heads; and the blue violet lies hid beneath the shade; the young goslings are running upon the green, they are just hatched, their bodies are covered with yellow down . . . The hen sits upon her nest of straw, she watches patiently the full time, then she breaks the shell, and the young chickens come out. The lambs just dropt are in their field, they totter by the side of their dams." "The butterflies flutter from bush to bush, and open their wings to the warm sun," Mrs. Barbauld concluded; "The young animals of every kind are sporting about, they feel themselves happy, they are glad to be alive—they thank him that has made them alive. They can thank him in their hearts, but we can thank him with our tongues." A diet of lyrical thought bruises prose, turning it purple, and after reading the *Hymns*, I swallowed a therapeutic dose of Jane West's poetry (1799). "My numbers are impeded oft," she wrote, "By peeping in the apple loft. / A chicken by the kite is taken; / The felon rats despoil the bacon; / The blackbirds on the cherries seize; / The pigs have rooted up the peas; / Away the unfinish'd ode is thrown, / And Clio yields to country Joan."

Mrs. Barbauld's elevated natural world to the contrary, little on my cards revealed Him. Instead, I am afraid, they reflected my own slatternly interests. Generally human nature is lower than poetic nature, lower even than that of the barnyard and loft described by Mrs. West. One year while studying in London I read a library of eighteenth-century novels. Many volumes were earthy. Maidenheads snapped like the bindings of cheap books. Sheets of water sloshed out of chamberpots and stained pages while wind broke through chapters in great fragrant gusts. Virginity and urine did not interest me, but farting intrigued me, for reasons which I shall not detail, and I began to collect accounts of those "natural perfumes," which as one novel put it, caused Lady Nicenose much "consternation." When acquaintances asked about my research, I said I was studying "matters dietary and medicinal." In *Chrysal; or, the Adventures of a Guinea* (1768), an alchemist refined the "spirit" of an "incorruptible mass" into life and voice. Feeling indebted to the alchemist, the spirit Chrysal recounted his history in order to prepare his benefactor "for the reception and proper use" of the "grand secret" of alchemy. Unfortunately for posterity, just before "*the mystick birth*" when the "*philosophick king*" was to rise "*in all the glory of the morning*" and reveal the consummation of human knowledge," Chrysal praised the alchemist for having listened to his long history without eating, even though, Chrysal said, he must have smelled the hot ox-cheek cooking in a nearby shop. "O doleful and deplorable event," the alchemist moaned, "never to be told without wailing; never to be read without tears. Just as the spirit had arrived at this most interesting point, human weakness, unable to suppress the impulse of internal vapour, which the mention of the fatal ox-cheek set in motion, in my empty bowels, by the longing it raised in my stomach, emitted an explosion that filled the room with a fetid steam.—The spirit started at the unpardonable offence to his purity; and looking at me with ineffable contempt, indignation, and abhorrence, vanished from my sight, without deigning a word more."

In *The Adventures of a Bank-Note* (1771), Dickey's grandmother was "a fine old lady." Although she "valued herself greatly upon her delicacy," she was sadly troubled "with a distemper," the author Thomas Bridges wrote, "called by the ancient Saxons, the ghormhanrhuttles" and "by the learned disciples of Galen" the wind-colic. "Not content with walking out at the fore-door of the old lady's tenement, with a gurgling kind of noise, called by the Froglanders belchabacumshaw," the distemper "would frequently issue out of the postern-gate with a noise like a crack'd trumpet." For a penny a day Dickey agreed "that when any of these crack'd blasts" occurred, his grandmother could rap him "on the pate, and say, sirrah, how could you dare f__t so?" At which Dickey was to reply, "I could not help it grandmamma."

As I read the novels, I became concerned about the soft impressionable heads of children. The "little, and almost insensible Impressions on our tender Infancies," John Locke wrote in 1693, had "very important and lasting Consequences." If the child was the parent of the adult, as Locke implied, then continued rapping upon children's pates would inevitably, I told friends, "influence the development of the rising generation." Out of an incorruptible spirit of generosity and educational concern, not bawdry, I assured acquaintances, I investigated the causes of and cures for wind colic. The notecards recorded the results. In searching for remedies, I took care in choosing writers to consult, heeding the admonition of John Cotta, who in 1612 warned that "swarmes" of "barbarous medicine-mongers" made a "gainefull traffique in botching in physicke." Not only "Taylors, Shoemakers, Weavers, Midwives, Cookes, and Priests, but Witches, Conjurers, Jugglers, and Fortune-tellers," he declared, covered and declipsed "the Sun-shine of all true learning and understanding," darkening "the very light of common sense and reason." In selecting cures for wind, I chose remedies that were both sound and readily available. Aware of the American penchant for pets, I paid particular attention to the recommendations of Humphrie Lloyd. "A Dogges toord that only eateth bones doth binde the belly mightily," Lloyd wrote in *The Treasury of Health* (1585). So that people who did not own a dog or know the daily routine of a friendly canine would not think themselves excluded from pharmocological concern, I copied down several of Lloyd's remedies. According to Lloyd, one dropping was almost as efficacious as another. If a sufferer made a bath and "put in all the sundrie drie toordes as may be found," he could, Lloyd stated, "resolveth windinesse." For people without access to clean water in which to bathe, Lloyd suggested applying hot compresses to the belly. "Dung of beasts that are kept up in stables verye ranke, even from the place where they pisse," he wrote, "dryde and layde to the griefe with frying Oyle doth appease the griefe wonderfully." Making an even better compress, Lloyd added, was "the doung of a Wolfe, if it bee newly made." Wolves having vanished from New England, this last cure would not help the flatulent of my state, Connecticut. The disappearance of the wolf, however, has enabled deer to increase enormously, so much so that almost every backyard in the Eastern Uplands is home to a herd of deer. Although the deer are a nuisance, destroying ornamental planting, the animals could become medicinally beneficial if pharmacists followed the prescription of Thomas Lupton. To relieve the wind colic, Lupton suggested in 1627 removing the "tender hornes of young Buckes" that were "covered with a thin hairy Skinne." Slice them into small pieces then boil them in a "well-covered" pot, he explained; next dry them then grind them into a powder. After mixing the powder with pepper and "Myrrhe," pour it into a "good wine," he concluded, and drink the result. Since the easiest way to remove the horns would not be palatable to sentimentalists suckled on *Bambi*, I searched for vegetarian remedies. Wormwood drunk with "Spycknarde," Anthony Askam wrote in 1550, "swageth the stomacke and wombe that are infested of wycked windes." Seeds of wood or briar rose, Gervase Markham recommended in his *Country Contentments* (1623), beaten to a powder, stirred into a "conserve of sloes" and then eaten, would cure both the "windines of the guts" and a "lask" or looseness of the bowels. I also recorded foods which caused wind, pears and grapes for example, although this last fruit,

Thomas Paynell noted in 1597, augmented the "rising of a mans yard." "Yard, front or back?" Vicki said when I read the card to her one night after dinner, "What sort of fill is he talking about?" "Yard," I answered, "is the old name for a man's big bamboo." "Banana," I continued when Vicki looked puzzled, "kielbasa, anaconda, redwood, tube steak." "Oh," Vicki said, taking an orange out of the pantry and handing it to me for dessert, before adding, "Lo, how the mighty have fallen. Where are the giants of yesteryear?" I almost replied that they had been banished by Tom Thumb but then I thought better of the remark and remained silent.

The cards contained a laboratory of medical lore. "*Ear-wigs that have crept into the ear,*" the *Cheap Magazine* noted in 1814, "may be destroyed by some friend dropping into the ear a little olive oil, sweet oil, or oil of almonds.—Or an Ear-wig may be enticed out alive, by applying a piece of apple (of which that insect has a peculiar fondness) outside the ear." Some lore was more intriguing than practical. In the eighteenth century peddlers wandered Britain selling chapbooks. Printed on rag paper and usually twelve to twenty-four pages long, chapbooks cost a penny or two each. Their subject matter was diverse, ranging from the high to the low, from the remnants of medieval romance to joke books and fortune-telling manuals. *Dreams and Moles with their interpretation and Significance,* for example, contained a recipe describing "*How to restore a lost Maidenhead, or solder a crackt one.*" "Take Mirtle-berries," the chapbook instructed, "beat them to powder; add to this the beaten flour of Cotton; being mixed, drink a little of the powder in a morning in a glass of white wine, and you will find the effects wonderful." In chapbooks moles revealed more about a suitor's worth than did a bank account. A lover with a mole on his right arm was a gambler. On the other hand if he had a single mole in the middle of his chest with a black hair curling out of it, he was inclined toward poetry. If a mole grew on a man's ankle, he was not the conventional stuff of marriage, *Partridge and Flamsted's New and Well Experienced Fortune Book* warned, for he was certain "to act the part of a woman, like Sardanapalus at the spinning-wheel." After urging maidens never to play "the wanton," Mother Bunch supplied advice to the lovesick. "She who desires to be satisfied, whether she shall enjoy the man desired or no," Mother Bunch advised, "Let her take two lemon peels in the morning, and wear them all day under her arm-pits; then at night let her rub the four posts of the bed with them: which done, in your sleep he will seem to come and present you with a couple of lemons; but if not, there is no hope." Instead of the worries of courtship, other chapbooks focused on the delights of marriage. In *Poets Jest or Mirth in Abundance*, a husband bestowed the pet name Warming Pan upon his wife. Forcing her "to go to-bed first in winter, to warm his place," he "turned her into the cold" when he came to bed. "At which she was vexed, and vowed revenge. So to-bed she went one night, and very orderly beshit it.—By-and-by he comes, bidding her turn out, which she did. Then he jumped into bed, and lying down was so besmeared, that you might have smelt him down stairs. On which he cried out You have beshit the bed; but she answered, It was only a cinder dropped from the Warming Pan." Despite my enjoyment of chapbooks, not everyone approved of them, and criticism appeared on several cards. In Arthur Dent's *The Plaine Mans Pathway to Heaven* (1601) Philagathus condemned them as "so much trashe," good "to kindle a fire, or to scoure a hotte Oven withall." "They were devised by the divel," Philagathus continued, "seene, and allowed by the Pope: Printed in hel: bound up by Hobgoblin: and first published and dispersed, in Rome, Italy, and Spaine. And all to this ende, that thereby men might be kept from the reading of the scriptures."

Although I did not copy down excerpts from the scriptures, material from godly books filled scores of notecards. Many early children's books were raised upon bricks of faith, and I wrote essays about them, particularly about books which focused on the "Joyful Deaths" of children. In *A Token for Children* (1720) James Janeway described the happy fate of a "certain beggar boy" who roamed the streets "running to Hell" as "a very Monster of Wickedness." Taken into service by a well-meaning Christian, the boy was transformed by "the Glory of God's free Grace." Unfortunately his "former Sins stared him in the Face, and made him tremble," and the "Poyson of God's Arrows" drank "up his Spirits." His "Self-abhorrency" grew so great that "he could never speak bad enough of himself," and the only "Name he would call himself" was "Toad." Not surprisingly it was not long before Toad hopped "into the arms of Jesus." Longing for "Robes immortal," Tabitha Alder cried out from her deathbed,

"Anon . . . I shall be with Jesus, I am married to him, he is my Husband, I am his Bride; I have given myself to him, and he hath given himself to me, and I shall live with him forever." "This strange Language," Janeway noted, "made the Hearers even stand astonished." The day before Lucy Cole died, Rebekah Pinkham wrote in 1830, Lucy asked for a looking-glass. "It being brought," Pinkham recounted, "she took it pleasantly, gazed upon her deathly countenance, and observed: 'Ah! lovely appearance of death.'" Just before she died Rebecca Jane Symonds requested that the door to her room be left ajar. If the door were open, she explained, she could look into the entry "and think how my coffin will look on the table there." "O that these poor weary arms were at rest!" Jane Evans moaned on her deathbed, "O that the arms of my spiritual body were playing upon that harp which is prepared for me above! 'tis strung and tuned for endless years, and it will never sound any other name but the name of Jesus." "Shout!" she cried to bystanders, "shout! why dont you all shout! let me hear you shout aloud, Victory! Victory!" Not all deathbed scenes were so dramatic. "Even in the midst of her feelings of strongest excitement," Ann Thane Peck "never for a moment forgot the delicacy and propriety expected from her sex. She even carried the feeling so far, that when on bidding farewell to her friends she had given a parting kiss to her parents, to her brothers and sisters, she refused to extend the same favor to her pastor, until she was assured by her mother of the propriety of the act."

In 1778 the *Arminian Magazine* described a preacher's "ranging and hunting in the American Woods after poor Sinners." Despite great hardship the man was "resolved in the strength of Jesus, to pursue the heavenly game more and more." In flipping through the cards, most of the game I turned up was domesticated. At home the doings, and misdoings, of George and Henry, cluttered the hours, turning my days into dog days. Experience determines interest, and I read cards detailing the antics of pets and farm animals. "Suppose a little dog were to go to school," the author of *My Little Primer* wrote in 1835, "and the teacher should try to teach him. That would be funny; don't you think so? But the little dog cannot learn; he cannot learn to read, and spell, and count as we do. He cannot learn any thing about the sun and moon, and pretty stars. No, the teacher would find it of no use to try to teach him these things. What is the reason that little boys and girls can learn?" the *Primer* asked, "The reason is, that every boy and girl has a soul, but that a dog has no soul. God has given me a soul, so that I can learn, and know a great deal. If I had no soul, I could only eat, and drink, and sleep like the dog. I could not think, and talk, and read, and spell as I do now."

The natures of both beasts and learning have changed. Soul plays no part in contemporary education. Only occasionally do teachers blame difficulties with reading on the slow development of soul. Rarely are students who need special help in arithmetic assigned a regimen of prayer. Moreover as humans have shrunk, losing souls and abilities to read and write, if national tests are accurate, the capacities of dogs have grown. In my house the children treat animals as diminutive, furry humans, racing downstairs in the morning to greet George and Henry before even acknowledging Mother and Father. "It would be terrible if George died," Eliza said recently; "he's my best friend. And I'd miss you, too, Daddy, if you died," she added as an afterthought. On the notecards, animals occupied a low place in most households; rarely did pets rate higher in the affection of a daughter than a father. After seeing the "pretty" lambs "frisking in the fields," Laura asked her mother for one as a pet. "My dear child," the woman replied in *Lessons for Laura* (1840), "that would not be a kindness to the poor creature, for it would grieve you to have it killed, when it grew too big to be in the house; for little lambs, when they grow up, will be great sheep, and sheep the butchers kill for us to eat, and when dead, it is called mutton, which is a meat you are very fond of, and love dearly when nicely boiled or roasted. And a great many of the young and harmless lambs are killed and sold at a great price, as it is a very tender and dainty food. It will seem cruel to you, that such pretty creatures as the sheep and lambs are, should be killed for man's use, yet the great and good God designed them for his food. Were they all to live, there would not be grass enough to feed them; so, when they are in a fat and proper state, they are slain: their flesh is eaten, their skin dressed, and made into parchment, for lawyers to write on, and many other uses. Of the lamb's, which is thinner and softer, ladies' gloves are made; and it is often used instead of kid skins, for the upper part of ladies' and children's shoes."

Not all the people who appeared on the cards were as sensible as

Laura's mother. In his *Ballads* (1805) William Hayley said that the "powers above" gave the dog to man as both "guardian and friend." When the "monarch of her breast," Edward, was posted to India, Lucy sent Fido with him, instructing Fido to make Edward's "life thy care." Lucy's wish was Fido's command. When Edward decided to swim in a river infested with crocodiles, Fido tried to warn him. Unfortunately Edward did not understand the canine tongue, and Fido could not break through the barrier of soul. Gallantly Fido raced to the river's edge before Edward and jumped into the water, having just enough time to whimper farewell before disappearing down the gullet of a hungry crocodile. Fido's sacrifice saved Edward's life. Although Fido was gone, he was not forgotten. Lucy commissioned an artist to make a statue of Fido, and on its completion placed it in her bedroom. On Edward's safe return, she and Edward were married, and Hayley wrote, "the marble Fido in their sight, / Enhanc'd their nuptial bliss. / And Lucy every morn and night, / Gave him a grateful kiss."

"Is it the best Method for the feeding and nourishing of the Bodies of young Children to bestow upon them Nuts and Almonds in hopes that they will taste the Sweetness of them when their Teeth are strong enough to break the shell?" Isaac Watts asked in 1730. "Will they not," he stated, "be far better nourished by Children's Bread, and by Food which they can immediately taste and relish?" By the end of the eighteenth century baking books for children was a thriving industry. The lessons beaten into books, however, were hard and nutty, at least in comparison to the soft truths cooked today. Two hundred years ago disobedience was not equated with creativity. In *The Holiday Present* (1787) Polly Ingrate's mother told her to stay far away from the pond in their garden. Polly did not listen, and one day when she was playing catch, she fell into the pond. On this occasion Fortune smiled at her, and she was rescued. Her mother next warned her to avoid "a dirty little yard" where pigs were kept. Once again Polly paid no attention, and soon after when she tried to pet a baby pig, a sow bit her fingers "so bad, that one of them was obliged very soon to be taken off." Polly's disobedience led to calamity. Despite being forbidden to approach open windows, Polly leaned out of a window in her mother's bedroom and falling to the ground below broke her back. "She is now a woman," Dorothy Kilner wrote, "and you cannot think how sadly she looks. She is never well: Her back sticks out worse than any thing you can imagine, and her shoulders are as high as her ears; and all this was the consequence of not minding what had been said to her."

Instead of being celebrated as a sign of lively intelligence, lying was thought the worst form of disobedience. A pupil in *The Village School* (1828), Ralph Breakclod, was an habitual liar, so much so that when a chaise ran over him and injured his back no one believed him. At school he was beaten for crying, and at home he was punished for complaining. Finally after he became bedridden, people realized that for once he had told the truth. "I am sorry as you did happen to speak the truth this time," his father said, "that I did not look at your back sooner; but, indeed it is your own fault, for having been so wicked, and given me reason to think, that you were falsifying. I do not think that you can ever be cured; but, if you should live, I hope it will teach you never to deceive any body again." His father's advice was well-taken, but unfortunately Ralph had little time in which to put it to use, for he died within the week.

More fortunate than either Polly or Ralph was Bella, "an indolent beauty," described by Richard Johnson in *The Blossoms of Morality* (1795). Because her father was wealthy and she was beautiful, Bella saw no reason to study. "What need have I of learning," she asked her mother, "when my parents are so rich, and you yourself acknowledge I am so pretty." When Honestus, "a young gentleman of fortune and character," met her, he considered "paying his addresses to her." Once he discovered she was "little more than an *ignorant beauty*," however, he changed his mind. Fortuitously for her, if not for the family, Bella was "instructed by misfortune." Her father died after going bankrupt and, forced to live modestly, Bella and her mother moved into a small cottage in the country. As consolation for the loss of wealth and position, Bella reminded herself that she was beautiful. Happily, as things turned out, this consolation proved fleeting as she caught smallpox and lost her looks. "Be careful," Johnson warned "youthful readers," how "you place too great a confidence in the possession of wealth and beauty, since they are as fleeting as the wind, and as unsteady as the vessel on the troubled billows of the ocean. Fortify your minds with religion and virtue, and a proper knowledge of the useful sciences; the storms and hurricanes of Fortune may then attack you, but you will always safely withstand their rage, and deride their fury." "Before she was a beauty without sense," Johnson explained, "now she had lost the charms of her face, but had found those of the mind, which are infinitely the most to be valued." Two years passed during which Bella educated herself intellectually and morally, and then Honestus, who happened to be nearby on business, stopped to pay his respects to Bella's mother. Bella was so scarred that Honestus did not recognize her at first, and after he did, he only began to talk to her "out of politeness." Conversation, though, quickly revealed the changes in Bella's character, and Honestus fell in love. Shortly afterward he proposed, and Bella accepted him.

I fancy myself less vain than the ordinary husband. Nevertheless, tales about beauty caught my eye as I looked through the cards. Perhaps appearance was on my mind because I was growing a beard for a part I had in a production of *The Magic Flute*. The beard was my first, and was not, I am afraid, celebrated domestically. Francis compared my face to a porcupine's bottom, and Vicki said that I resembled "something dug out of a cave in the Holy Land." These observations aside, however, *The Enchanted Mirror: A Moorish Romance* (1814) appealed to me. Leonora, one of two sisters, was "the most delightful creature in form and countenance that ever was beheld by mortal eyes." Unhappily, "her mind was at variance with her outward appearance. For she was so perverse, peevish, capricious, obstinate, and extremely ill-tempered and violent, that she usually went by the name of *Vixena*, which in the Moorish language signifies a perverse creature, from which our word *Vixen* is derived." In contrast the other sister Isabella was homely. Excluded by her looks from a fashionable life, she "took great pleasure in reading and improving her mind" and "paid great attention to instructions of her masters." As her mind developed so did her character, so much so that she was known as Euphrasia or Well-Beloved. One instructive day Leonora insulted Abu Ferez, the one-hundred-and-ten-year-old Knight of the Black Plumage. Immediately thereafter she found herself in "THE SALOON OF THE ENCHANTED MIRROR," where her figure was "reflected ten thousand times." Instead of being pleased Leonora "shrieked with horror," for her appearance had changed. "Her nose appeared flattened, her skin of a deep yellow, as if she was jaundiced, her eyes little and red, one side of her mouth was drawn down to the bottom of her chin, and her whole face was distorted; instead of the charming ringlets which fell down her bosom, her head was covered with white wool, and a serpent wreathed round her neck, and darting its forked tongue, hissed with unspeakable fury." From the Saloon Leonora was next transported to a wild forest where the giantess Urganda forced her into service. Warned not to contradict Urganda, Leonora said nothing when the meal of cold ham, chicken, and canary wine that Urganda offered her turned into black bread, onions, and muddy water. Leonora almost objected when the pink and silver robe that Urganda offered her turned out to be an apron and a brown stuff gown. Before she spoke, however, she overheard a conversation. " 'And so you are a black beetle for life, because you were too proud to wear a stuff gown, and a check apron; I do not pity you.' 'Do not approach me with my folly, but look at home,' pertly replied a black beetle; 'are not you become a cockchaffer, because you said you preferred green tea to bohea.' " Terrified that she might be changed into one of Urganda's creatures, Leonora endured humiliation silently. In the process her pride was curbed, and "habitual mildness" became part of her character. Because she suffered, she grew capable of pity and felt sorry for the people whom Urganda transformed. As Leonora's character improved the images in the Enchanted Mirror became less frightening. Finally when the mirror showed her inner beauty, Leonora was freed from servitude. Wiser and better, she now resembled Isabella, and she lived happily ever after, marrying Abu Ferez, who after being boiled in a cauldron turned into a handsome, desirable young man.

Abu Ferez was fortunate. Neither boiling nor shaving can make me handsome or desirable. Nothing can bring back my youth or even that older person who filled the study with notes. I reached few conclusions from looking at the cards. If placed side by side, they would, I reckoned, make a white line just over seven hundred and thirty yards long, a fact which like the line itself led me nowhere. At best the cards resembled mirrors, reflecting not present character but past, the interests of someone I used to know. I wanted the cards to reveal deep truth, and I longed for Tom Thumb's "Intellectual Perspective Glass." By 1815 Tom had retired from battling giants. Concerned about education, he mounted an exhibition of the "valuable curiosities" he collected during his adventures. Prominent in the collection was a "wonderful optic glass" which he "purchased from Mr. Longthought, its maker," and which made all objects viewed through it "appear in such a form as is most suitable" to their "natural qualities or probable effects." "If you was to make use of it in looking at a basket of unripe apples or gooseberries," Tom explained, "the fruit would instantly appear to be changed into a swarm of worms and other devouring reptiles, because, as I suppose, those who are imprudent enough to eat such unwholesome trash, must expect to have their stomach and bowels griped and tormented by those vermin." No matter, I thought, placing the card back down on the desk, "griping of the bowels is easy to cure." "The Oyle of the Figge tree of hell," John Frampton suggested in *Joyfullnewes Out of the New-found Worlde* (1596) was a good remedy for "the griefes of the Stomacke." In 1617 John Woodall recommended "horse-dung drunke in wine." Six years later Markham said water of rue was "good against gryping of the bowells." For the person who might have difficulty obtaining water of rue or oil from the fig tree, or who might think road apples unappetizing, the *Banner* advertised Zinsep in 1928. On sale at General Drug Store at Eighth and Church for $1.10 a bottle, fifteen cents below the regular price, Zinsep was, the paper stated, "guaranteed to relieve you." "Thousands of persons who have suffered from ulcers, indigestion, bloating, bad breath, sick headache, dizziness, nausea, vomiting, heartburn, sour gassy stomach and intestinal ailments" could, the advertisement assured readers, "testify to its worth."

9 Albania Alone

I missed the signs. "When I order new tags for the dogs," Vicki said one April night, "I'm going to omit our name and telephone number." "Oh," I said, dropping a term paper onto a pile by the right side of my chair, "what will you put on the tags instead?" " 'Henry: I'm Yours' and 'George: Please Take Me,' " she said, "then with luck we'll be free." "I wish someone would free me from these papers," I said, turning the first page of an essay entitled "Shadow of the Soul, or 'Other Me' in the Writings of Ralph Waldo Emerson." Four nights later I drove to Little Caesar's to get pizza for dinner, medium pizzas at $9.98 for two, the first one plain and the other splotched with pepperoni. While I was waiting for the pizzas, Henry peed on the floor in Eliza's room. "That's no big deal," I told Vicki later; "I have whiddled on the floor a few times myself. And the children," I continued, "have damn near flooded the upstairs. Instead of camp all three should spend their summers at pee-pee spray school. I'd be happy if just one could earn his marksman, never mind sharpshooter or expert." That comment, I thought, ended the matter. It did not. Actions mop up spills more effectively than words. When he was a boy, Mr. Harris our mailman had a pet dachshund. When handing us *World Wildlife* or *Time*, Mr. Harris often complimented Henry. That night while I was at Little Caesar's, Vicki, unbeknownst to me, had telephoned Mr. Harris and offered him Henry, stipulating only that he pick Henry up at eight the next night.

At seven that next evening I left home to attend a cast party for *The Magic Flute*. I was gone for two and a half hours, sipping wine and chatting about trees in Tasmania, rhododendron, Bo Diddley, Verdi, and not going to Woodstock in 1968. Once while I stood in the hall I heard a woman in the kitchen say to a friend, "She fell down the stairs and rolled under the table. She looked like a snail, and I laughed, then felt guilty." Later I dropped a piece of chocolate cake on the dining room floor and said, "Shit." No one heard me, though, and I dug all the crumbs out of the rug. When I got home, Henry was gone. I was taken aback. "This feminism," I declared, after thinking about things for an hour or so, "has gone too far. Put saltpeter into a man's beer. Chop his you-know-what off if you have to. But don't give his dog away." For two days I sulked. The next morning I went to the Cup of Sun by myself and ate tofu stir fry for breakfast, something I had never done before. "You had better watch out," I said to the children later, "your mother just might give you away, and not to somebody as nice as the mailman either." For six months I'd trained Henry. I wasn't completely successful. Still, I had not done badly. Unlike Vicki whom I have tried to train for thirteen years, Henry did not snap at me. To be sure he chewed paper and occasionally mangled his bed, but then Vicki was not particularly neat herself, recycling newspapers along the hall and cardboard boxes and bottles through the dining room, turning the whole downstairs, I occasionally shouted, "into a man-trap." "Yes," she invariably replied.

Aside from giving away Vicki who was superb at herding children from birthday to ballet and who could perform many startling tricks in the kitchen, there was little I could do to bring Henry back. Still, I did not think Henry should vanish without a yelp, so I decided to go to Albania. "If you can give my dog away without asking me, then," I said to Vicki, "I can go wherever I want without consulting you, and I can go alone." Because Albania had recently opened its borders to tourists and was still remote, and thus exotic, the country appealed to me. In high Albania I could bolt the kennel and bound free and howl. Little doings in Storrs ate at me like mange, leaving me hot and scratchy and always irritable. In the Albanian Alps I might escape my fatty, canned life and gnaw bone. "It's too bad your mother is not still alive," my friend Pat said when I described my plans, "I'd call her and tell her what you are thinking about, and she'd slap a muzzle and chain on you."

School was still in session, and breaking free would have to wait until June, probably until July when the boys were at camp. Three hundred and fifty-nine students were enrolled in one of my classes, and as the semester dragged to an end, packs of them surrounded me, barking about incompletes and extra credit, and driving Albania, indeed almost all thought of my life, out of mind and dream. At eleven-twenty the night before the final examination a girl telephoned. "What," she asked, "is a rite of passage?" "Right of passage," I exclaimed, "You have the wrong number. Call the Coast Guard Academy in New London and ask for a pilot. He will explain the phrase to you." That evening the family celebrated Francis's eleventh birthday. The children ate chocolate cake, and Vicki and I drank a bottle of Australian wine, a mixture of cabernet and merlot. "I have blended 80% Cabernet with 20% Merlot," the winemaster at Tyrell's vineyard explained, "as I believe most Cabernet needs filling out on the middle and back palate. While Cabernet gives great strength and lift to the nose and front palate, the Merlot serves to bring depth and length to the overall wine." By the time of the student's call the merlot was strong on the back palate, adding bite and darkening it like the mouth of a good hound.

Each fall I plant daffodils in the side yard. Because Henry's training absorbed many hours, I delayed buying bulbs this spring. After Henry's departure I suddenly felt energetic. As soon as examinations ended, I wrote the Daffodil Mart, ordering a hundred double daffodils, half white lion, half Winston Churchill, and then an assortment of split coronas, Francis's favorites, tricollet, sorbet, papillion blanc, and mondragon. Aside from mondragon, the blooms of which were orange and yellow, the split coronas were primarily white. Ordering flowers brightened days and made me generous. For Vicki I ordered fifty tulips, and as icing for the yard, six peonies to go with the nineteen already lining the walk to the front door: two white, two pink, and two red. In evenings Edward played baseball and Eliza took ballet lessons. Often the two events clashed, and instead of planning my trip I drove Edward while Vicki drove Eliza. I try hard not to put pressure upon the children, and because I wanted Edward to have fun, watching baseball was unbearable. One night Edward struck out four times and cried in the car while we drove home. Thereafter I did not watch the games. After delivering Edward to the field, I disappeared into the brush behind home plate and spent the innings wandering the woods surrounding Mansfield Hollow Dam. Most parents watched the games, and some thought my behavior odd.

"That's the strangest man," a mother said to Josh one morning in the Cup of Sun, pointing at me; "he brings his boy to baseball, but he doesn't watch. Instead he vanishes into the woods. What," she asked, "do you suppose he does there?" "Don't think about it. You don't want to know," Josh answered; "just be thankful he is not at the game. He is more than strange, and if I told you what he did in the woods, trouble would follow. Even worse, he despises people talking about him," Josh added, studiously looking away from me and talking out of the corner of his mouth. "Jesus," the woman said, "is he . . . ?" Before she could complete the question, Josh interrupted. "Yes," he said, "things are not what they seem."

Vicki's disdain for dogs was not what it seemed either. Over my protest she drove the family to Woodstock the next weekend for the Windham Dog Show. I expected a small crowd, parents and children happy with pet mongrels. I was naive. Cars covered the green hills like aphids. Dogs were everywhere, in runs attached to campers, in cages, and under tents. Oddly none barked, and there was no untoward sniffing. Only owners greeted each other, recognizing acquaintances and competitors from past shows. I felt sorry for the dogs and told Vicki that someone ought to get down on all fours and teach the fellows "a little hail hound well-met." "If you do," she said, "I'm going to Albania." Not packs but herds of dogs padded through fourteen rings: komondors resembling mops; wrinkled shar-peis, elegant borzois and Afghans, malamutes, hard Rhodesian ridgebacks; spaniels, weak-faced cockers and then confident field spaniels; samoyeds, barbets, vizslas; Gordon setters, comfortably black and tan and resembling cutouts sliced from the cover of an L. L. Bean catalogue; huge Irish wolfhounds; Welsh, Fox, West Highland, and Sealyham terriers; and poodles shaved and curried into Victorian dressing tables, cluttered with cut glass and sagging pink powder puffs.

When Mother was a girl, she owned English setters, always taking their names from Kipling: Tommy, Kim, and Danny Deever. Looking at the setters I imagined myself on the front stoop of a red brick house in the country, a dappled head resting on my thigh, boxwood to the left, magnolia to the right. Instead of a big house at the end of a dirt road in Virginia, I live by the side of pavement in a little house in Connecticut. Instead of box and magnolia I have daffodils and Breck's peonies. Too small for setters, the yard is just right for little dogs, and I spent most of my time at the show looking at dachshunds, kennels of them: standards, miniatures, short, long, and wire-haired. Henry looked the breed, but George did not. "I have decided," I told Vicki driving home, "that George is an Indonesian Rathound. They are much rarer than dachshunds and too useful to be exported. They catch rats. Instead of mangling their prey," I continued, "they carry it back to their masters. On Borneo members of the Canineite tribe cook the rats then chop them up and eat them on a tasty bed of rice, onion, green pepper, and human eyeball and tongue."

"Oh, Lord," Vicki exclaimed, "Not another screwy story. Maybe you should go to Albania; better yet go to Borneo." Henry's absence created a small hole in my life. For two or so weeks the hole gaped, making me morose and resentful. About the time of the dog show, though, I began to fill it with story, shovelfuls of cornball tales that irked Vicki almost as much as Henry's "accidents." Not long after Morris Hamper's death Googoo Hooberry met Hink Ruunt outside Read's drugstore in Carthage, Tennessee. Morris sold lard and grease and manufactured linseed oil, in the process fattening both himself and his wallet. Unfortunately he caught tuberculosis, and although his death left his widow comfortably padded, Morris was considerably thinner. "Consumption will," Googoo said, "scoop a fellow out." "Yes, indeed," Hink answered, "but it won't consumption what killed him but a hermitage of the lungs." "Still," Hink continued, "he was a useful membrane of society, active in the lodge and donating money to the Baptist Sunday School." "He could afford it," Googoo replied; "he was as rich as Creosote." "Be that as it may," Hink said, "he was a good man. Vester McBee told me he didn't complain once during his last sickness." Stoicism lay beyond Googoo's comprehension, and he dismissed the tribute, declaring, "Some people are braver than others, and some ain't." Both Googoo and Hink attended Morris's funeral at the Baptist Church. Used to the earthy ministrations of Slubey Garts at the Tabernacle of Love, they found Beagon Hackett's sermon too intellectual. "Beagon can preach, but to tell you the truth, Googoo, all that talk about Eve and sin seemed silly," Hink said; "the best I can make out is that Eve won't born in Eden but was some kind of lowlander or tourist.

If my old lady had been there she would have took up a rock and killed that serpent and made and end of the whole damn business." "Maybe," Googoo answered, "but I think that sinning was foreordained beforehand in advance, and there won't much Eve could do about it short of uncorking the heavens and calling down another delusion like the one what set up old man Noah in the boat-building business. Speaking of which, Hink, what do you think can help this drought?" For a moment Hink looked puzzled and rubbed his left hand along the side of his face almost as if he were a dowser, searching for a pool of words beneath the skin. When his hand reached the cleft in his chin it suddenly stopped, and digging deep with his index finger, Hink prodded up a response. "I reckon," he said, "a little rain would help just about as much as anything."

Carthage was familiar territory, and as I listened to the dozy foolishness of Googoo and Hink, Albania lost its appeal. One day Googoo and Hink got lost in the woods above Chestnut Mound. After wandering for four and a half hours, they stumbled out on to a dirt road and saw a sign reading "Carthage 18 Miles." "Eighteen miles!" Googoo exclaimed; "God almighty, that's awful!" "No, Googoo, that's not so bad," Hink said, trying to encourage his tired friend; "hell, it ain't but nine miles apiece." Hink spoke better than he knew. Travel often seems long when one is alone, but with a companion to share burdens of miles, and experiences, distances shrink. The winding trail from Tirana to Thethi and Kruja would, I now thought, wear me down and instead of invigorating me would strain my endurance. Suddenly the domestic became more attractive, even intriguing. One night as I read to her in bed, Eliza turned toward me and interrupted, saying, "There are many things you don't know about me." "What," I said looking up from the book. "I don't know how to explain," Eliza said, talking more to herself than to me; "even though you have lived with me for seven years and are my daddy there's a lot you don't know about me."

Albania's attraction was also tarnished by my failure to interest anyone in an account of my travels. For two thousand three hundred and sixty-five dollars a travel agency in Boston offered a trip to Albania. Included in the price were airfare from and back to Boston, transportation in Albania, then hotels and meals. Other expenses being small, consisting of such things as customs and visa fees, three thousand dollars would cover the whole trip. "Little enough to pay," I thought, "for one of my essays." I wrote first to *Gourmet Magazine*, proposing an article and including a copy of my most recent book as advertisement for myself. I did not sell. Next I wrote the *Hartford Courant*. "We'd really like an article," an editor told me, "but we can only pay two hundred dollars and you will have to furnish photographs." Finally I called the travel editor of a big southern newspaper. Unfortunately I telephoned at three-thirty in the afternoon, and he was tight. "What's your name?" he asked repeatedly. Once I told him, he exclaimed, "Goddamn, tell me more; that's a great idea." After I described the trip for three or four sentences, he interrupted, beginning the cycle again by asking, "What did you say your name was?" Our fifteen minute conversation did not climb past the rocky ledge of identity, and the next morning I wrote the editor. "Just to bring yesterday's fine chat back to mind," I began. Accompanying the letter were copies of my latest two books, one I thought resembling cabernet giving strength and lift to the mind, the other resembling merlot filling out the feelings, both conscious and unconscious. Alas, such subtlety lay beyond the palate of a confirmed topper, and the editor did not respond.

Although Albania no longer interested me, I still wanted to travel. Instead of crossing the Adriatic I decided to cross Route 195 and spend ten mornings roaming low Mansfield. The notches in the soft hills did not resemble the craggy mountain passes of dream, and the Fenton was not the Mot or the Drin. Unlike Librazhd and Bajram Curri, the beaver pond and sandy field eddied off the tongue, vowels and consonants slipping through the mind, never scraping the imagination. Still, unlike a tourist I had the leisure to see and to possess. I returned to sites and far from the din of guide and schedule pondered. Because I had roamed the hills before, I was aware of change and recognized loss. Behind the sheep barns near the power line loggers had cut red pine. They crushed roads through woods stripping out white oak. Where once a loose net of sapling and branch slipped and pulled in the breeze, great snags of branches clawed up out of welts, themselves sharp as brambles. Instead of pink azalea and damp new leaf, sawdust was dry in the air. Not just trees but stakes marking my world had been felled. Logging transformed the known into the unknown and like long time erased my presence. Not yet too old to adapt to change, I wandered the paths of the loggers until their footsteps became familiar and the woods again became mine.

After three or so days of travel I realized why my article did not interest editors. Like most travelers I was a bore. Each night at dinner I described the marvels of my morning to the family. As soon as I began, eyes glazed. Clearly, no one gave, to use one of Josh's favorite expressions, a flying crap about my adventures. Still, I persisted in the descriptions, modeling my behavior on that of Alonzo, Casper Higgerty's mule. Alonzo was not an ideal animal, and Casper was always trying to sell him. The price was low, and considering buying him, Googoo Hooberry went to Casper's farm in Buffalo Valley to watch Alonzo work. Alonzo ploughed well, and Googoo was ready to buy him until Alonzo ran into a big sugar maple in the middle of Casper's field. "Why that mule is as blind as a post," Googoo exclaimed. "No, he ain't," Casper shouted; "he just don't give a damn."

Spring was late this year, and although I traveled through the middle of May, dragonflies had not appeared and Solomon's seal had not bloomed. Trees had just begun to swell into color: reds, yellows, purples, and whites rising in a soft overture to summer. Around the new beaver dam in the Ogushwitz Meadow a prelude of greens glowed then deepened into song. Across the meadow winter cress bloomed, its yellow blossoms drifting above the ground, cooling the mornings. Great spurred and sweet violets turned my backyard into the sky, small white clouds blowing past sweeps of blue. At the start of my journey the flowers of white ash were bound in buds tight as knuckles; by the end of the trip flowers had shredded into purple then aged brown and soggy, leaves bursting through them in green fountains. In walking the woods I looked closely at trees, dusting myself with the yellow pollen of birch, much as sparrows bathe in dust beside a road. Near a gangly pitch pine, a cherry blossomed, its round flowers drawing bees like hives. Escaped from a garden, a purple leaf sand cherry bloomed, its pink flowers small faces pasted against deep red leaves. High in the Alps of northern Albania I would have looked across valley and tree and seen only a horizon jagged with mountain and cloud. At home I ran fingers across dogwood blossoms, thinking the folds at the tips of the petals pink spouts. Glistening in the rain was a stump as broad as the distance between my shoulder and wrist. Moss wrapped about the stump, near the top and down the sides silvery and light, around the roots thick and gold. Ground cedar clasped the roots like a wreath, and tablespoons of Canada mayflower grew up the sides of the stump in trays. Warblers piped around me, and from a dell in the woods a wood thrush sang.

I spent much time on my knees looking at plants, particularly the small blossoms of woodland and field: wild strawberry, dwarf ginseng, Pennsylvania bittercress, bluets, kidney-leaf buttercups, columbine, goldthread, and cinquefoil. All the books I have read state that wake robin has a noxious aroma. I smelled ten or twenty blossoms. Not one was unpleasant. Several reminded me of salt and the sea, long waves breaking on rocks, flowering up then falling back into the sun like red feathers. Most plant fragrances appeal to me. Cypress spurge reminded me of caramel, and although I refuse to eat anything containing caramel, I liked the fragrance of the blossoms. I enjoyed the local foods of wood and meadow, probably more than I would have those of far Albania. I chewed winter cress, wild mint, hearts of cattail, and sweet vernal grass. I dug crinkleroot, and bringing a bundle home, tossed it in a salad. Crinkleroot reminded me of horse radish; the flavors of most of the plants I munched did not bring grocery food to mind, however. Usually I thought they tasted green, or as in the case of sweet vernal grass, like a hillside damp in the early morning. In Carthage people described food less poetically but more accurately. Googoo Hooberry blinked when he first drank soda water. But then he said, "This tastes like your foots was asleep."

Not confined to bus or train, I ambled through mornings, noticing the jug-like blossoms of highbush blueberry, and then maidenhair fern, new leaflets rising above and circling tall red stalks like golden necklaces. Never before had I noticed that the stem of tussock sedge was triangular or that the stamens of sweet vernal grass resembled minute wooden clothespins. Unhurried I sat on a log and watched a beaver pull up handfuls of grass and daintily eat breakfast. A doe drifted out of the woods and crossed the meadow. In two minutes I counted twenty-eight frogs in the beaver pond, their throats yellow with music. When I looked up, I saw a barred owl staring at me from deep in an oak. A pair of rufous-breasted towhees scratched through underbrush near a stream. Catbirds mewed in the wet scrub, and from the distance a dove cooed and an ovenbird called. At my feet I suddenly heard drumming. A bumblebee was trapped in a narrow-necked brown bottle, on the base of which was stamped "Please Don't Litter." Under a piece of plywood I found a juvenile black racer, its skin mottled with umber saddles, black edging framing them. The snake shook its tail and darted at my hand, but I caught it and took it home to show the children. That afternoon I put it back under the plywood.

Because trees leafed late this year I saw birds that I only heard during past springs: a pair of scarlet tanagers high in an ash, veerys in the damp woods, and orioles, not one pair but half a dozen. Mockingbirds sang in scrub bordering the road running over Horsebarn Hill. Bobolinks and red-winged blackbirds fluttered across Valentine Meadow. Bluebirds perched atop the fence below the sheep barn. Tree swallows nested near the beaver dam; grackles hung in alders, guttering and squeaking. From a shaft of weathered goldenrod a song sparrow sang, the melody turning like a rusty wheel on a child's wagon. A red-bellied woodpecker dug through blisters on a beech. Rattling along a limb a hairy woodpecker disappeared into a rotten tree. Killdeers ran through the furrows of a pasture. Some mornings I seemed to see only birds: robins, goldfinches, sandpipers, vireos, cardinals, chipping sparrows, cowbirds, blue-gray gnatcatchers, phoebes, kingbirds, flickers, red-tailed hawks, and crows. A northern waterthrush bobbed through the shallows of a creek. A peewee called, and flycatchers fluttered above the beaver pond. Warblers swam through the brush: redstarts, yellows, yellow-throats, black and whites, myrtles; Canada warblers, black necklaces draped down their throats; chestnut-sided, and finally blue-winged warblers, a dark line running through their eyes like mascara and in the sunlight fairy-like, luminously yellow and green. While I sat silent, spring fluttered liquid and choiring around me. Hink's cousin Durham once visited Carthage, and after a long evening's drinking, he and Googoo Hooberry climbed Battery Hill. Unfortunately the night like the heads of the climbers was foggy, and they could not see much from the top of the hill. Still Battery Hill towered above Carthage, and the climb itself impressed Durham. "We are way up," Durham said, turning to Googoo; "can you see Lebanon on a clear night?" "Oh, hell," Googoo answered; "we can see a lot farther than that. When this here mist blows away, we can see the moon." Sitting in the woods behind the beaver pond, I, too, saw the moon. I also saw the sun, and the stars, and always the black earth.

The morning after I returned from Albania Vicki and I and the children drove to Essex. We rode the steam train then boarded a sightseeing boat and spent an hour and a half on the Connecticut River. Afterward we ate lunch and strolled through old Essex. Lilacs dripped sticky through the air, and antique shops bloomed like old-fashioned flowers: petunias for the shallow purse, hollyhocks for the deep. At Sweet Martha's Eliza ate a chocolate ice cream cone, and Francis and Edward had cups of yogurt, vanilla and lemon respectively. The sunlight was pale, and the hours seemed too clear for shadows. Off the docks sailboats bobbed, bright as lilies in a pond. "Daddy," Edward said, "don't you wish we were rich, so we could live in one of these big houses and own a boat?" "No, Edward," I said, "once I wanted such things, but not now, not after my trip to Albania." Edward looked puzzled, but I didn't explain. "Daddy," he said, "don't you miss Henry?" "Sure I do," I said, "but I'm happy. Aren't you?" "Oh, Daddy, I love you," he said, reaching out for my hand.

9 Trespassing

A heavy gate blocked the dirt road. Made from pipes painted white and banded with red warning stripes, the gate hung on two iron bars. Bolted to the middle of the gate was a white metal sign stamped with black letters. "STATE PROPERTY," it read, "NO TRESPASSING." I took the black racer I found on the road and after wedging its mouth open with a thick twig stretched it through the pipes so that the head gaped over the NO blocking two legs of the N from sight. No longer did the snake resemble a flattened branch. On the fence its body seemed to expand, coiling quick into odor and mood. Flies landed on the snake, and after perching for a moment on the twig in the snake's mouth, one crawled down the throat. Virginia creeper grew along the bank beside the fence. I broke off a bunch of new leaves and ground them into my palms washing off the smell of road and waste. I rubbed my hands up and down my thighs, drying them on my jeans, and then smiling, walked around the gate into the STATE PROPERTY.

For years I have trespassed. For me a closed gate is an open invitation to explore. Writers, of course, forever trespass, wandering beyond the margins of good behavior into off limits and then converting private property into public page. Indeed much of the attraction of writing is that it opens life. A writer must stray from path and turnpike, and so I roam days, clambering over fences and pushing through pasture and wood. Occasionally I snag trousers on a barb, but the cuts never tear the rich fabric of my hours. I can find snakes at the edges of woods, and I know where muskrats live. On Monday I brought a wood turtle home to show Eliza, and so far this July I have picked six quarts of wild raspberries. They grow in the field beyond the no trespassing sign, not only red and black raspberries but a third kind which seems a hybrid of the first two. The canes billow around a small rise in the field in thick green tufts, and in the sun berries glisten by the bushel, not by the quart. Yet I am the only human picker, gate and sign, I suppose, deterring other people.

Much as I pay little attention to fences and signs so I ignore those of decorum and push unseen into conversations. In June I traveled to Cape Cod and at a banquet for honors students talked about curiosity. Arriving early at my hotel I ordered a seafood Caesar salad at "The Pub." At a nearby table three lawyers discussed opponents in a recent case. "They have gone the sleaze route together for thirty years," one said. "Yes," the man at his left answered, "They'll stoop to anything. Phony documents, you name it, anything." Two weeks ago at six-thirty in the morning I drove to Manchester to have the brakes repaired on the Mazda. While the rear shoes were being replaced, I walked up Center Street to The Whole Donut. After I ordered a medium-sized cup of coffee and a chocolate doughnut frosted with coconut, I sat at a booth and taking out an orange pencil and a small CVS spiral notebook began to eavesdrop. Cars and dogs dominated conversation. A man in a blue tee-shirt with "SUPERCREW" printed across the front wanted to get rid of a white labrador puppy. His landlord disliked dogs and had hit the puppy with a rake. A young woman working behind the counter was interested. Her boyfriend owned "a greyhound and black lab mix." The dog was dopey and roamed the shore of a pond near where they lived, searching for dead fish. When he found a fish, the dog picked it up and walked around all day with it in his mouth. The white labrador appealed to her, the girl explained, because her sister once owned "a fuzzy white dog that was mostly Spitz." One afternoon when she was driving near Colchester, the sister saw a man throw a bag from a car window. Curious, she stopped. Inside was the Spitz. "It was a good dog," the girl recalled, "we had it six or seven years, and then one day it ran into the road and got kind of squished." "My puppy is good, too," the man said; "I have raised her right. She eats out of a stainless steel bowl. I don't believe animals should eat off plastic. With the dog," he continued, "I'll give you the bowl, her braided rope, a rawhide bone, some Puppy Chow, and a bottle of Pepto-Bismol. She has a little diarrhea, and every morning I give her a dose of Pepto-Bismol."

"You and the puppy," a bearded man said to the girl, "would look good in my Camaro." "Is it a four-door?" the girl asked; "I hate four-doors. The first car I had was a Lynx that my father bought me for three thousand dollars. It had four doors." A man driving a gray pickup with a red bug shield in front of the radiator bought a cup of coffee and the day's special pastry, a cherry doughnut. Sitting down across the aisle from me, he entered the conversation, saying, "Cars ain't that cheap any more." "I ought to know. I just spent two hundred and one dollars getting mine fixed," a woman smoking a cigarette burst out; "I didn't have the money and had to borrow from my mother." The doughnut shop was without fences, and people jumped in and out of conversations. Maybe the real attraction of trespassing is that it confines one to the present. Alert to the moment, people don't dig up the past, as the saying goes, or tote the future. "Working?" the bearded man asked a man in shorts who was drinking coffee and eating a squat doughnut filled with Boston Creme. "I worked my ass off yesterday," the man said; "I ripped a roof off, plywooded and shingled it in twelve hours. Just me and a kid. Of course it was a small roof, only seven squares, but, by God, we worked." "Did we get our hearing aids this morning?" one of the girls behind the counter asked. "I haven't seen them," the other girl replied, "or the two titsy rolls."

Many customers were in a hurry and did not talk. Often, though, their shirts spoke for them, advertising "Bob's Stores" or "The World's Largest Source of Natural Gas." Written across the chest of somebody's hall monitor was the declaration "Teachers Have Class." Above the letters stretched a line of eight ripe apples, each topped by a sprig of green leaves. Two women sat in the booth in front of me. They dressed similarly, wearing white trousers, white socks, and white sneakers. While one woman had removed the laces from her shoes, the other kept the laces in but left them untied. Both wore black tee-shirts. Printed in white up the right side from waist to armpit was "Narnia 1992." Stamped on the front of the shirt was the face of Aslan, the hero of C. S. Lewis's inspirational novels describing the imaginary kingdom Narnia. Instead of a great and terrifying lion, however, Aslan resembled a rumpled furry slipper. Although the women often laughed, they talked in a whisper. Still, I heard the phrase "fourth world missions." "Find people who believe in your vision," one said. The other nodded and said something I did not understand after which she added, "it's sort of lunar." "Yes," the other replied, "yes, yes."

' I stayed at The Whole Donut for an hour. Then I returned to the garage. My car was still on the rack, and so I went to the waiting room. A small man, his stomach bulging like a gourd, sat on a sofa reading the morning paper. He smiled, and I nodded and sat in a plastic chair. A coffee machine gasped, and the hostess of a television show gurgled from a set high on the wall. I drank too much coffee at the doughnut shop, and the television program bored me, the hostess appearing to be one of the missing titsy rolls. Eavesdropping determined my mood, and I could not sit quietly. I wanted to hoist myself over a gate and swing uninvited through a conversation. The opportunity soon arose. A tall, white-haired man with blue eyes and a hooked nose entered the room and sat on the sofa. "What's wrong with your car?" he asked the short man. Before the man could put down his newspaper and reply, the tall man continued, providing a joint by joint, gear by gear mechanical history of his 1982 Ford. Diagnosis of the car's sundry ailments always proved difficult, and this, he informed the short man, was the eighth garage to which he had brought the Ford. The speaker was a supply house of automotive information. Having replaced most of the accessories on his car, he next described stores where one could buy the cheapest parts in eastern Connecticut, places that sold lights, radios, mufflers, oil filters, alternators, and carburetors. "Last week," he said, "I found a place that will mount tires free." "Dear God," I interrupted, "who would want to do that for free? Why," I exclaimed, "I would not mount a tire for money, not even one of those cute steel-belted radials." For a moment the white-haired man paused, his eyes cloudy with incomprehension. Finally, awareness spread like the open sky over his brow, and he blinked and said, "No, I didn't mean. . . ." "I know what you meant," I said. "I wouldn't mount a tire, not even one wearing chains and studs," I continued, standing and opening the door to leave the room. "The very idea."

The conventional, particularly when it is detailed into the soporific, provokes the fence-climber in my nature. In May I spoke at Rock Valley College in Rockford, Illinois. Resembling great mills, pentecostal churches cover downtown blocks, their chapels, schools, community centers, and nursing homes blocking out the sun. At the beginning of my talk I alluded to the local fervor. "Never," I began, "have I seen such big churches." They were so large, I continued, that

I was giving "serious thought to moving to town and opening one of God's own businesses, a rattlesnake farm, so that true believers would never run short of serpents to toss around on Sunday mornings." Such remarks are the beginning of story, and I say them, in part, because I hope others will slide under sharp propriety and follow me to tale and observation. Of course, the truth is probably that I say such things because I am a foolish and impatient person. That aside, however, rarely do people trail after me into the forbidden brush, and such tales as I fashion are always episodic and their casts of characters thin, limited to myself and a series of flat, cartoon-like individuals. In April I visited my old college Sewanee. On the road outside Murfreesboro I stopped at the Firecracker Warehouse and bought a box of block busters. The box contained forty packs of firecrackers, each pack loaded with sixteen one-and-a-half-inch "Super Charged Flashlight Crackers." That night at one o'clock I set off the firecrackers. The noise flushed students from their rooms, many of them resembling the picture on the front of the box of Crackers: a blue dragon with yellow eyes, snorting fire and smoke, its red hair curling like a nest of angry worms. Wearing pajamas I mingled with the newly awakened and nodded in agreement whenever anyone expressed disgust at "such a silly undergraduate prank." Few people delighted in the disturbance, and fashioning the next episode was left to me alone. I did not disappoint myself. At a literary gathering the following afternoon a distinguished poet gave a public lecture. Before the poet spoke, however, I introduced him. I had done extensive research, and the introduction was detailed. The June bug was, I informed listeners, the poet's favorite insect. He drove a four-door Chevrolet Celebrity "with no bumper stickers." He owned four cats: Wanda Fay, Sammy Ray, Wayne Dwayne, and Rosebud Sue Ann. The redbud was his favorite tree, and the raccoon his preferred animal, these last being particularly fond of the cornbread the poet put out for them under his bird feeder. The poet himself fancied cornbread, and no meal made him smack his chops louder than cornbread, turnip greens, and a pot of pinto beans. At such a devouring little pleased the poet more than listening to music, especially his favorite pop songs, "Run Around Sue" and "Breaking Up Is Hard To Do." "Yes," I told the crowd, "the poet is a man of taste, discretion, and personality," although this last, I noted, "occasionally comes on a bit strong." "He is," I continued, "slightly addicted to fireworks as some of you may have heard last night. For that lapse he has nevertheless, apologized to both me and the administration of this college. We accepted his apology willingly, and we urge you to do the same. Allowance must always be made for true genius, for like a fly it only falls upon ordure to imbibe new life."

Rarely am I asked to make introductions. The form itself is so circumscribed by convention that it resembles a pasture, fenced and far from the sharp tooth of plough and man. Acquaintances know that if I introduce someone I am liable to batter at the structure of the form and then burst into the pasture and, as the saying goes, put my foot in it. No man is consistent however. While I forgive my own trespasses, thinking they have a boyish charm, I do not tolerate the trespasses of boys themselves. I have aged, and when I climb a fence, I do so with care, unlike rude, hormonal youth. When a student says "no problem" to me when he should say "thank you" or, better yet, "thank you great teacher," I immediately think of several problems to which I would like to subject him, most, I should add, of the high Aztec or Mohawk variety. In May I found a message in my box in the English department. A student who missed the final examination left his telephone number and asked me to call. I did so immediately. "May I please speak to Jim Watkins," I said when a boy picked up the telephone. "This is," the boy answered. The absence of *he* after *is* so trespassed against what I know to be polite form that I cared little for the boy's plight. Instead of murmuring long and sympathetically, I said crisply, "You must talk to the dean. The matter is out of my hands. Have a nice day. Good-bye."

In his first letter home from camp, Francis wrote that one of his counselors used "inappropriate language" and provided two scouring examples. On a camping trip the same counselor burned a leech, even though Francis asked him not to. "It wiggled around and suffered," Francis wrote, "then grew fat and wiggled one last time in agony before dying." Three minutes after reading the letter I talked to the director of the camp. In my conversation I used the expression "this is." Unlike the student, however, I forged past the verb and piled a mound of *in* and *im* words around the counselor's trespasses, words like insensitive, improper, and inappropriate. Thirty years ago I was a counselor at the same camp, and although boyish I did not use harsh language to children or harm the small things of this earth. The camp is a fine place, one fenced in by propriety and all those *no* signs I think necessary for the happiness of my little boys. "Bill," Francis wrote in his next letter, "is better. He is almost a different person."

To write a person must observe, and observation often provokes questions, turning one into a crank if not a trespasser. At a recent meeting of the school board an administrator stated that dealing with a particular matter "has been a time-management issue." "If you had said 'took a lot of time,'" I interjected, "you would have saved not only time but letters, twelve letters in fact, the difference between fourteen and twenty-six. And," I continued, "the angels rejoice in heaven whenever a letter is saved. They don't give a happy damn about people, but they are eager to convert alphas and omegas." Not only do cranks read and worry about children's letters, but they know leeches are annelids, members of a marvelous family of creatures including, among some fourteen thousand others, earth and blood worms and from the seashore bristleworms, the bodies of these last divided into more than a hundred segments. For the person willing to trespass far enough to marvel at the ordinary, days are a series of small joys, and life itself is wondrous. Late in May Vicki, the children, and I hiked up West Ridge Trail to the top of Cardigan Mountain, near Canaan, New Hampshire. The day was muggy, and in the woods black flies spun around us like cars rushing into a rotary, buzzing and sharp. I hardly noticed the flies, though, for I wandered from the path to look at flowers: Clintonia, wake robin, painted trillium, trout lilies, Canada mayflower, hobblebush, and then rose twisted stalk, its stem jutting out in jags and its flowers small pink bells. "The flies were bad," Edward said when we reached the top of the mountain, "but the view is great, and this is the high point of my life." "Yes," I answered, "three thousand, one hundred and twenty-one feet high." "No, Daddy," Edward said, "I climbed higher than that and so did you, looking at flowers."

Observance determines remembrance. Like a fence, detail protects experience from the hurly-burly of happenings that trample event out of memory. Oddly, in wandering beyond convention the trespasser preserves not a pasture or wood lot but his own life, and, against their wills, sometimes the lives of those nearest him. Along with wayside flowers I observe the doings of my children, locking what will become their remembered pasts behind a gate of words. Because I have described the cards they gave me the children will never be free to revisit this past Father's Day and trespassing against detail create memory. While Francis forgot Father's Day, Edward made a card, one and a half inches square. On the front Edward sketched a baseball diamond. Stick men wearing gloves played the positions. Despite the small size of the card Edward created motion; the catcher leaned forward behind the plate and the pitcher rolled toward him off the mound. The drawing was not centered, though, and Edward didn't have room to draw the right fielder. Consequently my team has only eight players. "To Dad. Happy Fathers Day. From Ed," Edward wrote in pencil, neglecting to put the apostrophe between the *r* and the *s* in Father's. Eliza's card was bigger, five and a half by four and a half inches. "To Dad," she wrote in red ink, "I hope you will like your moskita kalectsin." Drawn on the card were two insects, the first resembling a small beetle leaping into flight and spreading its front wings or elytra, the other a fat, goofy fly with a long snout and antennae thicker than sheaves of wheat. Pasted below the drawings were the leggy remains of stilt bugs that Eliza found beneath the storm windows in the upstairs bathroom.

Although Father's Day slipped his mind, Francis will remember this year's picnic at Northwest School. The day was wet, and the picnic was held in the auditorium. A mime performed, first by himself then with children. The mime selected Francis to play an imaginary baseball game. The mime was not successful. "A ball," Francis said later; "I thought he was throwing logs at me, and I pretended to split them, lifting the maul over my head then swinging it toward the ground." If Francis's acting mystified both mime and audience, my performance clearly irked Vicki. The first two acts went well and conventionally with grinder, potato chip, and fudge cake. Then at the beginning of the third act the woman sitting next to me said, "Oh, you're the famous Sam Pickering. I know," she said, smiling and thinking of the movie *Dead Poets Society*, "that you must get tired of people asking you." She got no further. "You're damn right I'm tired of it," I broke out; "the whole thing drives me crazy." And right here, alas, I vaulted over the gate and began to whoop and flap my arms, my voice rising like that of an owl on the *o*'s and falling with a spluttering *ploop* on the *p*'s. "You went too far again," Vicki said later, flicking her eyes at me like a snake's tongue; "I don't know why I ever married you." Vicki married me, of course, because when she sensed the time was right for her to marry I was the only person who asked her. And, in truth, she may have married because I trespassed. The old adage, "faint heart ne'er won fair lady," may be the bounder's motto, but it contains wisdom.

From a distance or before marriage trespassers appeal to people who chafe at convention and hope that their lives will differ from those led by parents and acquaintances. Young dreamers, though, are not alone in hankering after trespassers. Trustees of colleges often look back upon their student days fondly, to be sure with chagrin for some of their foolishness but mostly with admiration for the boyish doings of those few years before they became corporate. Thus when trustees begin searches for college presidents they will, at first, say they are looking for someone to exert moral authority or provide cultural and intellectual leadership. What lies behind the statement is the memory of a favorite teacher, both memory and man scrubbed and buffed by time. In the flesh, however, even the polished seem tarnished, and when a real teacher appears, he rarely shines. The real teacher educates himself by wandering and encourages others to do the same. Only platitudes come easily, and as the real teacher struggles to think for himself and fumbles through inappropriate words attempting to describe those thoughts, he makes others uncomfortable. In grasping for understanding he loses dignity and often seems a buffoon. Even worse, the attempt to be truthful can anger. Honesty threatens the fictions people erect to make social life possible. Belief, whether right or wrong, supports culture, and if people begin to wander from accepted paths and tear down *no* signs, community shatters. Then all those things done or accomplished past boyhood suddenly seem silly. In private, in an essay, one acknowledges the foolishness of accomplishment, maybe even the meaninglessness of life itself. In public one rallies to structure and buttresses the old fictions. My own explorations don't go far. Although I have tossed words over hedges, I have never really pushed through briars at the side of a path. I have not dug up a thought; instead I have wandered soft glades, places not visited by everyone but places familiar to people who read. And, of course, I have hammered *no* signs throughout my children's days. I want my babies to be happy. If they stick to well-trod thoroughfares, life will be easier for them, and maybe kinder to them, and so I batter them into correct grammar and appropriate language. Yet when they are asleep, sometimes I go into their bedrooms, kiss them, and whisper, "I'm sorry."

In my ambivalent behaviour I resemble college trustees. Instead of the real teacher they select the easy manager, a person comfortable with budgets and platitudes. In May Hampden-Sydney College began looking for a president. An all-male school with a thousand students, Hampden-Sydney is located near Farmville, Virginia. Founded in 1776 the school has enjoyed a long history of modest aspirations and quiet successes. Still, its reputation is parochial. Few people beyond Virginia know its name, and those friends to whom I mentioned the college confused it with Hampton University near Norfolk. The trustees wanted their school to be more than local, and in May I was asked to apply for the presidency. Reputation is often only bunting, and I applied not because I thought making the school better known was important but because I have a sentimental attachment to Virginia. Mother grew up in Richmond, and I spent many summers in Hanover Courthouse. I also thought my family would like the rural south and that I might be able to lead others, not to make their school "outstanding" but to help it rise from third or fourth rank to second. Dominated by extravagant claim and promise, most educational talk smacks of advertising, and I realized that modest intention would brand me a trespasser, someone not fit to "transform" a college. Nevertheless I flew to Virginia for interviews. In driving through Richmond I passed the building which housed my grandfather's store at the corner of Grace and Fifth. It was now a woman's shop called Hit or Miss. Both the surrounding streets and the store itself were empty, and the business seemed a miss much as I reckoned my interviews would be. Still, the premonition did not bother me, and I looked forward to seeing great-aunt Elizabeth and my cousin Sherry. At Aunt Elizabeth's house Chinese chestnuts bloomed in long fingers. On a rock a river otter groomed itself. At Cumberland Courthouse I ate a lunch that the poet would have envied: snap beans, black-eyed peas, turnip greens, and cornbread. I talked to one of mother's bridesmaids. She told me what she knew about Hampden-Sydney then asked about my children. "They are doing wonderfully," I said. "Of course they are," she said; "they are Katharine's grandchildren."

The people who interviewed me were gracious and generous, and I had fun. When asked what my personal goals were, I told the truth, saying that goals were for the young and that aside from seduction I had not had a goal since I was seventeen, adding that I wanted only to get through the rest of my days with a remnant of decorum and maybe live a little longer than an acquaintance or two. "Also I hope I won't be found out, but that," I said, "is a pipedream." On being asked over cocktails if I liked horses, I said I preferred gerbils and hamsters. A trustee took me to a picnic, and I changed clothes in a pasture. Under the trousers to my suit I wore boxer shorts decorated with small green cats. On seeing the shorts the man said, "I have seen it all now." "You've seen most of it," I responded, "but certainly not all." Or at least that's what I tell friends I said. What the truth is I don't know. I exaggerate so much that not only friends but even I think the truths I tell fiction. Indeed as I age, reality itself grows progressively vague and mysterious. Sometimes I think the things which have happened to me since my boyish days are just the dreams of a few moments. Instead of sitting at a card table writing, I know that I am stretched out dying in a ditch, my body crushed in a car wreck, and the events of the last thirty years are figments of a dis-ordered imagination. Other people have similar thoughts. "Daddy," Eliza said to me as we walked toward Mirror Lake holding hands, "life goes by so fast. I can't really believe this is my life. It goes by so fast that you don't really notice it."

Occasionally I think imagined life more real than actual life. I know that I telephoned Prince Edward Academy, a private school in Farmville, and asked about tuition, in the process learning that Latin had been dropped from the curriculum. But did I really say I would not accept the presidency unless the trustees gave Vicki a West Highland terrier? Did the man to whom I was talking answer, "Dog? Why not a Porsche? You'd like a Porsche." And did I say, "Porsche, hell! They are too low to the ground. Every time I got in and out I'd fart." What I do know is that I daydreamed about Hampden-Sydney. In my mind I roamed the campus running my hands raw across the red brick. Not only did I learn the names of all the trees

on campus but I climbed some. I wrote speeches and presented hon-
orary degrees to people whom I admired: to Mr. Rogers, heart of
the best neighborhood on television, and to John Sawhill, head of
the Nature Conservancy. I also awarded a degree to Little Richard
because he makes me smile. Little Richard did not deliver a speech at
graduation. Instead he sang "Tutti Frutti," and I joined him. Dreaming, of course, is done alone. Maybe the real trespasser is a solitary,
and genuine trespassing is interior, wandering mind instead of hill
and field. "Sam is too free a spirit to become a college president," a
dean said to a friend recently. The dean was right. In part I trespass
because I want to be alone, a desire, I am afraid, that has been passed
along to the children. In June Eliza began day camp. "I don't want
to make any friends," she told me before camp; "if I don't make any,
I won't miss them when camp is over." "Oh, Eliza," I began. "But
daddy," she continued, "sometimes I want to be solitary."

   To be in the middle of life maybe one has to be solitary or at
least drift from crowds and thoroughfares. Beyond "No Trespassing"
wonder thrives, and after a walk I wrestle with language, not shaping
phrases to win or fool but to celebrate. "You have had no adminis-
trative experience," a trustee said to me. "What makes you think you
could manage Hampden-Sydney?" "Arrogance, sheer arrogance," I
answered. What I almost said was that maybe the key to happiness lay
in avoiding managing. Instead of channeling words into distortion
perhaps the successful person allows himself to be managed, rolling
with the pitch of hill and creek, following the rain and then standing
silent like a root in a field, feeling sunlight clap warm through the air.
For an essayist a college presidency would be a long mistake, and so
I say odd things in order to remain free to wander the woods. From
a worldly point of view I would have been a successful president, one
of those admirable people remembered by portrait and building. In
being tacked into substance by convention, though, I would have
lost the ability to escape others, and myself. "Sam," Vicki said when
Hampden-Sydney fell through, "I don't know whether you are a sap
or not. Sometimes I think you are a jackass; other times I think you
are a little right, maybe even smart, especially," she added, pausing,
"when you find raspberries."

   On the kitchen table was a blue bowl filled with more wild raspberries. I discovered them growing in an abandoned field. With them

and the earlier quarts I picked, I brought home a peck of seasonal impressions. For the first two weeks in July I spent part of every day wandering beyond signs. For the first time I noticed moosewood or striped maple, its trunk streaked with green and its leaves big as hams and almost tropical. In the middle of a wood I found a dead white pine. The needles had turned pink, and bursts of long, thick flames flickered through the half-light. Seeds hung from ashes in gouts, each pod a drop of water streaming upward, not down, the wing of the seed dangling behind like a damp khaki trail. At the corner of a pasture stood two old apple trees, the green fruits gnarled as character, bumpy and bent, their sides sucked inward and wrinkled into ridges. May and June were cool, and flowers bloomed late this year. Several mornings I stood in a meadow amid fleabane high as my chest, the frayed blossoms pouring around me like milk. Winter cress had gone to seed, and the pods curled up in hangers like old-fashioned coat racks. Throughout the meadow Canada thistle bloomed, its blossoms gentle above the fleabane but its leaves spiny and tearing. Vervain rose in pitchforks, the square stems green and soft in the middle but hard and molded by red on the edges. Against the light the tines on the forks seemed sharp until they bloomed and blue flowers wrapped them in aprons. In the damp, Joe Pye weed was waist high. Starting at the tips, the new purple leaves turned green around creamy bundles of blossoms. Tall meadow rue grew frail along the Fenton River. In a breeze the stamens of each flower swayed like a squad of long soldiers, white and straight in parade dress, yellow bonnets on their heads.

The ringing of bees rose above milkweed while on the leaves red milkweed beetles doubled themselves. From the leaf axils of nettles green flowers tumbled out in cowlicks. In the abandoned bell of hornet's nest a nursery web spider clutched a white egg. Above the fleabane white butterflies spun upward in cylinders of air. A black-winged damselfly wobbled through an elderberry, and like salt and pepper shakers twelve-spotted dragonflies turned white and black above the beaver pond. A wren bubbled as it darted from a tree to hunt bugs in brush. In a sandy field birdfoot trefoil bloomed in yellow puddles, and ground beetles hid under rocks. Along a creek skunk cabbage splayed out and melted into the ground. The ribbed leaves of false hellebore collapsed and turned yellow then brown.

I picked flowers for Vicki, bundles so big that she did not arrange them in vases but set them around the house in buckets. I found a robin's egg for Eliza and mailed snake skins to the boys at camp. One morning I spent two hours kneeling on a rock in the middle of the Fenton River watching gnats swim through the air in currents, just above the stream. Around me water hurried and dug between rocks like screws twisting through soft wood. Beside the bank quiet basins resembled wishing wells, their bottoms coppery with rocks bright as pennies. Over them royal fern swayed yellow in the light. A towhee landed on a limb and began calling. The feathers on his head resembled a black cap, and the inside of his tail a white morning suit edged with black. For a moment I thought him a barrister, rising stuffy in a British court and incessantly saying "to whit."

Rooms and words can confine. Inside I often listen to myself and occasionally have thought I sounded knowledgeable. Outside amid the quiet of bird, leaf, and stream, I know better. I decided to learn the names of grasses. How could I swell so pompous about moral authority and cultural leadership, I thought, when I didn't recognize the grasses I saw every day? "Daddy, you are very nice-looking," Eliza said one afternoon when I returned from the woods, "but very old looking." Although wandering brightened my days, I was tired, and I limited myself to a handful of grasses. Next summer, I told myself, I could wander farther afield. Like a pink mist, red top hovered near the ground by the fence and ran along the road slicing up the side of Horsebarn Hill. Timothy bloomed lavender in the sun, its minute anthers dangling and shaking like purple clappers. By a wetland reed canary grass was shoulder high. The long panicle had expanded, and sharp purple lines cut through it like washes down a breaking slope. Smooth brome grass grew around a corn field. Like a series of ridges rising sharp above yet shadowing those below, sandy triangles climbed the tight spikelet. From the side of ray grass spikelets jutted stiffly out, their light green anthers yellow in the sun. Although I recognized deer-tongue, rarely did I mow through panic grasses to recognition. Much as they draw streams, wetlands pulled me, and for the first time I looked closely at rushes and sedges. With their spikelets clustered and joined by stems, the tops of meadow bulrush reminded me of bristly tinker toys. While the flowers of wool grass burst out in great sprays from the top of the stalk those of bog rush fell from the side. On my last walk I brought sedges home—hop, bog, and fringed sedge—and put them in a pitcher on my desk. I left them in the pitcher for several days, and Eliza asked when I was going to replace them. "Not for a while, honey," I said; "I'm resting."

Despite what I told Eliza, I won't rest much longer. Monkey flower and panicled tick-trefoil are about to bloom. Goldenrod is yellow, and I want to pick peppermint and bouncing bet for Vicki. Soon butterflies will hang on the big pasture thistles. Behind Unnamed Pond blackberries are swelling beyond green into red. By the time the boys return home from camp the berries will be black. Nailed to a tree on a hill above the blackberries is a red metal sign. Stamped on it in white letters is the warning. "TRESPASSERS WILL BE PROSECUTED." Someone sprayed black paint over the last word, and from a distance the sign seems to say "Trespassers Will Be." I thought about writing something over the black paint, but the words I considered seemed inadequate: FOOLISH, DISAPPOINTED, HAPPY, JOYFUL. At a time when *no* signs so stifle that people retreat from character into platitude, maybe it is enough just to assert that trespassers WILL BE.

9 Cool
Dude

*F*or a while in June I thought I might become head of a college in Virginia. Most college presidencies begin with words, speeches dry with hackneyed phrase and idea. I wanted to do better. Instead of tossing syllables light and brittle into the air, I wanted to brighten lives, and so I decided that if I were chosen president, I would donate garden carts of daffodils to the college. I would buy so many bulbs that the owners of the Daffodil Mart would drive over from Gloucester, Virginia, and supervise the planting. Come spring, blossoms would dance in the sunshine, making students and faculty pause. Amid the whites and yellows they would lose themselves, and forgetting blackboard and desk marvel at this fresh old world of ours. Even if I proved an inept administrator and had already packed my bags, I would have left a legacy of beauty behind and perhaps nurtured a bud of good cheer, maybe even hope. Alas, someone else was chosen president. Still, imagination is powerful. Not only had the daffodils bloomed through dream, but in my mind I had already withdrawn money from the bank to purchase them. Seeing the sum still in the savings account made me seem a hoarder, and so I decided to spend it and take the children on a vacation—one, I told Vicki, that would long remain green in memory.

At first I considered Cape Cod and islands off the coast of New England: Martha's Vineyard or Block Island. These I soon rejected. Not only would finding accommodations be difficult, but I suspected no place on a shore would be as beautiful and healthy as our farm in Nova Scotia. Instead of traveling somewhere new, we'd simply be visiting an inferior Nova Scotia. Next I looked through *Yankee Magazine*. Advertisements for two hotels appealed to me, and I wrote The Balsams in Dixville Notch, New Hampshire, and The

Mountain Top Inn in Chittenden, Vermont, asking them to send me brochures. With red and white clapboard buildings, The Balsams was pretty. Throughout the brochure, though, people whacked tennis balls and strolled golf courses. My days of athletics being over, I ruled out The Balsams and was about to make a reservation at The Mountain Top Inn when a letter arrived. The writer was a trustee of the college in Virginia, and he wrote to say he was sorry "things had not worked out." He was thoughtful and generous, and I had enjoyed talking to him in Richmond. Among other things we discussed the talks I made, and I mentioned that in the spring I was going to Sheridan, Wyoming, to address the Friends of Fulmer Library. In his letter the writer recalled our conversation, noting that in 1959 he had been a wrangler at a dude ranch outside Sheridan, Eatons' Ranch in Wolf, Wyoming. The summer, he said, had been wonderful, and longing to return as a dude, he envied even my short trip to Wyoming. Two hours later I spent the daffodils, and in truth several wheelbarrows full of manure—prime manure, too, not the common sort found behind barns but manure aged in oak like Tennessee whiskey. In place of the bulbs I had five airplane tickets and a reservation at Eatons' for the last two weeks of August.

I was excited. Only once had I been west, and that was to speak in Greeley, Colorado. Although I enjoyed the visit and on a clear morning saw snowy mountains in the distance, I spent most of my time in Greeley itself, sitting atop a desk in a square, windowless classroom, talking about adjectives and adverbs, gerunds and participial phrases. The family trip was six days off, and controlling my excitement was difficult. I struggled to maintain routine. In a downpour the next afternoon I walked to Unnamed Pond and picked three quarts of blackberries. The rain did not dampen my energy, and the following morning I took George and we spent the day roaming familiar haunts. Near the beaver pond a young green heron perched on a limb, its breast brown and white, streaks of yellow running down its back. Spider webs hung pearly on Timothy, and from the spikes of vervain, tattered strands of silk sagged wet with dew then glowed like necklaces of small prisms in the early sunlight. The stamens of blue curls swept upward then fell down toward a lobe which reached out and caught them like a tongue. Bundles of light green fruits hung from hop, bracts overlapping like new shakes. Bellflower escaped from a garden. Before blooming its buds puffed full, expanding so much that each resembled a five-pointed chandelier wrapped in purple cloth. Gathered and pulled back then bound tightly to the stem, the cloth resembled a dust-catcher, for a moment making me imagine a ballroom in a grand old house, its waxed floors silent and abandoned except for the soft, nervous skitterings of mice.

Thoughts of the west, of elsewheres, awakened my imagination, and instead of the ordinary, I saw the exotic, and my mind raced to metaphor. The red and pink clusters of groundnut were not the stuff of peas, but horns with curved stops in their mouths, goaty ceremonial horns, Persian in their ornateness. Because the trip was expensive, I decided not to mention it to friends. Enthusiasm soon betrayed resolve, however, and I discovered diffidence was silly. If booking the trip enpurpled my observations of flowers, just the mention of dude ranch turned conversation feverish. After learning about my plans, friends invariably seized the conversational bit and cantered into story. Because "Henry's" donkey brayed so much, recounted Tom, a member of the English department, Henry worried that his animal "suffered from a bronchial complaint" and took him to a veterinarian. After listening to Henry's lengthy description of the donkey's bray, its tone and texture, its very timbre, the veterinarian nodded and said, "I suspect you are right. This affliction is often inherited in equines, particularly from the distaff side of the family. Indeed," the doctor declared, pausing to light his pipe, "I'll wager that if you check into your donkey's immediate progenitors you will discover that he has an ass-ma." "In days long gone when fairies cavorted in the verdant glens and animals could talk," Mary, a poet, began, a black Arabian stallion married Lily, a snow-white mare. After the ceremony Lily curled her ruby red lips backwards and seized the mane of her mate between her milky teeth. "Hast thou," she said, tugging gently at her beloved's black crown, "hast thou forgotten the willowy Appaloosa of the plain?" "Yes," the stallion answered, placing his right hoof on his breast and rolling his big brown eyes. "And wilt thou ever be faithless to me again," the fair mare continued. "Nay, dearest," the black stallion replied. Whereupon she neighed.

I told friends that I was going to Wyoming in order to settle a disagreement with Edward. For years I have told Edward that I was "the coolest dude in Storrs, Connecticut." Each time I tell him, Edward shakes his head and replies, "Daddy, you don't have a tattoo or a mustache. You don't wear your hair in a pigtail. You don't have a ring in an earlobe. You don't own a motorcycle, and you speak correct English. You are not a cool dude." "After Wyoming," I said, "Edward will have to admit that I am a dude, maybe a warm rather than a cool one, but a dude nonetheless." Although the prospect of getting the better of an opinionated nine year old pleased me, what really lay behind my excitement was a lifetime of brushing against horses and things western. In Virginia Mother grew up on horseback, and she often talked about her horses: Princess, Nellie, Arab, and then Sam, who after falling asleep on his feet often collapsed with a thunk in his stall. When I was nine, Mother arranged riding lessons for me at a stable in Percy Warner Park in Nashville. The lessons did not take. Horses frightened me; after one became skittish and kicked up his heels, I bolted and refused to return to the park. Despite banishing real horses from my life, however, I did not padlock my imagination. Indeed matters western were so much a part of childhood that locking horses out of mind was impossible. Mother kept the Birthday, Get Well, Valentine's, and Easter cards I received as a child. Pasted in scrapbooks amid a menagerie of ducklings in sailor suits, kittens in skirts, big-eyed puppies riding tricycles, and Hummel-like children with pudgy thighs and marshmallow cheeks was a posse of cowboys. "HOWDY PARTNER! I'd like to LASSO You for My Valentine," said a bear seated on a fence railing. The bear had blue eyes and ears round as muffins; he wore a Stetson, a yellow handkerchief around his neck, a red and white checkered shirt, blue jeans, and white cowboy boots decorated with hearts. In his left hand he held a lasso. A round green cactus grew near his left foot; by his right a bluebird hopped. The cactus did not have thorns, and much too gentle to eat bugs, the bluebird looked up, begging for a treat. On another card Cowboy Joe wore blue chaps broader than the front of an automobile. On his head was a mountainous red hat. "A native of the wild and wooly West," Joe liked "breaking in wild horses." "Everybody" knew his "Faithful little pony" because Joe rode "the range from dawn till dusk." At night when he rolled up in his blanket around the campfire, he did not count sheep to help him sleep, but cows. Joe thought his life "swell." "Podner," he said, "I'll bet my boots, you'd like it here with me."

In imagination I escaped childhood in Tennessee and wandered the west, sometimes even joining Joe when he dined with hospitable Indians. In fact tepees appeared in four of fifteen pictures I drew in a pad during first grade, two yellow tepees with red door flaps, a black tepee with a yellow flap, and a brown tepee with a blue flap. Outside this last tepee stood an Indian with an orange nose and eyes. Two blue feathers stuck out from behind his head, and he wore green buckskin, topped off at neck and wrists by what appears to be pink ruffles. Accompanying images, as Joe put it, of "the Western days of old" in the classroom were matters equestrian. Although some note-books I used in first grade were green "Old Hickory" tablets, on the front depicting Andrew Jackson and the entrance to his home, The Hermitage, most were Blue Horse tablets. Near the top of the cover in a frame three and three-quarter inches long by four inches wide the blue horse stood in a corral, ears erect, nostrils flared, and eyes calmly intelligent, ready to trot the rocky paths of arithmetic and writing, assignments like four plus five and seven take away three, and sentences such as "Flowers bloom in the spring," "Mtoher likes flowers," "I like daffodils," and "I have a hen." Blue Horse tablets were popular, in part because they offered prizes to children who amassed quantities of covers. My classmates and I saved covers. Our interest rarely lasted long enough to win a prize, most of us collecting ten or twelve. Still, for the contest ending June 15, 1945, the manu-facturers of the tablets, Montag Brothers in Atlanta, offered 350 bi-cycles, 125 "R.C.A. Licensed Radios," 500 footballs, 500 Note Book Covers, "1,000 Victory Prizes and 13,525 Other Valuable Prizes." To become a contestant a child had to send the company "a mini-mum of 25 covers." "For many years Montag's has given prizes like these to children all over the South," the company stated at the bot-tom of the cover. "We know they're the kind of prizes you like and so we hope that all of them can be secured when this year's contest ends. As you know, the war has made it hard to get many things. If some of these prizes shouldn't be available, you will receive a prize of equal value or money equal to the cost. We hope no substitution will be necessary, but if it should be, we're sure you'll be pleased with your prize."

Along with misspelling *Mother* and claiming to own a hen, in the tablet I wrote, "I have a pony." Writing in first grade I unleashed my imagination, much as I now gave curiosity its head and instead of forcing a pace followed its lead through my scrapbooks. Slipped into the back of a red leather scrapbook were three programs. The first was the "1945 Edition" of the Ringling Brothers and Barnum and Bailey *Circus Magazine.* The magazine cost twenty-five cents and along with pictures contained articles on performers and then the history of circuses. I hurried through the articles and looked at the animals: Gargantua the Great Gorilla who was five feet seven inches tall and weighed 550 pounds, Paragon "the largest and most beautiful Royal Bengal Tiger in captivity," and Soudana, the "Tallest giraffe ever exhibited." In one picture elephants stood in a line inside a tent while people marched through, feeding them peanuts or taking pictures. At this, my first circus, Father bought me a bag of peanuts. Feeding the elephants thrilled me until one sneezed on me, and I began to cry. To stop me Father bought me a circus cane, a round wooden stick painted red with a gold knob at the top.

I glanced at the acts or displays as the program labeled them, but I remembered nothing about them. There were twenty displays, most of which used all three rings. The performance began with "A Rousing Series of Combative and Competitive Events by a ConGLAMORation of Girls in the Ancient Olympic Tradition." Following "AMAZONIA," as the first display was dubbed, was "a wild animal act featuring the six Leopard Women." Performing on the high wires were the Wallendas and Lalage, the lovely "Priestess of Rhythm Aloft." Tagadore Hilding led his boxing stallions through their paces, and the Loyal-Repensky family performed aerobatics while riding barebacked. Captain Roland Tiebor's sea lions juggled and blew horns. Yu's dogs pranced through a series of "canine capers," while the Lin Tang Troupe and the Galassos exhibited a "Plethora of Equilibristic Marvels from the Old World and the New."

Of more interest to me than the list of displays were advertisements in the program. In commercial cultures not event but products mark the passage of time. Instead of historical occurrence childhood becomes associated with advertising, a ditty or a saying such as "Call for Philip Morris." Tobacco companies bought much space in the program, advertising Chesterfield, Raleigh, Philip Morris, Kool, and Old Gold cigarettes; Bond Street, Revelation, and Briggs pipe tobacco, and then Beech Nut chewing tobacco. While the Coca-Cola Company urged patrons to "Have a Coke," Shell Oil warned people not to "drive a Booby Trap." "For Safety's Sake," the company declared, "get Shellubrication," the "answer to the effects of Wartime Stop-and-Go driving on your car." Snappy dressers appreciated "the Right Stetson" while any businessman bound to a schedule would certainly want a Longines Watch, the watch worn by Fred Bradna, the ringmaster responsible for "timing The Greatest Show on Earth." Johnson's Foot Soap relieved the "burning, tender, itching, perspiring feet" of parents who arrived at the circus early in order to take their offspring through the "Menagerie." For the adult who caught "Clothespin Nose" from a wheezy elephant, Luden's Menthol Cough Drops were sure to bring relief. For that rare adult to whom the circus did not appeal membership in the Book League of America was available. With membership came two free books, to be chosen from a list of ten including *Jane Eyre* of whose main characters the advertisement noted in black type, "A Terrible Secret Cursed Their Love!" On the back cover of the magazine, Elsie the Borden's cow prevented Elmer, her beloved husband, from storming out of the barn and shooting some "Black Market guys." The Black Market, Elsie explained patiently, was "hundreds of little things," not just one group of men. "It's every housewife who doesn't check ceiling prices," she continued; "it's people who count it a bargain when the butcher gives them a 12-point cut of meat for 8 points. It's the butcher who doesn't play by the rules." People needed to know which foods were not rationed, Elsie said, "like my *Borden's Homogenized Milk.* That's the milk with cream and Vitamin D in every sip." If a person broke the rationing rules, Elsie went on, he robbed someone else. "For instance," she said, if a person buys *"Borden's Evaporated Milk* without giving ration points, some baby may have to go without." Elsie forced Elmer to listen to a lecture on rationing. Although her "Fine Cheeses" were scarce at home because cheese was "needed for the men on the front lines," the "delicious chocolate food drink, *Hemo"* was plentiful. By the end of the lecture Elmer was weary, eager to put his gun down, and happy to follow Elsie's suggestion to "cool off with a dish of *Borden's Ice Cream* and *Milk Sherbert.*"

Beneath the *Circus Magazine* lay the *Score Book*, the program for a baseball game between the Nashville Vols and the Birmingham Barons played at Sulphur Dell in Nashville on June 6, 1952. The Vols and the Barons belonged to the Southern Association along with the Atlanta Crackers, Chattanooga Lookouts, Little Rock Travelers, Memphis Chicks, Mobile Bears, and New Orleans Pelicans. A seat in the grandstand cost men a dollar; ladies, eighty cents; children six to twelve, thirty-five cents; and children, twelve to sixteen, fifty cents. Both men and women paid seventy cents to sit in the bleachers while seats for children cost the same as they did in the grandstand. While a Gerst beer was thirty cents a cup and a Smith's Red Hot on a Holstein Roll, twenty cents, most items at the concession stand cost a dime. These included soft drinks, snowballs, peanuts, Swift's Ice Cream bars, and a bag of Blevins' Pop Rite Popcorn. For the person who wanted to take home a souvenir, caps were a dollar and bats thirty-five cents. Tax was included in the price of beer. For all other sales over fourteen cents, however, a penny of sales tax was added to the bill.

On the roster of the Vols were nineteen players, seven of whom were pitchers. Batting .344 Dusty Rhodes was in left field. In right Charles Ray hit .338, while Harold "Buster" Boguskie played second base and hit .322. I recognized the names of the players: Al Worthington, Pete Mallory, Rance Pless, and Ralph Novotny. Printed in red in the middle of the *Score Book* were two lucky numbers, A24406 and B29406. For prizes the holder of the first number received two tickets to a game, a car wash, two dancing lessons at the Arthur Murray Studio, a box of La Fendrich cigars, and six packages of Old Hickory razor blades. I grazed through the *Score Book*, chewing over the names of familiar streets and companies: Union and Demonbreum, Church, Lafayette, and then Keith-Simmons Hardware, Universal Tire, Smith Packing, and the Atlantic Ice and Coal Company.

A souvenir of the Gene Autry Show, the last program in the scrapbook brought me back to the horsebarn. My parents took me to the show on February 23, 1949. Along with the program they bought me an album of *Gene Autry's Western Classics* including, "Back in the Saddle Again," "Tumbling Tumbleweeds," "Home on the Range," "Red River Valley," and "South of the Border." Sometime later I received one of Tex Ritter's albums, my favorite song recounting the life of Billy the Kid. Except for puffs for *Western Classics* and Gene Autry Shirts and Jeans, the program contained no advertisements. Instead it contained sketches of performers on the show, most of whom were regulars on the cowboy's radio program, "Melody Ranch." In the center of the program were two pages of pictures, showing Gene and Ina Autry making "'Home, Sweet Home' their theme song." "Home loving folks," Ina sat on a sofa in one picture while Gene stood backside to the fireplace. In another picture Gene sat astride Champion who was bowing. Attached to the sides of Gene's saddle were large papier maché wings on which was printed "AIR FORCE ASSN." Champion, the program explained, "was the first horse to fly across the country in a commercial air liner," and when Gene became a charter member of the Air Force Association, Champion also received wings. The horse's flighty doings aside, the program now seems dull when compared to the *Circus Magazine* and the *Score Book*, reflecting, I suppose, the character of the cowboy himself, who when asked why he worked so hard replied, "Oh, I dunno. Maybe it's 'cause Champion needs new shoes." For a seven year old seeing Gene and Champion was a thrill, no matter the program. Although the show took place downtown at the Paramount Theater, I had long watched Gene at the Belle Meade Theatre. There at two o'clock every Saturday afternoon the Happiness Club met. For thirteen cents, children watched a movie, usually a western featuring not only Gene and Champion, but also the Cisco Kid, Hopalong Cassidy and Silver, Gabby Hayes, the Lone Ranger and Tonto, and then Roy Rogers with Trigger and Dale Evans. While much of my past has washed out of mind like scratches on sandstone, the Happiness Club remains pressed on memory, a hardy petroglyph depicting a childhood that now seems almost aboriginal in its simple joy.

The scrapbooks were filled with modern petroglyphs, photographs. In one picture I appeared dressed as a pirate. In another I was a wild animal trainer, mastering my cat Winkie. On Christmas Day 1948 I wore my new cowboy outfit. Holding a cap pistol in my right hand, I am smiling. Two of my front teeth are missing, and I am wearing a two gallon hat, a bandanna around my neck, and a vest and chaps, both of these last sparkling with ribbons and spangles. Behind the quiet images stuck to the pages lie story and family history. Stuffed in a box were loose pages from several scrapbooks. Fourteen pages contained photographs of and by Mother taken during a trip she made to Arizona in 1937. Mother did not attend college. She applied, she once told me, and was admitted, I think, to Bryn Mawr. "School," she explained, "didn't interest me and sending me to college would have wasted money, not something people did during the Depression." Years ago I found my grandfather's account books in a toolshed. He began his florist business with a loan. In the 1920s money bloomed about him like flowers in the spring. During the Depression his property wilted. By 1937, however, he had weathered the blight and had money enough to send Mother for three months to Castle Hot Springs and what appears in the pictures to be life at a dude ranch. The photographs pleased me. Almost unconsciously I clutch at the threads of the past. Would that I could weave a fabric linking past and present, a carpet of personality and family tale that will support my children and magically lift them beyond our unravelling society. I want the children to rise above sordid pettiness, and I don't want the clamor of discontent to jangle so loudly in their ears that they miss the soft music of ordinary life.

In going to Eatons' I repeated Mother's trip, something that would have given her almost as much pleasure as it gave me. At Castle Hot Springs Mother stayed in a large house resembling a dormitory. She played ping pong and swam in the "Cold Swimming Pool," as she wrote under a picture. She visited Tucson and bought souvenirs in Nogales, Mexico. On the trip to Mexico she wore a dark, pot-shaped hat, a full tweed skirt, sporty black and white winged-tipped shoes, and a heavy coat with a thick fur collar. Stacked on the sidewalk to her left were wicker baskets, big as stools and decorated with colored squares and triangles. In a window behind her were earthenware bowls and wide bands of beaded cloth. In Arizona Mother spent most of her time riding through the jagged scrub around Castle Hot Springs. Usually she wore jeans and riding boots brought out from Virginia. She rolled her long hair into buns and piled it around her ears, and in some pictures she seemed to have a pudding stuck to each side of her head. Sometimes she wore a Stetson and chaps, great flowing leather chaps that wrapped her legs from thigh to ankle. Some days she shot quail, but riding came first. Her horse was named Blondie. Blondie was small with a white mane and a broad white stripe running from the top of her forehead to the tip of her nose. In one picture Mother sat backwards in the saddle. Although Eliza did not see the photographs before we went to Wyoming, she insisted on having her picture taken while she sat backwards on Barney, her horse at Eatons'. In another picture Mother held the reins in her right hand, something I do, unlike most riders. On the pages were several photographs of Curly, Mother's cowboy sweetheart, a young man with wavy hair and a flat, open smile. In one picture Mother and Curly hunkered down, knees akimbo, before a campfire. In another Mother stood barefoot in the shallows of the Rio Grande, jeans rolled above her calves and legs spread, toes digging into the sand. Wearing boots Curly stood to her right front, left arm draped around her shoulders, right hand on his hip as if trying to balance himself, giving him a posed, uncomfortable appearance.

The landscape around Castle Hot Springs looked barren, files of saguaro cactus climbing lonely over the hills and the hard gulches and small canyons peppered with low bushes. Sharp rocks cut seams through the horizon, and as I looked at the pictures, through time itself. On the calendar fifty-five years had passed since Mother's trip. The pictures, though, were part of my present and the present of my family. For us, and the us includes Mother, our trip would continue a vacation started a short winter ago in Arizona. On August 18, we got up at 4:30 and drove to the airport in a sobbing rain. At three o'clock Rocky Mountain time or five o'clock Eastern time, we arrived in Sheridan. The day had been difficult. From Hartford we flew to Washington. Two flights left Dulles Airport for Denver at almost the same time, one departing at 9:15, the other at 9:16. Getting tickets had not been easy, and not until I tried to board with Vicki and the children did I realize that I was booked alone on the 9:15 flight. At Denver, Mesa Airlines overbooked the flight to Sheridan, and despite an hour and a half of seeing me stomp about and hearing me mutter about lawyers, the people at the desk were able to give me a seat only two minutes before takeoff. A Beechcraft 1900, the plane was small, holding nineteen passengers. Not without cause the inhabitants of Sheridan dubbed it the Vomit Comet, and when we landed in Wyoming, we were green Easterners, literally and metaphorically.

Eatons' was a wonderful tonic. Beyond the rates I knew almost nothing about the ranch. When I made the reservation, I asked about boots, learning that sneakers would not do for riding, but that we would not have to buy boots because the ranch had a room full of "loaner boots," worn and left behind by years of former dudes. I also asked if the food was good. "Some people say so," the woman on the telephone said. What I did not know was that the Eaton family started the dude ranch business in South Dakota at the end of the nineteenth century. In my ignorance I stumbled onto the grandfather of dude ranches, one that had entertained five generations of the same families and which let former guests do their advertising. Thirty minutes outside Sheridan, the ranch consisted of 7,000 acres of hill and meadow, canyon and valley. West of the ranch the Bighorn Mountains rose firm, not supple like the rolling hills of the Eastern Uplands of Connecticut. For pasture, for both cattle and dudes, Eatons' leased 150,000 acres in the Bighorn National Forest. Breaking down through the forest, Wolf Creek hurried through the ranch. Always on the verge of being tumbled and rolled the rocks in the creek seemed harassed, unlike the moss-covered stones that rest imperturbable in the Fenton River, resembling green eggs, the water trickling around them with no more force than tickling straw. The distance from the ranch's entrance to the cabins and barns was three miles. The entrance road ran beside the creek, and along it grew cottonwoods, some broad and lance leaf but most narrow leaf. I liked the cottonwoods, and some evenings walked the creek. Above me clouds rolled across the sky gathering the gray night, and breezes soughed through the trees. Cold gusts suddenly pushed against me then broke away, dumping me into still, warm pools. Bark on the cottonwoods was deeply furrowed and yellowish, sandy on the north side where lichens sprawled through the creases. Someone sawed a big limb off one tree, and the bark rose around the cut in triangles, the scar glowing like a dull sun. Instead of being scrubby with branches, cottonwoods split into heavy limbs, the leaves packed tightly together forming compact brushes, the better to withstand the winds and thick snows of winter.

I wandered days. By doing so I quickened the ranch for myself, much as I possessed Mother's trip and shaped memories of the circus by exploring the scrapbook. If I knew the trees and flowers, I thought, I would not be a soft, green stranger. Above Wolf Creek ponderosa pines reached high into the mountains. Broken into plates the bark resembled pieces from jigsaw puzzles, levelled then smoothed and piled into mesas. Between the plates cracks ran blond and pitch oozed out. I chewed a clot. The flavor was light, smacking of pineapple Lifesavers touched with tar. The pitch clung to the roof of my mouth. I couldn't scrape it off with a toothbrush, so I cut it out with a pocketknife. High on the slopes above the ranch grew Douglas and subalpine fir, limber pine, and rugs of creeping juniper. White drops of resin hung from the conescales of limber pine, resembling water slowly turning to ice. Shaggy orange bracts jutted out from cones of Douglas fir, making the trees seem Chinese, decorated with small festive lanterns, each containing a diminutive dragon flicking its tongue. Like magazine salesmen parceling out streets in a suburb then darting up driveways to hunt customers, red-breasted nuthatches worked through a ponderosa. On sunny days Clark's nutcrackers owned the tops of pines, and resembling busybodies, resenting yet intrigued by a new face in the neighborhood, called and gossiped when they saw me, making, I thought, the most unfair and unflattering remarks imaginable.

The driver who met us at the airport that first afternoon dropped us off by the barn, urging us to get our saddles fitted so we could ride after dinner. Just north of the ranch house the barn and accompanying outbuildings stretched in a line across the mouth of a small canyon. To the right of the barn was the blacksmith's shop, a tower of rusty horseshoes rising circular by the door like a piece of industrial pop art. The ranch dogs, blue heelers and Australian shepherds, liked parings from the hooves, and when the blacksmith was working, one or two dogs lingered outside the door. The dogs were countrified, and if they could not get fresh parings, they satisfied themselves with hunks of manure. Two hundred horses were in the pasture above the barn, and the blacksmith was often busy. Piled along a wall inside the shed were cardboard boxes heavy with silver shoes and long, thin nails. Bought at King's Saddlery in Sheridan, the shoes were manufactured at the St. Croix Forge in Forest Lake, Minnesota, while the nails were made by Capewell in Bloomfield, Connecticut, an hour away from our house in Storrs. To the left of the barn was a series of white clapboard sheds, joined together and resembling a chicken coop. Inside, atop a series of triangular roof-shaped roosts, saddles were stored, slightly more than two hundred saddles. Just under the pitch of each roof was a small, rectangular brass plate. Stamped on each plate was a number, making it easy for wranglers to identify a person's saddle. Our saddles rested on racks 90 through 94. The interior of the shed was dusty, but when I rubbed my hand across a saddle a hard leather fragrance arose, an aroma more imaginary than real, one moment smacking of sagebrush dry and minty, the next soft and wet as wild plum. Before going to Wyoming I had never looked at saddles, thinking them merely functional devices, the equivalents of car seats. Now I saw artistry, tooling that turned leather into landscape, pastures and hills, canyons through which imagination could roam and discover beauty: a rock wren hopping between stones, a grasshopper rattling through the air with its yellow wings snapping, and groves of aspen filling the folds between hills, the white bark blue from a distance but yellow as one rode through a grove, the sunlight first green behind the leaves but washed pale by the time it broke down over the trunks. Fittingly our saddles were not grand. Made in Sheridan by Otto F. Ernst, they were the workaday stuff of our slow wanderings over the ranch, of Indian Rock and Bozeman Point, of Chocolate Drop, the North Pasture, Black Canyon, and Soldier Creek.

Behind the barn were corrals. At night the horses grazed through the North Pasture and climbing over the hills wandered the badlands above Wolf Creek. Early in the morning wranglers rounded the horses up and drove them back to the corrals. At six o'clock clots of horses usually led by deer began dribbling over Rattlesnake Ridge. By six-thirty the dribblet was a stream as horses caromed through the canyon turning up a thick fog of dust. After lunch I often stood by the corrals. Sometimes I gave out horse cakes, round thumb-sized treats made from oats, molasses, and salt. I liked the way the big wet lips of the animals turned roughly across my palm. I liked their scratchy fragrance and the heavy, cloudy texture of their hides. I shut my eyes and listened to them, blowing and stomping and then switching their tails. The twisting and churning of their ruminations made me sleepy, and occasionally I dozed until one nudged me with his keg-like head, begging for a cake or a scratch.

The barn itself was white, tall, and narrow. Hay was stored in the loft, and wranglers stabled their horses inside. To the right of the front door was a coil of fire hose; to the left stretched benches. Wranglers sat on them, chatting, rubbing dogs, and waiting for dudes to return from rides. Conversation was slow, and instead of sparkling and calling attention to themselves, words ambled, moving from one point to another along the simplest, straightest path. I spent much time around the barn and sheds. The West was new to me, and I wanted to learn to see. I sat on the wranglers' bench and asked questions. Horse manure seemed wholesome, even sweet, and I smelled pieces, hoping that my nose could ferret out apt, descriptive words. "I don't know how to describe the fragrance of this," I said one afternoon as I sat on the bench turning a lump of manure over in my left hand. "Why don't you," a wrangler on my right began, then paused and gathered himself before starting again, "Why don't you just say it smells like shit?"

At Eatons' I asked many questions. Aside from being steered toward the barn to have our saddles fitted, we were told almost nothing on our arrival. That evening when we climbed aboard the horses for the first time, a wrangler showed us how to hold the reins. Then he mounted and without further instruction led us off to Indian Rock. Beside our places in the dining hall were napkin rings, flat wooden horses with holes cut in the center for napkins. If a dude did not stick his napkin through the ring when he left the table, he found his napkin tied to the back of his chair at the next meal. After a second oversight water was poured on the napkin before it was tied to the chair; on the third offence, honey. Only because we had been told little about the dining hall, not even the hours, did we watch the other dudes and avoid having our napkins knotted. After four days at the ranch I learned maps of the countryside were available in the office. By then I had roamed the pastures and seen grouse and sparrow hawks, and by a drainage ditch a golden eagle, driven down from the mountains by cold, rainy weather. Behind what appeared to be neglect, particularly at those chilling moments when I remembered what the two weeks cost, lay diffidence, the desire not to intrude, and then the belief that people did better if they made their own ways. Eatons', the trustee from Richmond wrote, was "a place people either love a lot or wonder why they ever went there in the first place." Having to fend for ourselves not only enriched the vacation but it made us feel part of the ranch. After six days I sometimes thought myself an oldtimer and enjoyed watching green dudes stumble through their first days. Oddly, the neglect fostered participation then loyalty, built upon knowing. No wonder, I thought, families returned summer after summer, generation after generation. People ache to form loyalties and to establish ties to place, particularly if the place seems unchanging. Too often people are bound to the corporations for which they work only by money, something that provides nourishment for the body but not necessarily for the spirit. The functional buildings in which people labor resemble funeral boxes, places in which one is confined, not where one grows, places where duties are mechanical and which do not appeal to the imagination, places in which sensibilities are constricted and life focuses not on living but on retirement, the end of employment and commitment. Often people are not defined by their jobs but by their hobbies, by their vacations rather than their occupations. Thus during the year dudes read the "Wrangling Notes" and look forward to the summer when for ten days to two brief weeks they can roam wide-eyed and imaginative, big-hearted, through the Bighorn Mountains.

We stayed in a log cabin with three bedrooms, two bathrooms, a huge living room with a stone fireplace, a porch, and closets so wide and deep that Vicki could undress in peace. No matter how I strained and leaned from my bed I could not glimpse even a hint of bare heel. Hung on the outside of most buildings on the ranch were trophies, skulls and racks of antler and horn. The bones had aged beyond the animal and resembled mats of heavy roots or branches, long dead and stripped of bark by cold wind. Hunting was not now the serious pursuit it once had been, and someone had plugged two dead light bulbs into the eye sockets of a skull over the door of a shed near the blacksmith's shop. Still, the trophies bothered me, both at the ranch and in Sheridan where the heads of elk, deer, bear, and wild boar stared from the walls of almost every store, including shoe and drug stores. "Only a sick animal shoots another creature then decapitates it and hangs the head on the living room wall," I said to an acquaintance at Eatons'. "Are you for gun control?" he asked. "No," I said, "gun confiscation." "Are you a communist," he said. "Yes," I said. "Damn," he answered, "what an interesting place. You meet all kinds here."

Each morning I got up before Vicki and the children. I lit the wood in the fireplace then went for a walk. Some mornings I climbed high in the Mountain Pasture or hiked the Roosevelt Trail into the National Forest. Usually, though, I followed Wolf Creek, at first identifying trees, box elder, river birch, rocky mountain maple, silver poplar or white cottonwood, the pale underside of its leaves twirling in the wind, making the trees shimmer and fade like mirages, peachleaf and sandbar willow, then pacific willow, the long leaves elegant and balanced, yellow veins cutting across their surfaces to the mid-ribs like streams slicing ditches through the shoulders of canyons to creeks below. Berry season had arrived, and fruits were thick on smooth sumac, poison ivy, wild licorice, and red-osier dogwood. Hips were red on Arkansas rose, and patches of snowberries scrubbed the vision, pushing color to the periphery of sight. On ninebark fruits hung in sprays, resembling cupcakes wrapped in brown paper. Heavy with ropes of dark red fruit chokecherries bent and stumbled earthward. Unlike wild plum liquid and cool with perfume, the berries dried the mouth, turning it into a gully dusty and clogged with gumweed and shrubby cinquefoil. Growing in rusty knots skunkbush berries were usually lemony. Occasionally, though, the flavor unwound and like a lariat snapping through the air, cut and burned.

From the hills above the ranch, sight ran free, north across the prairie into blue Montana, west into the National Forest, slipping clean between bluffs resembling chins, rocks falling beneath them like napkins. In Connecticut trees limit sight, and the small hills break the landscape into lots, neighborly plots which can be harvested by eyes, not only making it seem possible for one to own the earth but also enlarging man's stature. In Wyoming I was minute, not the lord of all I surveyed as I sometimes thought standing by the beaver pond in the Ogushwitz Meadow, but a fibrous clod, a weed whose roots ran shallow, barely touching a day, much less bedrock. In Wyoming I was often silent, for words which seemed so weighty and resonant in the small spaces of New England lacked body. In well-appointed, enclosed rooms in which stories dangle alluringly from knick-knacks and like curtains block out the dark and confine attention to the familiar, explanation and understanding come easily. Much as profound thought runs too deep for my strip-mining intelligence, so the vast, open living rooms of Wyoming lay beyond my capacity for analysis. The best I could do was furnish a mantle or shuffle figurines across a table. And so I watched birds and learned the names of flowers and trees. Maybe I could hang, I hoped, a print of Eatons' on my mind. Later, perhaps, I could see through the surface to idea, and affection, much as I did when looking at the prints of Jerusalem above piano and fireplace at home in Connecticut.

Like a pointillist I dotted the ranch with color, painting western tanagers red and yellow high in cottonwoods; pine siskins chattering through river birch, the yellow slashes on their wings blinking in and out of sight behind leaves; wild turkeys scrabbling over damp rocks along Wolf Creek; magpies black and white over a ditch near Indian Rock; a red crossbill along on a limb; and then in the badlands a nighthawk, gray against a stone, sheltering a fledgling under its right wing, the white wing bar so tempering the brown feathers that they flowed gently and unobtrusively into the ground. A pair of green-tailed towhees scratched through scrub hunting insects. A Cassim's finch swam into a bush, white stripes flowing down its neck like frothy water. Mountain bluebirds wandered a barb wire fence, landing then jumping into the air like pale clouds tossed by a sudden breeze. Near our cabin four calliope hummingbirds rested on chokecherries, their humped backs making them resemble pensioners worn and curved by time. When Vicki filled a glass feeder with sweetened water, two flew between her hands and fed before she could suspend the feeder from the porch.

By the steps of the porch sat a rabbit, the tops of its feet red. A wandering garter snake crossed a dirt road and vanished into grassy litter under a shadbush. Although I explored ledges in hopes of finding rattlesnakes, I didn't see any. Edward and Eliza, though, disturbed one on the path to Indian Rock and stood by while it hissed then curled into a mound and rattled. "Daddy," Eliza said, "it twisted into a cake then slipped away. I wish I had caught it for you." Although I missed the prairie rattlesnake, I saw prairie sun and cone flowers, the disks of this last rising ungainly from the middle of the blossom like the bodice of a young girl, the petals tumbling below, a yellow skirt too old and stylish for adolescence. Flowers streaked the hills: purple gayfeather, golden glow, showy asters, bluebells, sweet clover both white and yellow, tansy, rabbitbrush, wild lettuce, horsemint, and beardtongue. While virgin's bower had aged into soft spirals, Indian paintbrush still burst into starry slivers of red and yellow. Resembling durable rugs covering the floorboards of cars, rockmat dug into crevices and clung to the sides of stony canyons. I saw many butterflies: blueberry sulfurs, their yellow wings moulded with red; whites; checkerspots; swallowtails; and then fire-rimmed tortoise shells, orange and yellow flowing between black like those final bands of sunlight which ice the horizon and sweeten evenings. Most butterflies moved too fast for me to identify, and I spent more time examining seeds, fitting enough, I thought one morning after stumbling, trying to follow a fritillary. Let quick youth, I decided, chase flickering beauty. For a parent seeds were the more appropriate pursuit, at least for me, who years ago grew hard and spiny about my offspring in hopes of sheltering them from canker and the gnawing worm. Of course, miners and blotchers, borers, hoppers, and web-weavers are legion, and no parent can protect children forever. Around its seeds the yucca formed a thick, moist pod, a barrier resembling a small potato. Linked together in the center of the pod were six sections, each wrapped in a grainy membrane. When separated from each other the sections resembled small canoes, packed from bow to stern with half-moon shaped ebony seeds. Despite the plant's protection, insects deposited eggs amid the seeds, and small holes riddled the pods. On hatching, larvae bored across the struts of the canoes eating the middles out of the seeds and leaving black parings and tubes of gray droppings behind. Around the cabins goatsbeard went to seed, the swollen fruit heads resembling loose bundles of twine. Shaped like tiny bent cucumbers with jaws of small teeth running down their sides, the seeds dangled from furry umbrellas. Tied between the golden struts of the umbrellas were bows of cottony filaments. Gusts of wind lifted the seeds into the air, and they drifted buoyant and bright through the sun, raising my spirits and giving me hope for my own light offspring. Behind our cabin hollyhocks blossomed and grew knobby with seed. The squat fruits resembled mints wrapped in loose, green paper, so pinched above the candy that the paper bunched into ridges. Around a central core inside the pod was a circle of seeds. Each seed resembled the hoof of a horse, a small indentation in the back of the seed, around the front a silvery raised edge resembling an iron shoe. The hollyhocks were deep red, and I picked a handful of pods to carry back to Storrs and plant in the spring. I showed the seeds to the children, and, proud of my powers of observation, pointed out the similarity to horses's hooves. The children nodded politely; real horseshoes interested them more than imaginary ones. Indeed they had already collected a smithy of shoes to take home, to nail over the garage, Edward explained, and to remind them of riding, Eliza added. And riding, despite the green hours spent walking, is what I, too, enjoyed most in Wyoming.

If I had discovered horses before girls, I told Vicki after a week at Eatons', I would not have a family. Instead of a swing and slide in the backyard, I'd have a salt lick and a hitching post. Unless we went for five or six hour all-day rides, we rode twice a day, after breakfast and then either in the early afternoon or after dinner. We rode the same horses each day: Eliza, Barney; Edward, Rusty; Francis, Grayling; Vicki, Keemo, and I, Hannibal. Keemo was a rangy Appaloosa while Hannibal was a twelve year old red dun, fifteen hands two high and worth a thousand dollars. In the middle of his forehead was a white diamond, the right side of which bulged softly outwards. Although this was his first year at Eatons', he knew the lower fields well, having been ridden earlier in the summer by the irrigator when he made rounds through the pastures checking ditch and shunt. When I made the reservation, I said I wanted a dumpling of a horse, one that would fold around arthritis like a pillow. Although well-trained, Hannibal was hard, and would gallop at a touch, something I avoided unless urged on by Eliza. In the family Eliza had the best seat, and immediately comfortable in the saddle she always wanted to gallop. As I watched her, braids flying, red and white boots jammed into the stirrups and then swinging out to kick Barney in the sides, I saw Mother or the child I imagined Mother must have been. Eliza often went to the corral alone and was the first member of the family to saddle up in the morning. Only on one cold, rainy morning was she reluctant to ride. "I do think," she said as she sat on the floor in front of the fire, "that Barney would like to play today." We grew fond of our horses, so much so that Eliza and Edward cried when they said goodbye to Barney and Rusty.

As we discovered the schedule at Eatons' by ourselves, so we were told little about riding. At the end of two weeks, though, we rode, not well but with some confidence and much pleasure. On returning to Storrs Eliza declared she would prefer to study horses instead of the piano. None of us fell. I came the closest. On the second day, Hannibal shied, suddenly leaping to the right, his back switching back and forth, eyes rolling white and nostrils flaring. I thrust my boots deep into the stirrups, pulled back on the reins, grabbed the pommel, and held on. Across the pasture we spun, twisting, it seemed forever. When Hannibal finally stopped, his shoulders quivering and sweaty, I climbed off, handed him a horse cake, and sat down on the ground and hung my head between my legs. "Wow, Daddy," Edward said; "you're not a dude; you're a real cowboy." "No, Edward," I answered; "I'm a dude, and a hot, scared one." Later Edward told Vicki that Hannibal shied at a snake. "No, cowboy," Vicki said, turning toward me, "he just got a glimpse of your duds." My clothes were comfortable, if not western. With the loaner boots, I wore blue jeans and on warm days a tee-shirt with the trolley from Mr. Rogers' Neighborhood on the front. On cool days I slipped on a sweat shirt over the tee-shirt, one from the College of Wooster. Stamped on the sweat shirt was the college seal, in the middle of which was an open book, framed by the words HOLY BIBLE and then by a globe, a telescope, and what appeared to be a sprig of laurel. No matter the weather I always wore a work vest. Purchased from Forestry Suppliers in Jackson, Mississippi, the vest was bright orange. With nine pockets on the front and sides, the vest resembled the jackets worn by linemen working along the shoulders of state highways. Before riding I filled some of the pockets, stuffing them with pens, notebooks, pocketknife, hand lens, horse cakes, and clear plastic specimen containers. The rest I filled during the ride, collecting whatever interested me. On my head was a floppy Tilley sailor hat. Into a hole in the side of the cap I stuck a feather I found. Brown and white, the feather was fourteen and one quarter inches long and three inches wide. I thought it came from a hawk or an eagle, but two days before I left Eatons', a college student who worked in the kitchen said it looked like a turkey feather to her. "Turkey, this may be," I thought to myself, "but if you had seen me wearing this feather twenty-five years ago, your only thought would have been predator."

Aside from causing an occasional agonizing pain to gallop along the inside of my right knee, riding did not make me sore. In fact instead of tiring, riding perked me up, and I felt coltish. Unfortunately Vicki suffered, and there is nothing, I learned in Wyoming, to take a woman's mind off love like sore knees, aching thighs, and a bruised bottom. "I'm at the part of my essay," I said to Vicki yesterday, "in which I'm describing how amorous we were at Eatons'." "Jesus," she said, "you're not really writing about that, are you?" "No," I said, "there wasn't enough of it to fill half a saddlebag." "I suppose," she said, smoothing her nightgown down and stepping out of the closet, "I suppose if we had done it thirty-seven times you'd write about it." "Hell, yes," I said sitting bolt upright. "What a horse folks would think me." "A stallion," Vicki said, putting the top back on her hand cream and turning out the light; "Old Paint, they'd think you were a real bronco." To tell the truth I fancied myself a bit western, if not horsy, and one afternoon I bought a pair of cowboy boots in Sheridan. I got the most modest pair I could find, made from elk hide and with no ornate stitching. I did not wear them at Eatons'. The first morning back in Storrs, though, I put them on and mounting my bicycle cantered over to the Cup of Sun to show off. "Make way," I said, prancing through the door, "for The Urbane Cowboy."

During the two weeks at Eatons' we rode through volumes of *The National Geographic*, only our travels were not glossy but real, rich with sounds and smells, horses blowing and farting, coyotes crying, fog thick as fleabane and buttery with damp pine. I chewed mountain monardella and glancing back across a canyon, saw bald eagles riding thermals high above a ridge. An elk stood silent beside an awkward brooding limber pine. I refused to look over the edge of a switchback and prayed Hannibal wasn't contemplating suicide. A branch whipped across my face, slicing my cheek. In a pasture fringed sagebrush crept across the ground like moss. I picked some and rubbed the fragrance into my hair. I felt at home on the range and on the trails and in the mountains. For breakfast I ate sweet rolls, sausages, and omelettes bursting with mushrooms and cheddar cheese. At dinner I gnawed sides of beef. The second day home I went to Dr. Dardick's office and had blood drawn for a physical.

My cholesterol was lower than it had been in twelve years, and my blood pressure slid off the scale. Time has now passed, and I miss the creak of saddle and Hannibal hot under me. Come spring I will plant hollyhocks by the front door, and they will bloom long after the daffodils have folded limp beneath the grass. Maybe we will return to Eatons' next August. I'm not going to be president of a college, and I need loyalties beyond those of profession. Besides I want a pair of chaps. With chaps, my boots, and maybe a black Stetson tied to the top of my bicycle helmet I really would be the coolest dude in Storrs. And if the truth has to be known, Eliza and Edward were not the only Pickerings suffering from misty eyes when the family reboarded the Vomit Comet and saying goodbye to Wyoming and the Bighorns began the long trip home to Connecticut.

9 From
My Side
of the Desk

Not many children studied Latin at the Male and Female Select School in Smith County. To get enough students for the first year class Quintus Tyler visited Sunday schools around Carthage. Some of Jesus's best friends, Quintus told Sunday scholars, knew Latin well. In hopes of arousing interest Quintus described Pompeii on the first day of class and passed around an old *National Geographic*. Over the years the *Geographic* became tattered. One September Carolynne Foshee sneezed on the photograph of the House of the Silver Wedding at Pompeii while somebody stuck chewing gum on Hercules and Telephus, a wall painting from Herculaneum. The gum covered Hercules's behind. A stringy bit resembling a fishing line trailed down across the lion beside Hercules's right foot, then ran out to the end of the page before curving around and upward, back through the picture, ending in a small plop over Telephus's left eye. Although Quintus suspected Laney Scruggs, he never discovered who stuck the gum on Hercules. What he was certain about, however, was that the gum was Spearmint—Wrigley's, he told Turlow Gutheridge. "I pushed it about with a protractor and sniffed before it hardened," he explained.

Eventually the *Geographic* got so dirty that Quintus retired it. Although he searched the attics of Carthage, Quintus was unable to find another copy. A man of settled habits and years, Quintus enjoyed describing Pompeii, and so instead of changing the class, he decided to replace the *Geographic* with a volcano, one of his own creation. He bought a box of colored chalk and arriving early the first day of school covered the blackboard behind his desk with an extraordinary volcano. Big hunks of orange stone and a gray cloud of ash exploded toward the picture of George Washington hanging on the wall. Red lava gushed through a green countryside. Just ahead of the lava stick people fled along a road: two men in a pink chariot and a woman in a long blue bathrobe the end of which had caught fire. On the shoulder of the road lay an abandoned crib, two little paw-like hands tossing a spotted white ball into the air. Quintus was proud of the drawing, and after the first bell when students filed into the class he stepped from behind his desk striding over to the corner of the room near the stand holding the Tennessee state flag. Pointing to the picture with a yardstick, he asked, "What do you think this is?" When the children looked puzzled and did not answer, he persisted. "You don't know?" he said. "Look at this red flame. What does it remind you of?" For a moment the silence continued, the children studying carvings on their desks and the curious patterns dirt made under their fingernails. Suddenly awareness erupted. "Mr. Tyler, Mr. Tyler," Billie Dinwidder shouted, waving his hand and speaking before Quintus recognized him, "it looks like hell."

Billie and Quintus sat on opposite sides of the desk, and their views were not the same. The perspective from outside the classroom differs even more. Often people interview me about things educational. Although the questions asked are usually similar, they focus on matters I rarely think about. "What teachers influenced you?" reporters invariably ask. Because people want to believe education is a high endeavor shaping both moral and financial success and because reporters expect a platitudinous response, I mention one or two teachers. The truth is that home, heredity, and luck, not the classroom, have determined the course of my life. The question which ought to be asked is what teachers did I influence. Was fourth grade ever the same for Miss Bonney after I left, and how did I change Mrs. Harris's life in the eighth grade? Reporters interested in universities presuppose conflicts between teaching and research when the truth is that research invigorates my teaching. Between classes I roam wood and field collecting insects and wildflowers. One day early this past October I filled the pockets of my sport coat with animal droppings. "Tiffany," I said walking into a creative writing course and handing a furry hunk of raccoon scat to the most carefully perfumed student in class, "look at this." "John," I said, turning to a skinny boy wearing a tee-shirt with the Grateful Dead on the front, "smell this. Take a bite if you want. It tastes sweeter and is better for you than tobacco." The nitrogen I spread that day enriched the class, and during the semester essays bloomed bright, fragrant with natural observation well into December.

Escaping educational platitude is impossible. "Whatever you do," I heard a school psychologist say to kindergarten parents, "be consistent. When you make a decision stick to it." For a moment my stomach sank. Francis was five at the time and had long since battered me out of decisiveness. Suddenly, though, I realized that the psychologist got his ideas from a textbook, not from life. Firm decisive parents, I decided, raised quitters, children who taking *no* for *no* buckled under when the going got tough. I, on the other hand, was instilling drive, intensity, persistence, and the great American virtue of stick-to-itiveness. When the going got to no, Francis clamped down, and no matter how I or anyone else shook or twisted, he hung on until yes.

"How has television influenced students?" a writer asked me recently, expecting me to answer that television undermined literacy and morality. "Look," I said, thrusting my hand into my coat pocket "a hundred years from now people will long for the good old days when children watched television and stayed out of serious trouble. Besides," I continued, discovering an owl pellet in a fold in the pocket, "television is more dangerous to adults than children. How many children leave husbands or wives seeking the fleshly pastures of soap operas? Never have I heard of a child trying to perk up his domesticity by putting candles around the bathtub and then singeing his private parts when he tried to slip in alongside a mate. Ever since actors started bathing en flambeau on television, Dr. Jurgen here in Willimantic tells me," I said, "that sauteed bottom has become a culinary hazard of wedding anniversaries."

All too frequently reporters quiz me about teaching. "What," a writer asked last week, "makes a good teacher?" I did not answer. Blended in a good teacher are knowledge and personality. Both knowledge and personality, however, are various and the blend is mysterious and volatile. The person who is a wonderful teacher at thirty may be terrible at forty then good again at fifty-five. The teacher who stirs the top quarter of a class might not be effective with the lower quarter. Moreover, students often don't recognize good teaching until they have left school. The teacher who seemed incandescent to the twenty year old can appear ashen from the perspective of middle-age. Likewise the teacher whom the young student damned as dull and unimaginative might later be remembered as responsible, maybe provocative by the forty-year-old alumnus. Complicating attempts to define good teaching is the fact that the effects of a class vary according to students' personalities. The word one student does not hear echoes through another, ringing a carillon of associations. "Six years have passed since I was in your class," a girl recently wrote me from New Britain, "and I want to tell you that you handled me the right way. I did not think so then, but now that I am older and have thought about it for a long time I realize you were correct. Thank you for doing me such a service." I did not recall the girl until I looked at my grade book. She was one of fifty-four students and received a B in the course. She wrote three B+ papers, then a B, and finally a C paper; she made 86 on the final examination. In class she was silent, a faceless gray student who never talked. Indeed the semester passed without my speaking to her except when I returned her papers. From my perspective the handling that I accomplished so memorably did not occur. From her side of the desk, an offhand remark of mine must have seemed aimed at her and started thought striking across the years.

Last spring I taught a course in the short story. On the back row in the right hand corner of the room beneath a window sat a hard boy. He always wore a blue baseball cap with an orange bill. Printed across the front of the cap was "Danbury." Instead of removing the cap when class began, he pushed it around so that the bill pointed toward the wall. Then he leaned forward on his elbows and glared at me for fifty minutes, his scorn luminous and his expression never changing. This month he came to my office. He wore the same cap, but in his hand he carried an empty tin can, the top of which had been sliced off. The label still remained. Printed in yellow and white letters against a blue background was "Colossal Pitted Ripe Olives." Underneath the words were six dark olives and the trademark of Shop Rite stores: an overflowing black grocery cart, a commercial bullseye on a round red and yellow target. "Hope you don't mind," the boy said, sitting down then raising the can to his mouth and spitting into it. "I chew. I'll bet," he continued before I could reply, "you thought I was from Puerto Rico. I work at the beach in the summer and get dark. I am from Bridgeport, not Puerto Rico. I came to tell you," he said, "that your course was the best I had in this university. Funniest damn course in the world. Thought I would bust a gut laughing. Told all my friends to take it. I won't forget you," the boy said, abruptly standing and shifting the olive can to his left hand in order to shake hands. "I won't forget you either," I said, mechanically. Actually, now that I think about it, I know I will forget him, for my memory works as strangely as association does in the minds of students. "Incidentally," a man wrote me in February, "the story of you, the Dartmouth English department chairman, and the visiting Englishman has been in my repertoire for years." What story, what Englishman, I thought as I read the letter. I barely recall the years I spent at Dartmouth, much less any, if there were any, visiting faculty.

To know the effects of a class upon students or rather how students think a class affects them would be disturbing. Twenty years ago if I had known how my class affected Gail, my children would not be named Francis, Edward, and Eliza. I was young and unmarried. All I remember about Gail was that she had brown hair, sat in the first row, once wore a yellow dress, and that I was in love with her. I was so in love I could not bear to look at her, much less speak to her. Whenever she missed class, the room seemed empty. The semester ended, however, and Gail vanished. At a reunion eight years later George another student from that class visited me. "Sam," he said as we sat in the living room, "do you remember a girl in your class named Gail? She sat in the front of the room and had brown hair." "Yes, slightly," I answered, feeling uncomfortable. "God," George exclaimed, "was she in love with you! The whole class knew it. Some days she couldn't face you and wouldn't attend. Isn't that the darndest thing." "Yes, George," I answered, "the darndest thing."

The desk stood between Gail and me. Although I have long since emigrated from Youth and the volcanic landscape of passion, the desk still separates me from students. I have changed however. Missed connections hold no allure for me, and I am thankful the barrier exists. If someone my age, I warn students, wants to be your friend, watch out. I urge them to think of me as a father, kindly but stern.

Although many have lived through rich joy and sadness, students are too young to frame the narratives of their lives. Consequently, they don't interest me as much as adults. In part research attracts me because it enables me to wrestle with mature thought and pushes me to see and think, thus indirectly influencing the classes I teach. To students I pontificate, hoping for good discussion but rarely getting it. How effective an argument can an eighteen year old, no matter his intelligence, make to a middle-aged teacher who, more than likely, has heard the same points a dozen times before? Moreover the students' world does not attract me. "Go to Huskies," a girl suggested the other day, speaking of a hang-out at the edge of campus: "Wednesday is New Wave night." Instead of music the mention of waves brings death to mind. I don't imagine Bud Longnecks dancing with the St. Pauli Girl but Tennyson's sunset, evening star, and friends being swept across the bar and out to sea. Only then do I imagine the students, children drinking and misbehaving at Huskies, silly and unaware of the fragility of life.

One cold December Slubey Garts invited Pharaoh Parkus to preach at the Tabernacle of Love in Carthage. Pharaoh was a water-and-fire evangelist, and when he asked folks to "step out with Jesus," whole congregations waltzed toward the altar. At the Tabernacle of Love when Pharaoh called folks who had been smoking and drinking and staying out at night to come forward, half the congregation stood. "Tell it, Reverend," Dora Ludnum hollered from the back of the church; "preach it, Reverend. You're getting them." After Pharaoh asked men who had burning sinful thoughts about women and those women who had hot thoughts about men to come forward, almost all the rest of the congregation rose. "That's right, Reverend," Dora shouted; "you just preach it." When Pharaoh called those "captives" stung by bad thoughts about boys to come to Christ, Mr. Billy Timmons left the organ and joined the horde at the altar. "That's right, Reverend, amen," Dora shouted, sitting in her pew and waving her fan; "you done it at last. You done got them all." Pharaoh was silent for a moment. Then after eyeing Dora up and down, he said, "Now, I wants to see you old sisters who been walking around this here church, full of snuff and gossiping." "Damnit, Reverend," Dora shouted; "you done stopped preaching and gone to meddling."

Instead of men and women I see students as boys and girls, during the semester almost my adopted children. Last week Vicki and I were late for a meeting at Northwest School, and Vicki urged me to drive faster through the campus. I refused. "Vicki," I explained, "these students are other people's babies, and I have to be careful." Like Pharaoh I have gone to meddling, straying beyond textbook and assignment to sermon. On most days I am behind the desk fifteen minutes before class begins. As students drift in, I preach, warning them that I will lower their grades half a letter if I see them jaywalking. Riding a motorcycle without a helmet gets an F. 'Fools," I say, "don't deserve to pass, no matter their test scores." I bring knives and forks to class and lecture on table manners. I harangue smokers. Dangling modifiers and comma blunders might hurt a person's chances to get a job, but they don't cause lung cancer.

Because English is not central to the curriculum of the corporate university, I am free to meddle. No bridge collapses if I misinterpret Jane Austen. Still, I wish universities thought liberal studies valuable. Would that knowledge was more significant than credentials, all those certificates attested to as weighty by faculty committee but which float and tinkle like tinsel when real learning blows across them. "Don't be so down," my friend Josh said. "To be sure, these are lean times for English departments, but fattening things up would be easy. There is gold in mortars and pestles," Josh said, taking a deep breath and starting a sermon of his own. "English should change its name to Literary Sciences. Departments which once skimped by on scraps have grown round and sleek after changing names. Once the butt of jokes about stutterers and Dale Carnegie, speech has been treated with high seriousness ever since it became Communications Science. No pork-barrel bill could ever contain the crackling that Political Science has brought to Government. Gone is the seedy picture of back-slapping, booze-swilling witch-doctors. In its place is the image of white coats, stethoscopes, decency, sound learning, and constitutional law. Even Home Economics has come out of the kitchen and gussied itself up as Human Development and Family Relations. If you'd quit stuffing your pockets with manure in Valentine Meadow, you would see that the world has changed. Go to the library, but don't expect to find cheery Miss Puddleduck smiling behind the Reference Desk or old Mr. Bookbinder poking about in the Rare Book Room. Computers have replaced them. In fact if you say library, people will think you live out where the buses don't run. Libraries are extinct. Born-again educators have brought the Learning Resource Center to the university."

Once Josh bites into a subject, not even gristle slows him. Smacking of pipes, rumpled tweeds, argyle socks, and flatulence, the title *professor*, he said, ought to be dumped and something more tony like facilitator take its place. Unlike professors, facilitators don't fumble about but impact and interface. "Graduate students," he stated, "should be facilitators in training and the courses they taught practicums." Course names also needed changing. Bonehead English should be transformed into Interactive Elements in Informational Systems. The contents of the course would not change, he assured me; students would still learn parts of speech and compose simple sentences. In the catalogue, though, students would become clients and the word *simple* would be dropped. "In fact," he added, "the catalogue should be filled with mystifiers and awe-inspirers, words like kinesiology, morphology, and taxonomy," explaining that big words chopped money trees down faster than chain saws. "Good buddy," he said, "make the clear obscure. Don't be satisfied with half a fog. Import a northeaster. Between semesters baptize the Freshman English Committee and don't just dip it like some tottering weak-kneed serf or country-club Episcopalian. Toss it out into the shining river with the silver spray. Then watch it rise, wearing a golden crown and white robe and speaking in tongues, calling itself an Ongoing Curriculum Laboratory with a directive to emphasize Prethinking and Conceptual Complex Function." For a moment Josh paused and looked dreamily off in the distance toward the university's new twenty-eight million dollar basketball court. "Sam," he said, turning back toward me, "with a little effort the Literary Sciences could become Revenue Producing Agents, brokering the services of facilitators. Suppose the university franchised Diagnostic Centers calling them Mr. Sentence Shops. Folks having misplaced Elements in Informational Systems could visit a center. For a modest fee weary businessmen or inarticulate, lovesick swains could have their prose repaired while they waited."

Josh started to say more, something about turning the Ph.D. into a Doctor of Literary Science and then establishing a licensing board to police Learning Resource Centers and prosecute lax facilitators.

"Prosecute them," he said, "with the same fervor that the American Medical Association pursues delinquent members of the medical profession." Before Josh explained the workings of the board, however, a student appeared in the doorway and interrupted him. Since she didn't know what jaywalking was, she blurted out, she didn't think it fair for me to lower her mid-term grade. Josh looked at her, shook his head, and went to class. I told the girl that if she stayed off motorcycles, did not jaywalk, or smoke cigarettes for the rest of the semester, I might consider an adjustment to her final grade. The girl left, and I walked down the hall to the seminar room for lunch and the daily meeting of the Rump Parliament. Membership is not difficult for anyone over forty. First, the rumps of sitting members must measure at least fifteen inches from flank to flank. I, incidentally, better the minimum standard by two inches. Second, members must have been rendered powerless by academic trend. At ease with one another, Parliament enjoys good talk about real books. No member is ludic or dourly brilliant, and the house is pleased to let those more ideological run the university. "The happy geldings," Josh labeled us, but then Josh is thin and ardent. His outspokenness makes the house uncomfortable, and we wince when he rushes into the seminar room and interrupts debate to repeat one of his witticisms. "This morning I told the dean," he shouted, "that the whole of the English department was less than the sum of its private parts." As might be expected most members of Parliament are male. Indeed when recently asked to describe my approach to literary criticism and then being provided with a formidable list of forty or more approaches, most of which I could not pronounce, I simply wrote "white, middle-aged daddy approach." Family life reduces ideology to insignificance. Fears for my children and those other children whom I teach clang so loudly through my thought that I rarely hear the din of literary controversy.

Unlike me some members of Parliament observe trends, and on occasion Parliament discusses contemporary critical doings. Since our discussions like those of the British House of Lords will not influence matters in the English department or the corporate university, our chat lacks zeal and is pleasantly bloodless and genteel. All members of Parliament are effective teachers, however, and we keep abreast of student concern and activity. Managers of the university declared the second week in February "Sexual Awareness Week," and according to the student newspaper, a member of "the Health Education staff" said the purpose was not simply to "promote awareness of sexuality" but also to "introduce alternatives to sexual intercourse." Thinking this last subject provocative, Parliament went into extraordinary session, one extending fifty minutes, far past the usual quick bagel and cream cheese or sliced carrot sticks and tuna sandwich. Although many alternatives to intimacy were discussed, three rose to the top of the poll: Waldorf Salad, Parcheesi, and the foxtrot. Reaching a consensus in Parliament is rare. In general Parliament does not vote or sit in judgment. Instead members enjoy the higher pleasure of collegiality, benefitting from friends' worldly expertise. Last week a distinguished member showed us how to make a paper water bomb. The process was too intricate for most of us, so another member made a cootie catcher, in the mouth of which he drew four fat cooties.

The parliamentarians have served many honorable years behind desks, and I am very fond of them. They have aged beyond ambition and small loyalty to idea. For them, as for me, people and place are more important than guild. When I teach, I often look out the window. Horsebarn Hill rises swollen and mottled like old bread, reed grass growing mouldy up the slope beyond the parking lot. In Valentine Meadow Morgan horses gather in dark clumps, blowing steam. Lambing has begun in the sheep barn, and the bawls of the newborn crack the air. Seeing is not enough. I want to inhale place and transform it into muscle and bony thought. When I was young, I turned through libraries of books. Now I turn over rock and log, struggling to read the land. I want students to see beyond idea to particulars, rather than abstractions, clouds rising not like dream or hope but instead resembling sheep: the low, woolly clouds, southdown; the tall white ones, Dorset; the dark, black-faced ones Shropshire. I have modest expectations for my classes. Not for me high truths about existence but only the hope to fan curiosity. If students leave my courses willing to pause and turn over word and low stone, then I will have done enough.

After class I step from behind my desk, not to talk to students but to wander Storrs and find matter for the classroom. The past two winters have been Bluebird Winters, so called because the weather has been mild and bluebirds have thrived in eastern Connecticut, a flock of six living amid the brush and broken trees in the cut for the power line running behind my house. In February after classes resumed, I started roaming Storrs and Bluebird Winter. A tawny hunting cat prowled the sweet fern above the marsh behind the high school baseball field. Binding dried leaves to cocoons with dung, the orange larvae of small moths dozed through the winter in the fern itself. On cherry trees in front of the speech building were the eggs of tent caterpillars. In spring they would build nests, filling them with their droppings. The droppings discourage most predators but not green stinkbugs who bore through the dung and suck the juices out of the caterpillars.

This winter I spent days looking at trees: the hawthorne with its chalky limbs and spiked twigs topped by glistening green buds, the bold, stubby buds of the ginkgo, the fringe tree, its modest buds giving no sign of May's white bunting. In the middle of February pussy willows became noticeable, silver fluff creeping out from under the dark beetle-like scale. After I started looking, I realized that for years I had walked blindly past forests on the way to class. Never did I notice the katsura, for example. Along twigs remnants of seed pods swayed upwards in groups, swelling at the upper end like minute cobras bewitched by the cool music of a mild winter. Occasionally identifying a tree took a long time. For a while I thought the green, rolled calyxes of witch hazel were early spring blossoms instead of the remnants of fall flowers. Although I walked miles, I often sat still in the woods, typically studying lichens filling pits in granite rocks with orange or just looking at a hornbeam, a few pink leaves hugging branches and folded inward making fragile, papery pockets.

Near the end of February the wind freshened; gray drifted out of the gunny sky, and days turned blue. The light seemed tinted with spring, first colors that brought plants to mind, followed by the plants themselves: peach and cherry, dogwood, shadbush, and autumn olive. On the first of March the last winter snow fell. Heavy and wet, it caked trees and shrubs. At ten-thirty at night I went for a walk with George, my dachshund. We climbed the side of Horse-barn Hill and then dropping down along the horse trail behind Bean Hill wandered the Fenton River. Shrubs drooped low over our path in thick, moist patties, obscuring the familiar, and twice I lost my way. The night was silent and blue, and the pain in my arthritic hip throbbed, more noticeable than in the day. Early the next morning I explored the campus. The snow that turned the big ashes into lattices clogged highways, and people seemed out of sorts. For many snow was an inconvenience. Instead of changing the landscape so that one saw and maybe thought anew, the storm disrupted schedule. I crossed the Gurleyville Road and followed the creek through Valentine Meadow. Against the snow vervain stood out dark and wiry, goldenrod galls bulged, and reed canary grass gathered the meadow in rippled tufts. The snow pushed brambles over into half circles, exposing highbush blueberry, winged euonymus, red seed pods still spotting its branches, and then nannyberry, the flower buds resembling the dried skulls of diminutive crows, swollen at the base but tapering long and beaked.

In the low pasture behind the sheep barn was the body of a deer. In leaping a fence the deer snagged its right hind leg between woven wire and a strand of barb wire, twisting then cinching woven wire around its ankle. I tried to free the deer, but the wire had cut through the hide and into bone. The deer had been dead a long time; animals had eaten its entrails and white oak leaves had drifted and piled up under its ribs. Later that morning on a stony slope just north of the abandoned ski tow, I found the skull of a small animal, lodged between a rock and a fallen tree. Unlike the deer the skull was fresh. In the eye sockets specks of red shone, and the brains were uneaten. I thought about taking the skull to class and identifying it, but the snow was deep and some creature, I knew, could make a meal out of the brains. The snow remained on the ground only two days. Bluebird Winter was almost over. On the eighth of March I noticed that red maples had broken into bloom. That afternoon I saw a dead groundhog on the Chaffeyville Road. For weeks I had seen bodies of raccoons and opossums. Their bodies revealed little about the weather. That of the groundhog, however, told me winter was over. Above the groundhog a flock of starlings pulled across the road. Resembling a question mark on its side, the flock flowed suddenly up in a hump over the pavement then rolled downward, sliding rapidly through the stem of the question mark across a field bristly with corn stubble.

"What makes a good class?" a reporter asked me last month. In discussing education tough, sensible people become soft. Instead of honesty they want sentimentality. Knowing the writer expected a vague scientific metaphor describing a reaction between student, teacher, and material, I poured him a beaker of palatable humbug, a simple, ideal mixture glowing and syrupy. The truth is that the success of a particular class depends upon my mood, something that texts and students rarely influence. My knowledge of the books I teach is thorough and constant. What varies is the topography of my days, the hills and long, low creek beds not simply of the Eastern Uplands but of life itself, the very ages of man—dreamy youth imagining a light at the end of the tunnel and happiness beyond, middle-age knowing that the only thing at the end of the tunnel is the end—and then more fleetingly those little happenings that blow across an hour turning mood green toward the blushing south or blue toward the pale north. Three times a week I swim before class. During winter many people swim, and the pool is crowded. Four weeks ago as I was leaving the pool, I noticed an older faculty member walk out of the men's locker room, step on to the tile, and stride toward me. Over his shoulders hung a red towel. The towel was gathered neatly and was almost dashing. Clearly the man arranged it carefully. In his left hand he carried a striped athletic bag. The man's air was jaunty, and he was pleased with himself. Unfortunately, he had forgotten to put on his bathing suit. "Well," I greeted him as he approached, "aren't you the bold lad?" He looked puzzled, and I continued, "You are doing something I have wanted to do but have never been able to muster the nerve for." When he looked irritated, almost contemptuous at my unexpected familiarity, I said, "Only a real man would be brave enough to come out here bare ass and fancy free." An hour later my class was a success.

Not all unexpected events are jolly. Last Saturday the local newspaper interviewed me. My birthday was mentioned in the article. Monday morning when I was in the Cup of Sun, pouring half and half into a coffee mug, a stranger introduced himself. "We have the same birthday," he said, "September 30. Have you ever thought," he continued, "that you were conceived on New Year's Eve and your parents were probably drunk as hell?" Although the thought had never before crossed my mind, it beat a path through my brain during class thirty minutes later. No matter what students said I could not push the picture of Mother and Father out of my imagination, eyes glazed, tossing streamers to the ceiling, little red party hats falling down over their ears.

Because I write essays I study my life. Many of the ordinary events I press into memory might drop silently out of another person's mind. Not only does the clutter influence my courses but sometimes it prefaces the books I teach. Today before class and Sherwood Anderson's *Winesburg, Ohio*, I described George, the dog, who can't pee down. George has a low rib cage, and whenever he urinates, he sprays his chest, making picking him up somewhat unpleasant. In truth most events which influence my mood are domestic. "Daddy," Eliza said, pulling up her leotard, "I want to be a famous ballerina." "Oh," I said, having just returned from a speech in Colorado and feeling full of myself, "as famous as your daddy?" "Well, not exactly," Eliza said slowly, "a little more famouser than you." For the teacher the classroom can be unhealthy. Treated as an oracle the teacher can lose perspective and maybe humanity. At home I'm daddy: a silly, flawed, ordinary man, a realization which accompanies me to the classroom. In my writings I celebrate the everyday; in my teaching I urge students to notice the ordinary. In January Vicki, the children and I visited her parents in Princeton. Roads were icy and the drive back to Storrs was difficult. Recollection of the drive, however, warmed my mood yesterday. Aside from the usual family doings, nothing happened on the journey. A Roadway truck broke down on the George Washington Bridge, and traffic backed up into New Jersey. We sat on the bridge for twenty-five minutes, and Eliza's allergies bothered her. "Jesus," Vicki exclaimed after Eliza sneezed for ten minutes, "this is like living in Booger City." "Booger City, where?" I said trying to inch in front of a silver Volvo in the left lane. "Booger City, South Dakota, where else?" Vicki answered, reaching into a sack on the floor and pulling out an apple. "These are empires, good for the nerves. Do you want one?"

Not long after my father died, a family friend said Father envied my life. "Roberts and I," Father told her, remembering his college roommate, "always wanted to be free spirits like Sammy." Father was wrong. Affection and its consort responsibility have bound me so close to others that the concept of freedom has always seemed beside the point, an abstraction too cold for Bluebird Winter. The love and fears I have for my children make me worry about students. Dawn suffers from bulimia and after eating a meal often forces herself to vomit. The bile she throws up burns her skin, and dark channels run searing from the corners of her mouth over the sides of her chin. Last week she wrote a story describing a girl suffering from bulimia. One afternoon the girl went to the grocery store and starting to shop lost control of herself. Frantically her hands crammed food into the grocery cart: Lender's Raisin Bagels, Philadelphia Cream Cheese, a six pack of Reese's Peanut Butter Cups, a bag of double stuffed Oreo's, an Entemann's cheese danish, a half gallon of Ben and Jerry's "dastardly mash" ice cream, sacks of Barbara's Pinto Chips and State-line Potato chips, a box of Pepperidge Farm Chesapeake "Chocolate Chunk Pecan Cookies," and lastly a quart of diet Sprite. While driving back to her apartment, the girl ate the Oreos. Once home she gorged, aware of nothing except "a buzzing in her head" until she noticed her stomach was distended. Stumbling into the bathroom, she balled her left hand into a fist and with her right forced it into her diaphragm. She pushed until she vomited. To make sure no food remained in her stomach she guzzled a quart of water and punched herself again. She repeated the cycle until all she vomited was yellow bile. The story ended sadly. On the last page the girl prepared a celebratory banquet for herself. After setting out silver and covering the table with a lace tablecloth her grandmother brought from Germany, she put on the white dress she wore to her senior prom in high school. Then she lit a candle, played a recording of "We've Only Just Begun" by the Carpenters, and began to eat. "Savoring every bit," she ate everything. Afterward she walked into her bedroom and sat down on the bed, smiling at her reflection in the mirror. Then she opened the drawer in the bedside table and took out two bottles of Nytol. She removed the tops and "one by one swallowed the sweet tablets." The story frightened me, and I came out from behind the desk. That night Edward had a nightmare and woke up crying, "I've lost my daddy," he said, "and I can't find him." "I'm here, Edward, honey; I'm here. Daddy's here," I said pulling him to my chest and rubbing his head, almost as if I were trying to squeeze fear out of him, and me, forever. As I held him, I thought of Dawn, her left fist hard against her stomach, and I wondered if I had done the right thing.

The next morning was bright and clear. It was Edward's birthday; he was eight years old, and Vicki had stayed up late blowing balloons and hanging them in the kitchen and dining room. When Edward awoke, he bounced downstairs. He had shadows under his eyes, but he did not remember the nightmare. That afternoon Vicki and I picked him and Francis and Eliza up at Northwest School. Edward had invited ten of his friends to a bowling party at Lucky Strike Lanes in Willimantic. The car was packed, and the children barely had room to sit. Piled in the trunk were party favors, napkins, plates, balloons, ice cream, popcorn, and trash bags. The cake was on the floor of the back seat under Eliza's feet. We were late, and I drove quickly through Mansfield's winding roads. As I turned on Route 32 toward Lucky Strike, Eliza suddenly grunted and then threw up on herself, Edward, the back seat, and the top of the cake box. "Oh, Jesus," Vicki cried, turning around and grabbing the box then wiping the top with a Soft & Dri. I made a U-turn and took Eliza home and washed her in the tub. Vicki and the boys went to the party. "How was it, gang," I said three hours later. "Great," Edward said, "just great." "Great," Vicki echoed, smiling wanly as she sat down and asked for an apple. "Well," I said after the children vanished upstairs, "how was it really?" "I survived," Vicki said. "Didn't anything awful happen," I asked. "Not really," she said; "the son of the second grade teacher threw a bowling ball at the school superintendent's son, knocking him over the ramp for the ball return. He's a big boy, though; he bounced and wasn't hurt. In any case it was all in the school system, sort of like family."

PLAYING BY THE BOOK

The evening was warm. Silver and gold rumpled the horizon, and dark fall seemed distant. A pair of pearly brown wrens fluttered through the underbrush behind us; a yellow-bellied flycatcher swept up from the woods and perched on the end of a thin, curved branch. Earlier in the day I saw buzzards circling low over Pleasant Valley, so low that I noticed spaces between their feathers, ruts, I thought, harbingers of the gaps that would soon twist high through the trees, paths leading to cold and snow. Winter, though, was far from my mind as I sat in the stands at Spring Hill watching Edward play soccer. Michael sat next to me. His son Ari was on the opposing team. Careless in the spring of their lives our boys seemed to ride the wind, looping and spinning, then turning to dash straight as arrows on compasses, pointing not to the old north but to the young south. Michael and I talked about our lives, marvelling that a doctor charged ninety dollars to freeze a plantar's wart on a child's foot, then wondering what a September would be like without soccer. Once our children vanished from the playing fields how, we asked each other, would we get through the long evenings. When Ari brushed Edward aside and darted goalward we cheered. When Edward spun Ari around and slapped the ball toward the sidelines, we clapped. We did not care who won, for we had seen many competitions: swimmers pulling themselves heavy through water, bicyclists hunched into hillsides, joggers pumping along roads, beside them fields yellow with winter cress and dandelion. We applauded good play and encouraged boys who did poorly. The teams were evenly matched, and we hoped the game would end in a tie, so that on this night, at least, no one would win or lose.

Behind the stands Eliza picked flowers. Around the neck of Violet, a small stuffed snow leopard, she hung a wreath of purple clover, goldenrod, and Queen Anne's lace. "Gosh," Michael said, "Eliza has grown. She looks like a young woman." "Yes," I thought, "but thank goodness she's still too soft for the games ahead." The truth, though, was that Eliza had already begun games. Two nights a week she also played soccer, and she was a toughy, becoming angry when teammates lost concentration or neglected their positions. Flowers and stuffed animals soften a sideline, but when Eliza was on the field, she wanted to win. Last week I urged her to spend more time on her homework, saying, "I have a smart little girl, and I want her to do well in school." "Actually, a clever little girl," Eliza said, almost before I finished the sentence; "smart is too simple a word. Clever is better."

"That was a great game, Edward," I said, as we walked off the field; "both teams played so well I wish it had ended in a tie." "What," Edward exclaimed, "didn't you want us to win? I wanted to win." "Yes," I answered, "but Ari tried so hard that I didn't want him to lose. When the game is over," I continued, paraphrasing something Grantland Rice wrote years ago and Father quoted to me when I was a boy, "it doesn't matter whether you won or lost but how you played." "Maybe," Edward said looking up at me, "but we're the best team in the league, and last week I heard you tell Mommy that you were the best essayist in the country. If being best is not important, why did you tell Mommy you were so good?" Vicki has not read my books, and although in a moment of domestic exasperation I might have tackled the truth a little roughly, knocking it out of bounds into exaggeration or perhaps even into a lie, my literary conversation is usually more temperate. "After I'm dead," I often remind Vicki, "you are going to read my books. Then you'll see what a terrific guy you missed."

I did not answer Edward's question. When we got to the car, I fussed over his seat belt, and he forgot about my essays. That night, though, after the children were asleep, I thought about writing. On paper I play hard. I like getting the point of my pencil behind a sentence and seeing words sail aloft. I enjoy cutting in from the margin and bounding into swift ideas, dropping them to the earth in a tight bundle of phrases. Even the aches and pains of erasing give me pleasure. Yet, I write not to win, but so I don't lose the moment, both the present that passes in a flicker and then that series of flickers, life itself. "Give it all you've got, Edward. Keep them away from the goal," I yelled, "there are only five minutes left in the game."

Edward played his best, and when the whistle blew at the end of the game, he grabbed his left side and dropped to his right knee. Then he stood and smiled. Here and there, I, too, have struggled through minutes, trying to preserve experience by sweeping it off the field, transforming it into language. In September, I flew from Hartford to Kirksville, Missouri. I changed planes in Chicago. The first flight was crowded and uncomfortable, and the commuter terminal in Chicago was drab. As I sat waiting for my second plane, I thought the day lost, even dead. But then, I decided to dig my cleats in and taking out a pad and pencil began playing. I read the list of cities to which Great Lakes Airlines flew. The names were alluring, even poetic: Springfield, Quincy, Sterling, Rhinelander and Iron Mountain, Waterloo, Mason City, and Fort Dodge. A caravan of small red ants wandered across the carpet in the waiting area, each ant carrying a crumb larger than its head. "Look at these ants," I said to the young woman checking tickets. "I'm sorry; I can't see them," she said, stepping out from behind the counter and trying to bend over. She was pregnant and her baby, I learned, was due in four weeks. "I have trouble," she said, "looking at things on the ground. I have put on thirty-eight pounds. My mother says it is too much. What do you think?" "Thirty-eight pounds is nothing," I said; "my wife put on forty-five with each child, and she and the babies were just fine." "Oh, that's so good to hear," she said smiling, then asking, "are you an antologist?" "Sort of," I said, sitting down. Two baggage handlers sat nearby, eating lunch. I listened to their conversation. "I don't know but if I was in your boat I'd get divorced from one of them," the first man said; "that's a bigamy." "A what?" the second man asked. "A bigamy," the first man replied, gesturing with his sandwich, crumbs falling on the carpet for the ants, "if you marry two, that's a bigamy."

In Kirksville a linguist told me a story and I wrote it down so I wouldn't lose it. Among the Circassians living in the mountains above Antioch in southern Turkey, the tulip is known as "Joseph's Coat." Before casting Joseph into the pit, his brothers stripped him, tossing his coat of many colors onto the ground. The coat covered a patch of tulips. Until that moment tulips had been undistinguished, gray flowers. The coat, however, changed the tulip. Those flowers which lay under red cloth suddenly turned red, while those under yellow became yellow. Beneath the coat blossoms bloomed in rainbows. When Reuben picked up the coat to dip it in the blood of a goat, perfume rose in a cloud, and "the sons of Israel were sore afraid and rent their clothes and put sackcloth upon their loins."

One afternoon shortly after returning from Missouri I went for a walk. The sky was overcast; neither Edward nor Eliza played soccer that night, and the day seemed a loss until I began to play with my pencil. Suddenly the land was clothed in color, and delight. At the edge of a brown field leaves on a black tupelo shined red and green. A silver maple exploded into loud yellow stars while a butternut hickory stood silent, its bark pinstriped and formal. Dodder wrapped around Joe Pye weed. Raspberry canes were blue, and vervain turned mouldy, its spires ghost-like, rising, it seemed, through a fog of its own creation. A black blister beetle hurried through the grass, and beside a path clumps of puffballs-in-aspic bloomed, the bright red fruit bodies rising on stalks surrounded by saucers of gummy jelly. Swamp dogwood opened up, and sprays of blue berries tumbled out. A red-tailed hawk sat on a dead limb at the edge of a marsh. Smartweed was pink; sweet everlasting resembled creamy peat moss, and field milkwort bloomed in droplets at my feet. The leaves of stinging nettles curled and the hair along the stalks drooped, wilting out of irritation. The seed pods of beardtongue resembled small red turnips and smelled like sour milk. The jagged leaves of beggar ticks had turned purple, and the calyx and seedpods of wild indigo shined formal and black. Rain fell, and like a wash swept through trees, bringing back greens that had begun to drift out of sight. Near the Fenton River pin cherries glistened, the fruits resembling newly-minted coins, brighter even than the orange shirts worn by Edward's soccer team.

"Daddy," Edward said when I came home, soaking wet, "what were you doing outdoors?" "Playing, Edward," I answered, "just playing." "Did you win?" Eliza asked. "No, Eliza," I said, "but I didn't lose." November has now arrived. Soccer has ended, and the children are taking ice-skating lessons. I'm still playing my game, though, roaming fields and eavesdropping on conversations then tossing sentences onto pages. Maybe these very words will warm those inevitable soccerless Septembers that lie ahead of me and Ari's father, indeed lie ahead of all parents and children. Maybe after I, too, have vanished from the field this book will roll into another's present and bouncing high draw him kicking from the bench, helping him enjoy a summery moment or two.